# LOSING THE RACE

## ALSO BY JOHN H. McWHORTER

*The Missing Spanish Creoles:*
*Recovering the Birth of Plantation Contact Languages*

*Spreading the Word:*
*Language and Dialect in America*

*Towards a New Model of Creole Genesis*

*The Word on the Street:*
*Fact and Fable About American English*

# LOSING THE RACE

## SELF-SABOTAGE IN BLACK AMERICA

## JOHN H. MCWHORTER

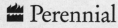 Perennial

*An Imprint of* HarperCollins*Publishers*

A hardcover edition of this book was published in 2000 by The Free Press, a division of Simon & Schuster, Inc. It is here reprinted by arrangement with Simon & Schuster, Inc.

HarperCollins books may be purchased for educational, business, or sales promotional use. For information please write: Special Markets Department, HarperCollins Publishers Inc., 10 East 53rd Street, New York, NY 10022.

First Perennial edition published 2001.

*Designed by Leslie Phillips*

Library of Congress Cataloging-in-Publication Data

McWhorter, John H.
    Losing the race : self-sabotage in Black America / John H. McWhorter.
      p.  cm.
    Originally published: New York : The Free Press, 2000.
    Includes bibliographical references (p.  ) and index.
    ISBN 0-06-093593-6 (pb)
    1. Afro-Americans—Psychology.   2. Afro-Americans—Social conditions—1975– .
3. Afro-Americans—Education.   4. Success—Psychological aspects.   5. Self-defeating
behavior.   I. Title.

E185.625 .M38 2001
305.896'073—dc21                                           2001024092

04 05 ❖/RRD 20 19 18 17 16 15 14 13 12 11

# CONTENTS

# PREFACE

In January 1999, David Howard, the white ombudsman to the newly elected mayor of Washington, D.C., Anthony Williams, casually said in a budget meeting with two coworkers "I will have to be niggardly with this fund because it's not going to be a lot of money."

*Niggardly* is a rather esoteric word meaning "stingy." Its resemblance to the racial slur *nigger* is accidental. It has been used in English since the Middle Ages, when black people of any kind were unknown in England, and had been imported to the country by Scandinavian Viking invaders in the 800s, in whose tongue *nig* meant "miser."

Howard's coworkers were a white person and a black person. The black coworker immediately stormed out of the room and would not listen to Howard's attempt to explain. Shortly thereafter, Mayor Williams curtly accepted Howard's resignation, his official position being that in a predominantly black city with a history of racial tension, Howard's choice of words was grounds for dismissal, akin to being "caught smoking in a refinery that resulted in an explosion." Black talk radio was abuzz with indignation, almost unanimously in support of Williams's decision. A former president of the National Bar Association, a mostly black group, was uncompelled by the fact that the word is not a racial slur, fuming, "Do we really know where the Norwegians got the word?" Meanwhile, David Howard was contrite, considering his dismissal deserved. "You have to be able to see things from the other person's shoes," he explained, "and I did not do that."

*Niggardly* is, to be sure, an awkward little word. Its chance resemblance to *nigger* is such that many of us might quite justifiably choose to avoid it in favor of *stingy, parsimonious,* or *penurious.* There are words like that—the original meaning of *horny* was "rough or calloused," and one formerly had this word at one's disposal in describing, among other things, voice quality. In the twentieth century the word happens to have acquired the slang meaning of "sexually aroused," though, and as such it is now gracious to avoid using it in its original meaning.

Yet it was difficult not to ask whether a man deserved to be cast into unemployment because of this innocent and passing faux pas, especially a man who had dedicated his career to a troubled, predominantly black administration, and who had never shown any sign of racist bias. For many black observers, however, this was beside the point. "How would another ethnic group react if you came close to the line with a phrase inappropriate to that group?" asked the former National Bar Association president.

That rhetorical question cut through the whole issue in its way, because in fact, there is no other ethnic group in the United States today whose sensibilities would lead to someone's summary dismissal for a mere unintended allusion to a racial epithet applying to them. If Howard had made the equivalent slip-up in a Jewish, Asian, Latino, or even gay association, he would have been dutifully taken aside and informed that such a word was not the most felicitous choice and that he would be best advised not to use it in the future. He would then have been allowed to continue in his efforts to do good work.

Whatever our opinions on what happened to David Howard, only in an African-American context is the image of a man cleaning out his desk for such an evanescent little flub even processible. In other words, the firing of David Howard was "a black thing."

Like Howard's gaffe, the *niggardly* episode in itself was a minor flap, which will surely be all but forgotten by the time this book is in your hands. Yet it was symbolic of larger things, whose significance comes through in a thought exercise.

In the 1970s, an anecdote used to circulate in which a man is killed in a car accident but his son lives and is taken to a hospital where the surgeon says, "I can't operate on him—he's my son." Most people were more likely to puzzle over how the boy's father could be both the doctor and dead than to even consider that the surgeon was in fact the boy's mother, and thus a woman.

Now, keeping that in mind, imagine if a Martian came to our planet and asked to interview a representative member of several leading nations, and the representative of the United States was chosen by lottery, and that the person who came up was an African American.

The fact is that for most of us, this would require the same polite adjustment needed to spontaneously imagine a female surgeon. We know that, theoretically, black Americans are "Americans." However, it's a rather intellectual point for both blacks and whites. When writers like Shelby Steele and Stanley Crouch wax eloquent about black people being Americans and perhaps even the most American of Americans, they are pushing the envelope, stretching the boundaries, attempting a transformation of thought, not simply stating a truism. The reasons such statements are more transformative than observational is because in all of our hearts, black Americans are perceived as a "case apart" in a way that almost no other native-born ethnic group in the United States is today.

Our archetypal sense of the representative "American" would be a WASP male, for example. However, a female WASP would be perceived as no less "American," nor would a white Catholic male or female. Except for an increasingly small fringe of fixated anti-Semites, no one would perceive Jewishness as refracting the American essence to any substantial degree. Although the Irish would have strained most Americans' sense of "American" a hundred years ago, today, even Irishness worn on the sleeve would arouse no comment, nor would being Italian, a Pole in Cleveland, an isolated rancher from Wyoming, or even a poor Appalachian. Whatever their individual heritages, all such people are processed as being a fundamental "part of the fabric."

The native-born people who strain our sense of who representative Americans are include Latinos, who often speak Spanish natively and have strong ties to other countries; Asians, for whom the same factors apply; and American Indians, who also often speak another language natively, are descended from indigenes torn from this land, and are now often relegated to the margins of society, and as such often have only a hesitant sense of being "American."

In this light, it is significant that black Americans are as difficult to process as representative "Americans" as many Latinos, Asians, and Indians. This is perhaps unremarkable in the case of inner-city youth. Crucially, however, our sense of dissonance would persist even if the black American chosen was an upper-middle-class corporate manager living in a manicured suburb. Somehow, all of us, black and white, can imagine this person representing the American soul as a whole only after an awkward little pause. And yet, unlike many Latinos, Asians, and Native Americans, this person speaks nothing but English natively, as have all of his ancestors and relatives alive while he was. He has no ties to another country: His distant ancestors came from not one but a number of distinct African nations, and which nations these were is probably lost to history; meanwhile, he is unlikely to have even traveled to Africa. This man is an American: there is certainly nothing else that he could logically be. And yet to all of us, what this man is first and foremost, regardless of his tailored suit, Volvo, and walk-in closets, is "black." Certainly this is how most whites see him—but crucially, this is also how most blacks see him. As the *niggardly* episode demonstrated, almost forty years after the Civil Rights Act, "black" is profoundly and incontrovertibly "different," drowning out all considerations of class, income, or accomplishment.

When someone asks "Why does everything always have to be about race?" the usual subtext is that whites keep this torch burning while black Americans are increasingly frustrated in their attempts to be accepted simply as "people." But this book is written in the belief that the idea that white racism is the main obstacle to black success and achievement is now all but obsolete. Today, ironic accidents of history have created a situation in which black Americans themselves are forced into the dominant role in making it so that most of us have to think twice to remember that even a black corporate lawyer living in the suburbs is an "American."

This is due neither to opportunism nor deliberate obstinance, despite frequent claims to the contrary. It is instead an externally imposed cultural disorder that has taken on a life of its own. As such, it no more justifies an indictment of the black community than a flu epidemic would justify censuring the administration of a city. However, we can only eradicate an epidemic and heal a community by identifying it—trace it, face it, and erase it, as one hears in twelve-step programs. Along those lines, I will show that black America is currently caught in certain ideological holding patterns that are today much, much more serious barriers to black well-being than is white racism, and constitute nothing less than a continuous, self-sustaining act of self-sabotage.

Importantly, my conception of black American well-being incorporates anything any black American might subsume under that heading. For some, the main index of black American well-being would be integration. In that light, I believe that the black community today is the main obstacle to achieving the full integration our Civil Rights leaders sought.

Yet I am aware that integration is now a tired, distant, and fraught notion for many if not most African Americans. This is encapsulated as I write in a sitcom called *The Hughleys,* in which a black man moves his family to the suburbs and finds himself uneasy at the prospect that they will lose their cultural blackness in the course of daily contact with whites. Whatever the wisdom or folly of this anti-integrationist trend, for such people, black well-being would be less a matter of integration than basics like financial success and psychological well-being. Crucially, however, the main thing today keeping even *these* goals elusive for so many black Americans is the very mindset with which history has burdened the black community.

The ideological sea of troubles plaguing black America and keeping black Americans eternally America's case apart regardless of class expresses itself in three manifestations.

The first is the Cult of Victimology, under which it has become a keystone of cultural blackness to treat victimhood not as a problem to be solved but as an identity to be nurtured. Only naiveté could lead anyone to suppose that racism does not still exist, or that there are not still problems to be solved. However, the grip of the Cult of Victimology encourages the black American from birth to fixate upon remnants of racism and resolutely downplay all signs of its demise. Black Americans too often teach one another to conceive of racism not as a scourge on the wane but as an eternal pathology changing only in form and visibility, and always on the verge of getting not better but worse. Victimology determined the *niggardly* episode: The basic sentiment that racism still lurks in every corner led naturally to a sense that the use of a word that even sounds like *nigger* was a grievous insult, in alluding to a raw, relentless oppression and persecution still beleaguering the black community from all sides. The black coworker's bolting from the room deaf to appeal illustrated this, with the implication that the mere utterance of a particular sequence of sounds was an injury beyond all possible discussion, regardless of its actual meaning. More than a few black Washingtonians even surmised that Howard was using the word as a way of slipping the epithet in the back door, under the impression that racism this naked is still typical of most whites in private. Only in a community concerned less with solving victimhood than nurturing it would a mayor compare Howard's harmless little blooper to "being caught smoking in a refinery" and deny a man his job, instead of informing him of his mistake and allowing him to move on with the business of running the city.

The second manifestation is Separatism, a natural outgrowth of Victimology, which encourages black Americans to conceive of black people as an unofficial sovereign entity, within which the rules other Americans are expected to follow are suspended out of a belief that our victimhood renders us morally exempt from them. Because of this, the sad thing was that Anthony Williams *was* in a sense engaging in the business of "running the city" in accepting Howard's resignation. At the outset of his administration when the *niggardly* episode happened, the low-key, Ivy

League–educated Williams was widely suspected of being "not black enough" in comparison to former mayor Marion Barry. He had first been chief financial officer on the control board that had taken over the city from Barry by order of Congress. He had gone on to be elected by whites and successful blacks, and had then brought a great many whites onto his staff. As such, Williams felt compelled to let Howard go in order to show his allegiance to the predominantly black constituency he had come to serve. Importantly, showing that allegiance meant firing a man for an innocent mistake. This irony was due to the fact that the Cult of Victimology has a stranglehold upon most of the black Washington community, and conditions various local rules considered appropriate for blacks in the name of victimhood, i.e., a Separatist conception of morality. One manifestation of this sovereign morality had reelected Marion Barry after he had run the city into the ground despite billions of dollars in Federal aid and been sent to prison for drug use. The idea that a white official uttering a word that sounds like *nigger* must be fired regardless of his intent was simply one more manifestation. In other words, for Williams, part of running Washington, D.C., was showing that he was rooted in Separatism.

Separatism spawns the third manifestation, a strong tendency toward Anti-intellectualism at all levels of the black community. Founded in the roots of the culture in poverty and disenfranchisement, this tendency has now become a culture-internal infection nurtured by a distrust of the former oppressor. As I will demonstrate in this book, it is this, and not unequal distribution of educational resources, that is the root cause of the notorious lag in black students' grades and test scores regardless of class or income level, and this thought pattern, like Victimology and Separatism, rears its head in every race-related issue in the United States. "Do we really know where the Norwegians got the word?" I recall the former president of the National Bar Association asking in reference to *niggardly*. Yet the Scandinavians are not exactly well known for their role in the slave trade—the Danes and the Swedes tried their hand briefly but never made much of a mark. This man might object that racism spreads nevertheless, but even here, a question arises: Blacks have been unjustly stereotyped as being many things, but "stingy" is not one of them. As such, how likely is it that *niggardly* would ever have referred to black people? How plausible is it that people picked up the slur *nigger* in a region where few people had ever even seen a black person until a few decades ago? Even if we somehow allow this, why exactly would they then proceed to apply the word to people who are tight with

their cash? ("Come on, Sven, don't be such a nigger—buy me a beer.")
But this past president of the National Bar Association obviously did not
pause to even briefly consider any of this, even before making statements
to the press. A minor thing in itself, to be sure, but symptomatic of a general sense in much of the black community that to dwell upon such
things as the origins of arcane words and, by extension, books, is "of another world," specifically the white one.

One of the most important things about these three currents is that
whites in America do nothing less than encourage them. This is partly, as
Shelby Steele argues, out of a sense of moral obligation that leads most
whites to condone Victimology, Separatism, and Anti-intellectualism as
"understandable" responses to the horrors of the past. More than a few
whites have come to see the condescension inherent in this, but only the
occasional few dare express their opinion openly or at any length, since
such an act is as likely to attract excoriation from other whites as from
blacks. Whites also unwittingly encourage all of these currents via well-intentioned social policies like open-ended welfare and permanent affirmative action, which are intended to help blacks overcome, but in practice
only roil the waters under all three currents. Whites are now implicated in
nurturing black self-sabotage not because of racist malevolence, but because of the same historical accidents that have encouraged blacks to embrace these thought patterns. Yet the fact remains that interracial relations
in America have congealed into a coded kind of dance that unwittingly encourages black people to preserve and reinforce their status as "other,"
and a pitiable, weak, and unintelligent "other" at that. This, too, was evident in the *niggardly* episode, in which David Howard actually accepted
the condemnation rained upon him by most of black Washington. Howard
thought that he deserved to be fired for innocently uttering a word that
even sounded like *nigger,* even though what he was doing while uttering it
was helping to improve the lives of the city's citizens.

One misconception about these three currents is that they are merely
fringe phenomena, minor overswings of the pendulum that need not
concern us in the long run. However, adherents of Victimology are in no
sense limited to the likes of melodramatically opportunist politicians
such as Al Sharpton, academic identity politics mavens such as Derrick
Bell and Lani Guinier, or sensationalist cultural demagogues such as
June Jordan. On the contrary, Victimology has become, less fervently but
with profound influence nevertheless, part of the very essence of modern black identity. It now permeates the consciousness of a great many

black Americans in all walks of life, most of whom in a recent poll were under the impression that three out of four black Americans lived in ghettoes, as opposed to the actual figure, which is one in five. Similarly, the furious and militant separatism of people like former Nation of Islam official Khalid Muhummad is but the tip of an iceberg. The general sense that the black person operates according to different rules was eloquently demonstrated, for example, by the muted concern with the open sexism of the Million Man March—what group in America could any of us even begin to imagine convening an all-male march in 1995 other than African Americans? The Anti-intellectual current is often thought to be primarily an inner-city problem typical of underclass youth alienated from poor schools, but is in fact a tremendous impediment to black culture as a whole, as shown by the little-noted fact that even middle-class black students tend to make substandard grades even in well-funded suburban schools where teachers are making herculean, culturally sensitive efforts to reach them. In short, these three currents are neither only inner-city ills, mere cynical ploys by politicians, nor just smug fantasy churned out from the ivory tower by the brie-and-Zinfandel set. They are so endemic to black culture as a whole that they are no longer even perceived as points of view, but rather as simple logic incarnate. In other words, these defeatist thought patterns have become part of the bedrock of black identity.

The most serious misconception about these three currents, however, is that there is nothing wrong with them, and even that they are an evolutionary advance that other identity groups would benefit from adopting. On the contrary, these three currents hold black Americans back from the true freedom that so many consider whites to be denying them. Victimology is seductive because there is an ironic and addictive contentment in underdoggism. However, it also inherently gives failure, lack of effort, and even criminality a tacit stamp of approval. In addition, because focusing on the negative debases the performance of any human being, focusing on remaining aspects of victimhood rather than the rich opportunities before us is a ball and chain restraining any effort to move ahead. Separatism promises the balm of a sense of roots, and offers an escape from the vicissitudes of making our way into realms so recently closed to us. But the wary social remove that Separatism encourages blacks to maintain from whites regardless of actual experience is a much more powerful factor than white racism in making blacks less likely to be hired, or especially, promoted. Black Anti-intellectualism can often seem like a jolly and even healthy alternative to sterile nerdishness, but it is also, as I have noted, the main reason blacks underperform in school. On a broader level, a race permanently wary of close reasoning and learning for learning's sake is one not only spiritually impoverished, but permanently prevented from forging the best techniques for working toward a better future.

I have written this book under the conviction that it doesn't have to be this way, and that more to the point, it absolutely must not. Black America is currently embarked on a tragic detour. Accidents of history have condemned us to miss an unprecedented opportunity to reach Martin Luther King's mountaintop. In the first four chapters of this book, I will discuss the operations of these three currents in modern African-American thought. In the next two chapters I will show how these currents have shaped two race-related issues of wide impact, the affirmative action debate and the controversy over whether or not the in-group speech of black Americans is an African language called "Ebonics," which ought to be used in classrooms as an aid to teaching black children to read. The last chapter will outline suggestions for getting back on the track that our Civil Rights leaders set us upon. Following that track will require some profound adjustments in black identity, which today would feel nothing less than alien to most African Americans under the age of seventy. Nevertheless, these adjustments are not only possible, but most importantly are the only thing that will cut through the circularity and fraudulence infusing so much of interracial relations in America today, and bring African Americans at last to true equality in the only country that will ever be their home.

# LOSING THE RACE

# 1

## THE CULT OF VICTIMOLOGY

The fact of slavery refuses to fade, along with the deeply embedded personal attitudes and public policy assumptions that supported it for so long. Indeed, the racism that made slavery feasible is far from dead in the last decade of twentieth-century America; and the civil rights gains, so hard won, are being steadily eroded.
—DERRICK BELL, *Faces at the Bottom of the Well,* 1992

Tyson is in the pen now. Strange fruit hanging from a different tree. Yet the strangest of all walk among us—as long as they're free, white, male, and twenty-one. The greatest of these qualities is the freedom. I wonder how it feels? I am trapped and can only say "Nooo" and hope my scream is loud enough to discourage the monsters and keep them back until I am strong enough, powerful enough, to fight my way free. Powerful enough to slip the noose from my neck and put out the fire on my flesh.
—RALPH WILEY, *What Black People Should Do Now,* 1993

What more do they want? Why in God's name won't they accept me as a full human being? Why am I pigeonholed in a black job? Why am I constantly treated as if I were a drug addict, a thief, or a thug? Why am I still not allowed to aspire to the same things every white person in America takes as a birthright? Why, when I most want to be seen, am I suddenly rendered invisible?
—ELLIS COSE, *The Rage of a Privileged Class,* 1993

These quotes are from books written in the 1990s by successful black men. The conception of black American life they represent is considered accurate, or at least a respectable point of view, by a great many people black and white of all levels of class, education, and income, one indication of which is that all three books were published by major mainstream houses, all were soon released in paperback, and none was even the author's first book.

Yet most of us would be hard pressed to match these portraits with the lives of most of the black people we know. Are we really afraid that, as "civil rights gains, so hard won, are steadily eroded," Macy's is on the verge of refusing black patronage? Do all the black people we see at the movies, on planes, copping sports trophies, graduating from college, and eating in restaurants appear, even metaphorically, to have fire on their skin? Do we ruefully consider a home, a car, or a college degree—"things every white person in America takes as a birthright"—all but out of reach for the middle-class black people we know, who are the subject of Cose's book? How "invisible" is an author who manages to have books of his opinions regularly published by top presses? How many of us can truly agree with these authors that the Civil Rights revolution has had no notable effect upon black Americans' lives?

Without falling for the line that racism is completely dead, we can admit that these quotes reveal a certain cognitive dissonance with reality. Yet they are anything but rare, and are one of myriad demonstrations that there is, lying at the heart of modern black American thought, a transformation of victimhood from a *problem to be solved* into an *identity in itself*. Because black Americans have obviously made so very much progress since the Civil Rights Act, to adopt victimhood as an identity, a black person, unlike, for example, a Hutu refugee in Central Africa, must exaggerate the extent of his victimhood. The result is a Cult of Victimology, under which remnants of discrimination hold an obsessive, indignant fascination that allows only passing acknowledgment of any signs of progress.

## What Is Victimology?

The charge that blacks engage in "peddling victimhood" is not new, but many might wonder how one could possibly criticize a group for calling attention to its victimhood. In this light, we must make a careful distinction. Approaching victimhood constructively will naturally include calling attention to it, and is healthy. However, much more often in modern black American life, victimhood is simply called attention to where it barely exists if at all. Most importantly, all too often this is done not with a view toward forging solutions, but to foster and nurture an unfocused brand of resentment and sense of alienation from the mainstream. This is Victimology.

Two contrasting examples will demonstrate. Marva Collins saw that inner city black students in Chicago were posting the worst grades in the city year after year. She founded a school combining high standards with rich feedback, celebration of progress, and a focus on self-esteem and upward mobility. Its successful techniques have been adopted by schools elsewhere in the nation. This is addressing victimhood as a problem.

On the other hand, Susan Ferecchio, a reporter for the *Washington Times*, visited the Afrocentric Marcus Garvey School to report on its progress in 1996. Asked to show her notes before she left, she refused according to journalistic protocol. For this, the principal Mary Anigbo told her to "get your white ass out of this school" and led a group of students in taking her notebook and then pushing, smacking, and kicking her from the premises. Anigbo first accused Ferecchio of pulling a knife on a student, then denied the episode ever happened, and then claimed that Ferrechio had deserved it. This was Victimology. What Anigbo did was meant not to allay victimhood but simply to express unfocused hostility: The physical violence Anigbo incited will do nothing to enhance the upward mobility of her students.

In leading black American thought today, Victimology, adopting victimhood as an identity and necessarily exaggerating it, dominates treating victimhood as a problem to be solved. Most black public statements are filtered through it, almost all race-related policy is founded upon it, almost all evaluations by blacks of one another are colored by it. Derrick Bell prefers couching his therapy disguised as reportage as allegorical "stories." Here are some of my stories, only they are real.

## Stories of Victimology

### The Story of the Party Shelby Steele Is At

A black academic at a predominantly black conference in 1998 once recounted how typical it is at parties thrown by people affiliated with universities to meet "white racists" who say "Oh, there are black people I like, but . . ." Needless to say, the audience ate it up with a spoon, amidst which she added, "Shelby Steele is at those parties. . . . "— "Shelby Steele" having become synonymous with "unthinkable sell-out" in black discourse. Yet the audience empathy came at the cost of plausibility. Her scenario so strains reality that we can only take her on faith via condescension. As a black academic, I myself have now spent twelve years attending these very same parties, and I can attest that I have never found myself peering over my glass of Chablis realizing that my evening will entail negotiating a minefield spiked with "white racists." Can we really accept this professor's contention that white Ph.D.s and professionals in the year 2000 regularly say things remotely like this? How many white people has this professor met in the academic/professional world who even gave any indication of *thinking* this way since about 1974? Perhaps one here and one there, but certainly not enough to imply that such people are *par for the course*. It is significant that the professor used this as an ice-breaker—because Victimology is part of the very fabric of black identity, there is no better way to signal your allegiance with "black folks" than to couch a story in it.

### The Story of the Bigoted Math Professor

I will never forget a gathering of black students at Stanford in 1991, when a black undergraduate stood up and recounted that a white mathematics professor had told her to withdraw from a calculus course because black people were not good at math. Quite frankly, I don't believe her. Where the black professor in the last story exaggerated, this student went beyond this to fabrication. I choose that word carefully, to allow for some possible rootedness in reality: This professor may have told the student that *she* wasn't good at math, and may perhaps even have displayed some subtly discriminatory attitudes in the classroom. However, frankly, the chances are nil that anyone with the mental equipment to obtain a professorship at Stanford University would, in the late 1980s in as politicized an atmosphere as an elite university, blithely tell a black student that black people cannot do math. Even if he were of this opinion, he would have to have been brain-dead to casually throw it into a black student's face, possibly risking his job, reputation, and career.

Yet the student was vigorously applauded for airing this demonstration that nothing has changed, by hundreds of black students most of whom who owed their very admission to Stanford to affirmative action, a product of the very societal transformation that Victimology forces them to dismiss.

### The Story of the Minstrel Smile

At a conference on black performance I once attended (ironically in the same room that the episode I just described took place in), one audience member claimed during the question session that she is tired of having to put on a happy face and adopt an insouciant, bouncy demeanor whenever she leaves her apartment, otherwise being in danger of harassment by the police since "white people think a serious sister is a criminal." This observation was greeted with applause and comments of support from black people in the audience.

Inappropriate and abusive racial profiling is a problem in this country, as I will discuss later in this chapter. Yet what this woman said was nonsense. A quick look at the black women walking down any street in the United States will easily disprove that black women labor under a burden of putting on minstrel smiles in public, and to my knowledge, no police officer interviewed about the cues they seek in stopping-and-frisking people has stated that one of the things that get their antennas up is "black women who aren't smiling." Indeed, black women around the country have valid stories of having been detained and humiliated by police officers—but to claim that racism in America is still so tragically omnipresent and inexorable that all black women are required to grin and shuffle their way through any shopping trip on the pain of arrest is an arrant and callow exaggeration. Furthermore, this woman did not have the excuse of having grown up in an America where profiling and harassment of minorities were more open and accepted and had yet to be publicly decried. She gave her age as twenty-five, which means that her mature life had taken place almost entirely in the 1990s.

This is not to say that this woman may not be occasionally trailed by salesclerks, or that a police officer may not have once stopped her for a drug search. Injustices such as these show that we still have some distance to travel. But transforming them into apocalyptic embroidery does not address victimhood but instead simply celebrates it. Of course, if she were airing a concrete grievance this would be one thing: we certainly must identify problems as part of solving them. But crucially, this woman's charge was a fantasy, and as such, logic dictates that her aim was not to decry actual injury. Rather, her aim was to dwell in a sense of victimhood as a ritual.

She underlined the essentially ritual, rather than grievance-based, nature of her claim in following it up with an unsolicited performance of a lengthy "slam" poem she had written in hip-hop cadences detailing her dissatisfied *Weltanschauung*. Crucially, much of it was about aspects of her personal life that concerned neither racism nor black performance, and this was not only a time-consuming pit stop in a setting devoted to discussing the invited scholars' presentations, but also included some naked profanity that was particularly inappropriate given that there were many small children present (including one she was carrying on her back). One could not help considering that the conference was being broadcast on public access and that many of the presenters were professional performing artists. Cloaking herself in the genuine moral grievance that Martin Luther King marshaled to help free us, what this woman was really doing was trying to snag herself some DJ gigs in a quest to become the next Lauryn Hill. In essence, there was no moral

distinction between this incident and someone donning a neck brace after a fender-bender to seek a big settlement in a court case.

And yet of course she brought the house down. To be sure, there were
some more constructive approaches to victimhood at this conference.
Yet we might ask why this hyperbole and profanity was processed as compatible with the proactive proposals and reality-based expressions of
grievance, rather than as an awkward intrusion. The reason was that
adopting victimhood as an aspect of identity rather than addressing it as
a problem has become an accepted form of black American expression.

All three of these stories spring from a conviction held by many blacks
that forty years after the Civil Rights Act, conditions for blacks have not
changed substantially enough to mention. Yet basic facts speak against
this claim.

In 1960, 55 percent of the black population lived in poverty—that is,
every other black person and then some. A substantial band above that
were working class; the middle class was a quiet and lucky minority, and
the upper class all but statistical noise. A mere 3.8 percent of black men,
and 1.8 percent of black women, were managers or proprietors, a situation that had remained essentially unchanged since 1940, when a mayoral report in New York City noted that business outside of Harlem in
New York could be divided between "those that employ Negroes in me-
nial positions and those that employ no Negroes at all." Lawyers num-
bered 1.8 percent, doctors, 2.8 percent. There were exactly four black
congressmen. Of black people twenty-five to twenty-nine years old, just
5.4 percent had college degrees. Today, we associate the Great Migration
of blacks from the South with sepia-tinted photos and people now in
their nineties, but as late as 1964, of 1.1 million blacks in New York City,
no fewer than 970,000 had come in 1945 or after, and 340,000 of them
only in the past ten years—in other words, almost every black person in
New York was just a step past sharecropper.

That world would be all but unrecognizable to anyone under forty-five
as I write. Today (2000), under a quarter of black Americans live in
poverty—instead of every other black and then some, today fewer than
one in four. Hardly the ideal, but then hardly the steady erosion of the
Civil Rights victories Derrick Bell bemoans either. By 1990, one in five
blacks was a manager or professional; to put a point on it, by 1996, about
one in ten of all female managers in America were black. and about one
in twelve male professionals. Twice as many blacks were doctors in 1990
as had been in 1960, and three times as many were lawyers. By 1995,

there were no fewer than forty-one black people in Congress, and 15.4 percent of black people had college degrees (if that number seems small, consider that only 24 percent of whites did). The unofficial slavery of sharecropping is now something most black Americans dimly associate with their great-grandparents, and we are no longer a country folk as we were in 1960, when those born in cities were distinguished as a new group "born on concrete." The blacks who migrated north in rags starting after World War I would have been flabbergasted, and the ones still alive indeed are.

The signs of progress are stark, relentless, and certainly cause for celebration. In 1940, only one in one hundred black people were middle class, with "middle class" defined traditionally as earning twice the poverty rate. The Victimologist response here is to question whether twice the poverty rate is truly "middle class." This is not the book to dwell upon that point, but for these purposes note that twelve times that proportion of whites were middle-class by that same metric in 1940. By 1970, 39 percent of black people were middle-class by this metric, while 70 percent of whites were. Today, Ralph Wiley screams "Nooo," but almost half of African Americans are middle class today, having increased by 10 percent since 1970—while the white middle class has increased by only 5 percent.

The social landscape of modern America also incontrovertibly shows that something significant has been afoot since 1964. In the early 1960s, when the Civil Rights victory was just over the horizon, the author of the play *A Raisin in the Sun,* Lorraine Hansberry, and her white husband, Robert Nemiroff, were often refused service in restaurants in New York City—in Greenwich Village, which had been the most notoriously bohemian, open-minded area of the city for fifty years. Even when I was a child in the late 1960s and early 1970s, an "interracial couple" like Hansberry and Nemiroff was a curiosity, their children automatically "torn." Today, black-white relationships and marriages are so common in many parts of the country that they do not even arouse comment. Certainly this is not the case everywhere—yet most people reading this can think of a number of black-white couples they know for whom the race question has been barely an issue if at all for them, their families, or their friends, and what is important is that this would have been all but impossible just twenty-five years ago. The film *Guess Who's Coming to Dinner* is increasingly a period piece rather than topical, and it is not accidental that there have been no moves to "remake" it—the shock that the interracial relationship arouses in an educated liberal white couple simply would not make sense today. In 1963, a minuscule 0.7 percent of black Americans were not married to other black people; in 1993 the figure was 12.1 percent, about four times what it was even in 1970 (2.6 percent). I don't think I personally have referred to a black-white couple as "interracial" since about 1983, and George Jefferson's hostility toward the interracial Willises on the old sitcom *The Jeffersons* is today quaint.

The institutionalized housing segregation so searingly depicted in Hansberry's play is still occasionally encountered, but only marginally. Much of it that remains is due to self-segregation in the name of cultural fellowship by working and middle-class blacks themselves, a largely harmless phenomenon. (My family moved to the all-black New Jersey town of Lawnside in the 1970s from a very peaceful integrated Philadelphia neighborhood because it reminded my mother of the warmth of black Atlanta.) Hansberry was the first black woman to have a play produced on Broadway when *Raisin in the Sun* premiered in 1959, but today, there are barely any "firsts" left to be. African Americans now hold, or have held, so very many top-echelon positions in American life that to even begin the usual list headed by Colin Powell would be a cliché. These leaders are now far too numerous to be dismissed as tokens—note that even "token black" is becoming a rather hoary concept—and importantly, the holding of these positions by black people would have been all but unthinkable as recently as 1970.

## The Foundation of Victimology: The Articles of Faith

To be sure, none of these things mean that race has no meaning in America. Neither, however, do these things mean all but nothing—and it would be difficult for any intelligent person not to wonder upon what basis the latter could be said.

Yet Derrick Bell, Ralph Wiley, Ellis Cose, and a great many black Americans would consider that question as to why a black person would still consider America a racial war zone too obvious to merit an answer. What do these writers and their ilk know that we don't?

What Bell, Wiley, Cose, and all of the subjects of my stories consider themselves to know is that the statistics, the marriages, and the success stories are all just so much glitter, and that people like me just don't "get" the truth. "What's really goin' down," according to this perspective, consists of a certain seven Articles of Faith carefully taught and fiercely resented in the black community. They are so deeply entrenched in

African-American thought that any argument outside of the Victimologist box falls largely on deaf ears, white as often as black.

These Articles of Faith are not the famous street conspiracies such as that whites have infected blacks with AIDS. These Articles of Faith are much broader and less fantastical indictments of white America, but all of them are either outright myths or vast exaggerations and distortions, born via the filtering of a subtle and always improving reality through the prism of Victimology, with its seductive goal of aimless indignation over solving problems.

## Article of Faith Number One: Most Black People Are Poor

In a 1991 Gallup Poll, almost half of the African Americans polled thought that three out of four black people lived in the ghetto. This reflected that one can be certain that a good number of black people one talks to assume that most black people are poor or close to it.

This conception is mistaken. The number of black people who lived in ghettos in 1995 was a low one in five. The number of black families who were poor in 1996 was roughly one in four (26.4 to be specific). One statistic often heard is that 41.5 percent of black children are poor (as of 1995). This understandably leads one to suppose that about 40 percent of black people as a whole are poor, but the figure for children is skewed because of the high birthrate of unwed inner-city mothers.

The inner cities are, in my view, America's worst problem. However, this does not gainsay the basic fact that *most black people are neither poor nor close to it.*

## Article of Faith Number Two: Black People Get Paid Less Than Whites for the Same Job

In 1995, the median income for black families was $25,970, while the figure for whites was $42,646. The figures were quickly translated into the claim that "black people make 61 percent of what white people make" and taken to mean that black people are regularly paid less than whites for the same work, so that, for example, the black assistant manager takes home a salary about 40 percent smaller than the white one working in the office next door. This is naturally read as indicating a deep-seated racism in the American fabric far outweighing the significance of increased numbers of doctors or interracial couples or black characters on TV.

But the figure is extremely misleading. The black median income is dragged down, again, by the extenuating factor of the low income of un-wed mothers living on welfare, a larger proportion of the black popula-tion than the white. The median income of black *two-parent families* is about $41,307, as opposed to about $47,000 for whites. Even here, the gap is extremely difficult to pin on racism. In 1995, 56 percent of black Americans lived in the South, and wages are lower there. Finally, as of-ten as not today, black two-parent families earn *more* than whites—they did in about 130 cities and counties in 1994, and in the mid-90s, their median income was rising faster than whites' was.

Thus it simply is not true that black people are paid less than white people for doing the same work, on any level. The proportion of black poor unwed mothers is a problem, but no one would argue that they get less welfare than their white counterparts; they do, however, pull down the aggregate figure for black American earnings as a whole.

The famous 61 percent figure is another thing that many people, shak-ing their heads in disgust, see as an incontestable rebuke to any argument that black people are not still in chains. This Article of Faith is a fiction, but Victimology, which primes black Americans to hear and pass on bad news instead of good, has rooted the figure in black consciousness.

Black Americans are no strangers to paying close attention to the treachery of statistics when the moral absolution of perpetual victim-hood is threatened. A standard defense against the charge that too many blacks were on welfare, for example, used to be that greater *num-bers* of white people were on welfare nationwide even if a greater *pro-portion* of blacks were. This continued to be a community mantra even long after it was no longer true, whereas the 61 percent figure has been subjected to no such scrutiny, because doing so would not feed the flames of Victimology.

## Article of Faith Number Three: There Is an Epidemic of Racist Arson of Black Churches

Between January 1995 and June 1996, thirty-four black churches were burned. Since then, it has become common wisdom in black America that these burnings are part of an imminent return to the naked white persecution of blacks in the past. The burnings were seen as reminiscent of the burning of the 16th Street Baptist Church in Birmingham in 1963 in which four black girls were killed; by 1997, Spike Lee had filmed a wrenching documentary about this earlier tragedy (*Four Little Girls*).

The burning of a church is an unspeakable evil. However, the idea that there is an epidemic of *black* church burnings is, like the 61 percent figure, pure fiction. From 1990 to 1996, about eighty black churches were burned. During the same period, however, over *seven times* that many white churches were burned *every year*. Thus during a typical year, six hundred white churches burned while only about fifteen black churches did. In other words, there is a regrettable practice afoot in America of setting fires to churches, period. Because black people live in America we certainly would not expect such an epidemic to mysteriously bypass black people entirely—however, the epidemic has no racist source.

Furthermore, investigators have been able to turn up no racist motivations for these burnings, and church burnings in general have been decreasing steadily since the 1980s. Finally, in South Carolina, eighteen arsonists have been apprehended, and of these, eight are black.

Victimology, however, has ensured that the black community heard only the initial misleading report without the figures for white churches.


## Article of Faith Number Four: The U.S. Government Funneled Crack into South Central Los Angeles

In 1996, Gary Webb wrote a three-part report for *The San Jose Mercury* describing how the Central Intelligence Agency had deliberately sold crack cocaine to dealers in South Central Los Angeles to fund the Nicaraguan contras in the 1980s. Later that year the newspaper retracted the story, because it turned out that Webb had never found anything even resembling proof of this arrangement. Yet Congresswoman Maxine Waters has continued to demand further investigation of the case, convinced that the inner-city crack epidemic could only be explained by racism.

The chances that the CIA, by the 1980s notoriously inept, could have managed such an endeavor are slight to say the least, and the notion of officials in Washington openly devising, endorsing, and putting into action such a blatantly racist policy strains credulity, seeming no more likely than white doctors injecting blacks with AIDS.

Yet a great many blacks find such ideas plausible nevertheless, and assume (with many whites) that the editor of the *Mercury* was simply caving in to coercion from the Powers That Be. For the sake of argument, let's say that the CIA was actually guilty as charged.

The first problem is that if they did this, they were throwing a match into a blaze that had been raging for decades—the inner city was created through the confluence of white flight, deindustrialization, and the expansion of welfare benefits. The first of these factors, white flight, was racism but hardly directed from Washington, and made possible by a general suburban expansion which was indeed encouraged on the Federal level, but for financial reasons unconnected with racial concerns. The second, deindustrialization, has been a matter of faceless economics (no one would argue that corporations have moved to the suburbs and overseas to escape black people). The third, the expansion of welfare, can only be interpreted as benevolence. Even if the CIA were caught red-handed, this would not indicate that the horror of the inner city was a deliberate creation of racists in the U.S. government.

Second, even if the CIA had channeled crack into South Central, how do we explain the same inner-city horrors in all of the other American cities, like Philadelphia, New York, Detroit, Atlanta, St. Louis, Oakland, and dozens of others? Unless we believe that the CIA also funneled crack into each and every one of these cities, then the question arises: If conditions got to the point they did in all of these other cities, then what makes it necessary or even worth pondering that South Central resulted from CIA intervention?

And finally, even if with great effort we could somehow find a smoking gun proving the implausible scenario of the CIA devoting its overextended energies to carefully funneling crack into just the black communities of over a hundred American cities, then *what would that do for the people suffering in South Central today?* Wouldn't Maxine Waters be better serving her constituency by focusing on concrete efforts to better their lives? The aimless obsession with this is a waste of precious energy, but it makes sense as yet another demonstration of how addressing racism constructively has taken a backseat to simply crying racism to savor whites' humiliation.

Importantly, all that has been found is that a few CIA operatives looked the other way and allowed some drugs into South Central as part of the wider effort to aid the Nicaraguan *contras*. Altar boys they were not, but this hardly constituted a targeted effort to hook inner-city blacks across the nation on crack. The latter has yet to be proven by Waters or the reporter who could rescue his career with a smoking gun. If the issue were something black people had done, we can be sure that the case would be long considered closed, its very mention by the white press considered racist. Victimology, however, will ensure that even educated and successful black Americans like Bill Cosby will continue to trace the crack epidemic to the CIA.

*Article of Faith Number Five: The Number of Black*
*Men in Prison Is Due to a Racist Justice System*

In 1995, one in three black men in their twenties was either in jail, on probation, or on parole (the statistic is often distorted as "one in three black men" period, rather than in their twenties, but the truth is awful enough). More to the point, almost half of the United States prison population is black.

This is generally interpreted as evidence that black people are arrested out of proportion to their numbers in society, since they constitute only 13 percent of the population. However, the figures must be seen in light of the fact that as sad as it is, nationwide blacks commit not 13 percent, but 42 percent of the violent crimes in the country. In other words, contrary to the idea that blacks are arrested disproportionately, their proportion of the prison population neatly reflects the rate at which they commit crimes. The *reason* they commit more crimes is surely traceable to racism, which left a disenfranchised people on the margins of society and most vulnerable to antisocial behavior. However, this does not mean that the percentage of the black prison population above 13 percent were put behind bars for no reason.

Yet the general feeling is that even if blacks are arrested in proportion to the crimes they commit, that there is a bias in the severity of their sentences. However, one study after another, even by scholars expecting their results to reveal racism, show no such bias. When prior records, gravity of the crime, and use of weapons is taken into account, there is no sentencing bias against blacks. Contrary to another piece of common wisdom, black people are not sent to death row disproportionately. Their numbers there also correspond with the proportion of crimes blacks commit, 40 percent in 1994 (also, whites are more likely than blacks to be executed).

Thus the black community sentiment, nurtured by white comrades-in-arms, that the railroading of Mumia Abu-Jamal represents life as usual for black men in America is wrong. All evidence does suggest that crucial exonerating evidence was barred from Abu-Jamal's trial and that he does not deserve to be in prison, much less to die. Yet without minimizing the unspeakable injustice of his incarceration, Abu-Jamal's story is today a freak tragedy, not business as usual. He was cursed by a combination of variables: having been a Black Panther in a city with a particularly racist police chief, having then been a particularly effective gadfly journalist, and falling under the jurisdiction of a particularly racist judge. But the facts above remain: Mumia Abu-Jamal is one person, and studies show that blacks are not discriminated against in general under the legal system. The vile Judge Albert Sabo who sentenced Abu-Jamal is an exception, not the rule. Many would vigorously disagree, thinking about some other racist judge they have heard about, but certainly there are individual racist judges—we're not on the mountaintop just yet. The point is that if the justice system was racist overall, then the proportion of blacks in jail would be greater than the proportion of crimes they commit—but it isn't, and no amount of justifiable sympathy for Abu-Jamal can erase that fact. Sabo is also elderly, i.e., a relic of the past, and the incident that entangled Abu-Jamal in this web was in what is now virtually another time, almost twenty years ago.

The prison statistics are also widely attributed to the disparity in sentencing for possession of crack cocaine versus powdered cocaine, which according to common wisdom in the black community was instituted in order to corral black people, who mostly use crack, into prison.

Yet how racist can a law be which the Congressional Black Caucus vigorously supported and even considered too weak? If we had asked these black congresspeople in 1986 why they supported these laws, they would have said that they were aimed at breaking the horror of the crack culture, which had turned inner cities into war zones by the mid-1980s. Indeed, the sentencing laws were *not* designed to catch white users even though there are more of them—because the whites were not part of the murderous culture that was decimating blacks young and old in the inner cities. The people who put these laws into effect—prominent blacks among them—were quite explicit about having the inner-city crack culture in mind rather than the white investment banker doing some lines after work in his apartment.

And what we must keep constantly in mind as we evaluate the appropriateness of these laws is something very simple that is tellingly almost never mentioned when the issue comes up: namely, they worked. The world depicted in films like *Colors* and *Boyz N the Hood* is quickly becoming history: Crack no longer terrorizes the inner cities as it once did. Of course none of us rejoice at the spectacle of so many young black men behind bars. But let's face it, they didn't get there for playing jacks. Because their being put there solved a problem, our question is whether having them out of prison would be worth going back to the world of *Boyz N the Hood*.

It is true, however, that these sentencing laws have *now* outlived their usefulness and beg revision. Because they succeeded in breaking the crack culture, today we are seeing increasing numbers of people quite unconnected to the warring crack trade of yore thrown into jail for ten years, or even life, for possession of small amounts of drugs, and this burden falls disproportionately upon lower-class people, a great many of course black. I perform on stage as a hobby, and recreational drug use is par for the course among many of the twenty-something white people of the theater world; it often sobers me to think that the only thing stand-ing between me and ten years in jail if I happened to be pulled over while carrying a bag of something would be the possibility that the status of my job as a college professor and my "middle-class" demeanor *might* incline a prosecutor to get me community service instead of jail time. However, the fact remains that fifteen years ago, the laws were instituted not sim-ply to give black people a hard time, but as an emergency measure— openly and heartily supported by the Congressional Black Caucus—to break the crack culture terrorizing black communities nationwide.

Yet apparently, to critics of the crack policy, young black men being ar-rested in large numbers is such anathema that they would rather have seen these guys be allowed to stay on the street and do their business. But how might these professors, lawyers, politicians, and journalists cry-ing "racism" feel if it had been *their* children and family and friends be-ing iced while walking down the wrong street on the wrong evening? Are these people really this cold-blooded?

Certainly not. In the 1970s and 1980s, the New York City police de-partment were walking by drug transactions in cold daylight, hamstrung by liberal enforcement rules favoring the criminal. At the time, it was fashionable to say that whites were hoping that black people would just kill each other off. But now that whites have dedicated themselves to getting these people off the streets and succeeded, they are charged with trying to decimate the black male population. What exactly, then, do these critics want?

That's not a rhetorical question, because it is clear what such people want. Their refusal to be satisfied stems from a guiding commitment not to any concrete plan to rescue the inner cities, but to crying "racism" whatever the circumstances. Victimology strikes again, so powerful that it perverts us into seeing the taming of a murderous scourge as a reversal.

## Article of Faith Number Six: The Police Stop-and-Frisk More Black People Than Whites Because of Racism

Unlike the 61 percent and church-burning myths, it is true that black men are more likely to be stopped by the police than white. It is also true that as often as not, police tend to be discourteous and sometimes even physically abusive during these encounters.

There is no excuse whatsoever for police brutality, an important subject that I will discuss shortly. Here my focus is on stop-and-frisk encounters, with the unpleasantness they often include, but not those involving physical abuse, which I will discuss in the next section. Even so, neither is there justification for someone being screamed at or unduly detained in the process of a police check.

Many people claim, however, that regardless of whether harassment or violence is involved, to focus at all on minorities in preventing crime is based on "racist stereotyping." However, there are some unpleasant but vital realities that we must keep in mind when addressing this issue for the future. I will give two examples.

In 1989 the New York police department conducted an antidrug effort at the Port Authority Bus Terminal. Indeed, 65 to 75 percent of the people they stopped were black or Latino, while only 35 percent of those stopped were white. According to the wisdom that the concentration on blacks and Latinos was racist, they should have been a much lower percentage of the people actually carrying drugs than 65 percent, and certainly no more than 75 percent. The actual figures: the blacks and Latinos were 99 percent of those found to be carrying drugs (208 out of 210). Obviously their being stopped in larger numbers guaranteed that they would constitute a larger portion of those on whom drugs were found: but the fact that almost *no one* carrying drugs was not black or Latino was significant.

In New York City in 1999, four policemen shot and killed an unarmed Guinean immigrant named Amadou Diallo in the course of interrogating him during a search for a rapist, allegedly because he somehow appeared to be armed. This killing took place within the context of a citywide crackdown on crime instituted by Mayor Rudolph Giuliani. Based on William Bratton's "Broken Windows" theory of crime-fighting, the crackdown emphasized stiff penalties even for small infractions like jumping turnstiles and defacing property, on the assumption that such things discourage more pernicious behaviors from settling in a neighborhood. Clearly, Amadou Diallo's killing took this punitive approach much, much too far, and in general the New York City police were rightly considered to have been much too harsh in their dealings with minorities in general.

Nevertheless, after Diallo's death, under the glare of the media the

New York City Street Crimes Unit started making many fewer arrests (291 in the seven weeks after the shooting, compared to 705 during the same weeks the previous year). The number of shootings promptly went up within the Street Crimes Unit's area of operation: that is, more people, most of them black or Latino, died or suffered serious injury.

What these episodes show is the following:

> Even a police force devoid of racism, and never abusive or discourteous in stop-and-frisk encounters, would in some areas have to stop more black people than white to prevent crime effectively.

The ultimate reason for this is, of course, racist disenfranchisement in the past (or, depending on how you view the inner city, even the present). But *in* the present, let's face it—crime is crime.

What this means is that in certain areas where certain kinds of crime are rampant, a police officer can, quite reasonably, stop more young black people, especially males, than any other type of person without being racist at all; on the contrary, to do so is often the only logical way to effectively fight crime. This is not a pleasant thought. But if this attention to minorities were unfair, then the minorities checked would almost always come up empty-handed. But as we have seen, all too often this is not the case. All of us know that, especially since the 1980s, there has been a violent drug trade run by urban minority men. Certainly this would lead black men in certain places to be more likely to be carrying drugs. Figures like the ones from the Port Authority, which are quite typical, prove this empirically.

One of many things showing that "profiling" is not proof of the eternity of racism is that black police officers are as notorious for it as white. "I mean, you're a cop. You know who's committing the crimes. It's your neighborhood. That's how it works," one in Philadelphia has said. How many of us could look this man in the eye and tell him he should concentrate on the Latina mothers pushing baby carriages and the white Temple University professors waiting at traffic lights driving to work? At Baltimore's main train station, a black police officer unhesitantly notes that young black women who favor certain accoutrements are known for delivering drugs and money for New York dealers. Especially since the "profile" is but a subset of the black female population (middle-aged black women with their children are not focused upon), is this man a "racist" for concentrating upon these particular women in trying to stanch the degradation that drugs wreak upon the New York City black community? How likely is it that the black dealers in Harlem have also incorporated paunchy middle-aged white businessmen in gray suits commuting from Washington into their networks? Many black police officers are as disenchanted with the analysis of profiling as racist as white ones are; as this Baltimore officer says, "The problem with black politicians is that they think the cop is automatically guilty."

This is certainly not to say that there have not been areas where profiling has gotten out of hand. This is particularly true of one kind of profiling, the concentration on black people when making random stops of cars to check for drugs. For example, it has been discovered that while 75 percent of the cars New Jersey police officers had been stopping were driven by minorities, an average of only 13 percent of the drivers had been found to be carrying drugs, while 10 percent of the white drivers had. Similar evidence has come forth in other states, such as Florida and Maryland, and suggests that randomly stopping black drivers on the "D.W.B." (Driving While Black) charge is ineffective, and thus inappropriate and wrong.

However, there are two things that tend to get lost on the "D.W.B." issue when it comes to deciding whether racism rages eternal in America. One is that the officers guilty of this practice were working under the pressures of quotas, stopping more black drivers out of a sense that they were more likely to be carrying drugs. It was concretely documented in one state, for instance, that minority stops were concentrated during the last two weeks of any given month, just as parking tickets traditionally are. Even though the profiling was inappropriate and has since been prosecuted, our issue is whether or not these officers were motivated by racism, and in that light, what motivated them was in fact pragmatism, misaimed though it turned out to be—based on the fact that it is true, regardless of its cause or the justice of that cause, that black people do commit crimes in this country in disproportion to their numbers. This is indeed what officers have often stated on the subject. We need not pretend that there is no racism among some of these officers, *but even if there were none whatsoever, the result would have been the same,* especially since black officers have been as guilty of profiling as white ones. These officers black and white were overgeneralizing on the basis of concrete experience, as all humans black and white tend to. Clumsy and cynical, yes. But racist? Life is more complicated than that.

This brings us to the second issue. Stopping cars is but one form of profiling, not its totality. This is important because it returns us to the fact that profiling by officers patrolling certain neighborhoods or public settings and stopping people on foot has resulted in rooting out a significant amount of criminal behavior, as we have seen in the Port Authority case and in New York after the Diallo shooting. What has been discovered is not that racial profiling serves no purpose in fighting crime. It was instead found that concentrating on blacks in fighting crime via the particular method of highway pullovers was inappropriate, and thankfully, the practice was condemned and changed (this in itself yet one more instance of the ebbing of racism in American institutions).

This is hardly to say that there are not times when the police have overstepped their bounds in profiling black people on foot, as in a notorious case when middle-class black boys were arrested at a shopping mall clothing store for shoplifting when one was wearing a shirt he had bought there previously. But cases like these are individual ones; it has not been shown, for example, that concentrating on young black men in intercepting drugs on the street in North Philadelphia turns up no more contraband than if people were stopped randomly. There will always be some bad cops—there are bad black people and good black people, bad white people and good white people. Life isn't perfect. But just as one black person's bad conduct cannot be interpreted as an indictment of the race as a whole, isolated incidents of excess from whites cannot be taken as evidence that a whole system is racist. Only the *prevalence* of excess could be interpreted this way, and as we have seen, 99 percent of the people caught carrying drugs at Port Authority were minorities, and black-on-black crime went up immediately in the districts of New York City where officers relaxed their patrols after Amadou Diallo's death.

Significantly, even in the case of these excesses, progress is being made. As the ebbing of racism would lead us to predict, we are in fact getting ever closer to the hypothetical ideal police forces mentioned at the outset of this section. Tragedies have a way of forging change. In the wake of the Diallo tragedy Mayor Giuliani, while not exactly a model of tact in his public statements, submitted the police force to sensitivity training and replaced fifty members of the 380-man Street Crimes Unit with minorities. In a similar crackdown effort in Boston a few years before, events had never even reached a point of crisis. The police certainly focused on minorities in their searches, but also forged links with inner-city communities and trained officers in restraint and cultural sensitivity. Such things are concrete evidence that stop-and-frisks are yet one more realm where racism is abating. It would be quite impossible for anyone surveying the national scene on this score in the year 2000 to construct even a tentative case that in this area racism is holding firm, and to show that it was getting worse would be utterly hopeless.

Yet at the end of the day, it must always be remembered that even though blacks do commit more crimes than whites, most blacks *don't* commit crimes. Our goal must be that those detained be treated with the utmost of respect, with not the slightest assumption of guilt without just cause. However, to detain more black people than white in many neighborhoods and settings is sadly nothing less than necessary, because black people commit proportionately more crimes than whites.

This is particularly important given that we often lose sight of the fact that the criminals in question mostly ravage the lives of *other black people*. Unfortunately but urgently, crack is likely to have a nastier effect on demoralized inner-city residents (and their children and the younger siblings who look to them as models) than on the affluent investment banker on Wall Street who likes to snort up before a party. What this means is that current realities are such that, *unless we approve of drugs making their way into inner-city black lives,* in certain neighborhoods young black men must be checked more often than their white equivalents. They must be treated with the utmost civility when stopped, because indeed a great many, even most, of them will turn out to be innocent. But to refrain from stopping them at all is to put more black lives at risk. To eliminate profiling entirely would be to deprive not as much white as *black* people of their right to as much protection as possible from the depredations of criminals. To ignore this is to unintentionally turn a cold shoulder to true suffering.

Maybe I sound a little callous here, and the reader might be wondering "Has it happened to him?" Well, yes, I do have my story, although not one as unpleasant as many black men have. One night at about 1:00 A.M. I was walking to a convenience store. I was dressed not in my usual Gap/khaki clothes but in jeans, sneakers, and a short-sleeved button-down shirt open over a T-shirt, with my hands in my pockets; I had a few days' worth of stubble. I crossed a two-lane street far from the traffic light or crosswalk, and when I saw a car coming at about twenty-five yards away I broke into a quick trot to get across before it got to where I was (I am a Northeastern city-bred street crosser, and must admit that I do tend to be rather independent in crossing the street, especially at one in the morning).

I hadn't realized that the car was a police car, and the officer quickly turned on the siren, made a screeching U-turn, and pulled up to me on the other side of the street. The window rolled down, revealing a white man who would have been played by Danny Aiello if it had been a movie. "You always cross streets whenever you feel like it like that?" he sneered. "I'm sorry, officer," I said. "I wasn't thinking." "Even in front of a police car?" he growled threateningly. My stomach jumped, and I realized that at that moment, despite being a tenured professor at an elite university, to this man I was a black street thug, a "youth." I simply cannot imagine him stopping like this if a white man of the same age in the same clothes with the same stubble had done the exact same thing; he was trawling through a neighborhood which, unfortunately, does sometimes harbor a certain amount of questionable behavior by young black men on that street at that time of night, and to him, the color of my skin rendered me a suspect. I explained again as calmly as I could that I had meant no disrespect. I frankly suspect that the educated tone of my voice, so often an inconvenience in my life, was part of what made him pull off—"Not the type," he was probably thinking. But if I had answered in a black-inflected voice with the subtle mannerisms that distinguish one as "street," the encounter would quite possibly have gone on longer and maybe even gotten ugly. He pulled off, and left me shaken and violated.

I cannot say, however, that I walked away from that episode furious that I had just been swiped by the long arm of white racism eternally tainting all black lives. I felt that what had happened was a sign that the black underclass is America's greatest injustice, and that I ought take it as a call to action to do as much as I can to help rescue the underclass so that such encounters with the police won't be necessary. Yes, *necessary*—because under current conditions, whether we like it or not, they are. If I had gotten *beaten up* by that officer and his partner, then I would have felt different—see the next section. But while we can certainly trim the excesses—such as the highway stops—if we complain about being singled out *at all* in such searches without offering any alternative strategy, we are giving in to victimhood—not only ours but that of the increased number of minorities killed in New York after the Diallo incident—rather than working to eradicate it.

## Article of Faith Number Seven: Police Brutality Against Black People Reveals the Eternity of Racism

Police brutality is the only issue out of all of the ones the Articles of Faith concern which does demonstrate racism. The disproportionate police brutality against minorities is not a myth, nor is it a sad but inevitable by-product of historical inequities like the crack and stop-and-frisk issues are. There was no excuse for Amadou Diallo's death. There was no excuse for Haitian immigrant Abner Louima having a plunger stick shoved up his rectum in New York. Rodney King was no saint, being drunk and quite belligerent when stopped by police officers in Los Angeles, but the savageness with which the officers beat him into submission went far beyond necessity and revealed, on videotape for all to see, primitive barbarity in the name of detention. The transparent antiblack fervor that the Los Angeles Police Department had barely bothered to conceal over the decades also made it clear that a white belligerent drunk would have been much less likely to suffer the same treatment.

Thus there is no question that police brutality is racism. However, my point in this chapter is not whether or not racism exists; we all know it does. My point is whether or not it is gradually disappearing. In this light, police brutality is not a demonstration that, as Derrick Bell has it, "slavery refuses to fade."

The traditional view of police brutality is that it is "one more thing" showing that racism reigns as strongly as it did in 1950. However, as we have seen, blacks have made great strides in all areas of American life, blacks are part of the American social fabric to a degree unthinkable forty years ago, most black people are not poor, black people are not paid less for the same work than whites, there is no epidemic of black church burnings, the CIA did not funnel crack into South Central, black men are not sent to prison out of proportion to the crimes they commit, and black people are not stopped for drug checks out of proportion to their participation in the drug trade. Clearly these things mean something, even if the reader disagrees with a point or two.

In that light, police brutality is not "one more thing"—it is the *last* thing—or even if you disagree with one or two of my points, one of the last things.

Importantly, police brutality is exactly what one would expect the last major type of racism to be, and as such, is one more demonstration that racism is on its way out, not holding firm. Most police officers are working-class people from tight-knit communities, of modest education. As Orlando Patterson notes in *The Ordeal of Integration,* these are just the white people most likely to retain a degree of racism now all but absent at "the parties Shelby Steele is at" and in most of American society, the kinds of people who would make me uneasy walking through a white working-class neighborhood in the "Great Northeast" region of my hometown of Philadelphia at night. Furthermore, the nature of police work brings out the mob mentality, making the police behave more violently and impulsively than they might otherwise.

Yet the tendency among a great many is to view the tape of Rodney King and think "the only difference between them and all white people is the uniforms." This tendency, however, is based on the Articles of Faith, and therefore does not square with modern reality. If those officers really did represent white America as a whole, then we can be sure that a lot more than one in four black people would be poor, that interracial couples would still be a beleaguered oddity, that there really would be an epidemic of racist church burnings—in other words, it would be 1960. We need be under no impression that white America would not be capable of keeping us in that state, because after all, it did for 350 years.

What happened to Rodney King, like what happened to Mumia Abu-Jamal, is not the state of the art—it is a remnant. We could predict, in other words, that racism would make its last stand. That racism is a minor factor just about everywhere in American society except among such undereducated, parochial churls is, in itself, one more proof that it is on its way out in America. When a house burns down, often the only thing left standing is the chimney, whose materials resist burning. Often one has to go break up the chimney by hand before clearing the site and building a new house. Yet no one takes the chimney as evidence that the house didn't burn down, and certainly not as a sign that the house is on its way to reconstituting itself. In fact, a standing chimney surrounded by wreckage is, in itself, an indication that the house burned down.

Some might reject the chimney analogy and object that police brutality signals not the end of racism, but just a way of expressing it eternally when other channels have been closed—"if they have to pay us, live near us, eat with us, and hire us, then they're gonna make damned sure they can at least beat the hell out of us whenever they feel like it." This is a tempting notion, but in fact, police brutality, like all other racism in America, is *on the wane*.

Our tendency, for example, is to freeze in time the LAPD that caught Rodney King. This, however, was almost ten years ago by the time you read this, and by the mid-nineties, the LAPD had cleaned up its act in response to the harsh glare of world opprobrium that the King episode focused upon it. Racist police chief Daryl Gates is history. In 1996, the department was no fewer than 53 percent women and minorities, and 15 percent of the police officers were black (a higher proportion than blacks even represent in Los Angeles as a whole). Police brutality and bias complaints are increasingly rare; a 1998 survey by the U.S. Justice Department found that 82 percent of Los Angeles black people are satisfied with the police force. The claim that racism is *not* on the wane would predict that the LAPD today would be business as usual, with the status quo returning as soon as the news trucks packed up and went home. But that prediction is not borne out. Instead, Rodney King's beating and the officers' exoneration were so appalling to the American public that the department was completely overhauled, despite having for decades been virtually unaccountable to the municipal government by the dictates of the city's constitution. The officers who beat Rodney King got off—life isn't perfect—but the LAPD was never the same again. Even as I write this, the department is still revisiting evidence of injustices of the past to redress them where possible—this was not happening in 1991.

On the subject of New York, as I write this, the assault there on police brutality is proceeding so briskly that it continually outstrips my ability to submit a final draft of this chapter. When Officer Justin Volpe beat Haitian immigrant Abner Louima and then sodomized him with a broomstick and held the stick to his face, Volpe claimed innocence and assumed, along with racism-forever advocates, that the traditional blue wall of silence would protect him from punishment. Yet once again the facts went against Derrick Bell and Ralph Wiley's smug fatalism. One by one, officers came forward at Volpe's trial and confirmed what Volpe had done so incontestably that he was forced to take the stand and plead guilty in sniveling humiliation; he was sentenced to thirty years in prison. One would search the news archives in vain for a similar scenario—the times are changing. Even Volpe himself, in all of his ignominy, presented a more nuanced picture of the state of race relations than one might expect. On the one hand, one cannot help suspecting that he would not have treated a fellow white Staten Islander, or any white person, so brutally. On the other hand, Volpe, born not in 1947 but 1972, was engaged to a black woman.

The battle surely is not won yet. But today's events must be seen in historical perspective. In 1953, Congressman Adam Clayton Powell, Jr. launched a major effort to expose police brutality against black people in New York City, but even one of the most brilliant and effective Civil Rights legislators in American history, at the very top of his game, couldn't break down the blue wall of silence. Clearly, it is significant that today there are stories like Los Angeles, Boston, and New York.

Police brutality against minorities has not evaporated; however, it is on the wane, fast, and most important, there is no other manifestation of racism left in this society that even approaches it in force or spread. Police brutality is a fact, but it is not evidence that racism overall is impregnable, and therefore does not make Pollyannas of the increasing numbers of people noting that so much of the news in black America is good.

## Transition Versus Backslide

In 1992, I saw Spike Lee's *Malcolm X* with a college student born in the Czech Republic. After the movie, she said to me, "I can see how bad it was for black people years ago. But now they're in the schools, they can go anywhere they want, they can have any job they want, and it's practically illegal to say anything bad about them in public. So what's the problem?"

Obviously the question is naive, stemming from her status as a partial outsider to American culture. She knew little of ghettos, and it would have taken an afternoon to explain to her the subtle forms that racism can take even in the absence of signs on water fountains.

Nevertheless, it is significant that forty years ago a Czech who had been in America for a week would not have had to ask that question, even in the North. Whites, privately haunted by more informed versions of the Czech's question, but cowed by the insistence of so many black people that the country is still a racist war zone, tend to assume that there are things that they will simply "never know," and blacks tend to support them in that feeling. Yet most of what blacks assume whites "don't know" is founded upon seven Articles of Faith which are all either outright myths or distorted readings of historically based discrepancies, none of which give any indication that racism is unchanged, and certainly not that it is back on the rise.

Thus my point is not that bad things are not still happening; all one has to do is open a newspaper to see that this would not correspond with reality. Yet the popular stance, reigning from the Halls of Ivy down through boardrooms, barbershops, and barrooms, that nothing has changed or that things are getting worse does not correspond with reality either.

Neither mired in 1960 nor on the mountaintop yet, African Americans are currently in a state of *transition*. In a transition between one phase and another, there will inevitably be transitional points. "When do you want freedom for your people?" Ruth Buzzi asked black Johnny Brown (later better known as Bookman the janitor on *Good Times*) in a blackout sequence on *Laugh-In* in the late 1960s. "Now would be fine!"

Brown quickly answered. But this was a *joke:* how could racism have possibly vanished the morning after the signing of the Civil Rights Act of 1964? Because we are at a point of transition, nasty episodes, although occurring more often, are nothing less than inevitable, such as the dragging death in Jasper, Texas, of James Byrd in 1998. These things must be identified, condemned, and stamped out. That is what we are doing: For example, Byrd's killer was swiftly apprehended and convicted, with whites from Jasper, traditionally thought to be a bigoted backwater, joining the Byrds and the Jasper black community in mourning Byrd's death. One would die searching newspapers before roughly 1970 describing any such scene.

There are no logical grounds whatsoever for reading any of these increasingly occasional glitches as a slide backwards, as so many seem so inclined, even eager, to do. After an hour in the freezer, a glass of water will still contain some unfrozen pockets, but we do not decide on this basis that it will never freeze, and certainly do not watch it get harder by the hour and yet complain that it is on its way back to water. If someone puts down mothballs in a closet swarming with moths, if he encounters a couple of stray moths in the closet three days later, he does not claim that mothballs do not work. Yellow passes through green to become blue, but if someone held up a blue-green Crayola crayon and told us it was "yellow" despite its appearances, we would suspect some perceptual disorder. In the same way, the professional pessimism maintained by so many African Americans in the face of a miraculous social revolution has fallen so starkly out of sync with reality that it reveals itself to have become a self-perpetuating cancer. As cancer eats away healthy tissue, this Victimology cult, obsessed with what the Man did last week, expends energy that would be better devoted to moving ahead and figuring out what we are going to do next week.

## The Roots of the Plague

Why has this mode of thought become common coin in black America? Contrary to appearances, the cause is not simply a sorry case of arrant self-righteousness. Much of it is traceable, ironically, to something miraculous, the forced desegregation of the United States in the 1960s. It is historically unprecedented that a disenfranchised group effected an overhaul of its nation's legal system to rapidly abolish centuries of legalized discrimination. The country as a whole can congratulate itself on this.

One result was that a context was set up in which black Americans were free to confront whites with their indignation and frustration on a regular basis and be listened to—Jews, the Irish, turn-of-the-century Asian immigrants, and other formerly disenfranchised groups never experienced such a stage in their journey to equality. White Americans have surely learned some long-needed lessons from the endless harangues they have had to suffer at our hands over the past forty years. I grew up watching my mother, who had participated in sit-ins in segregated Atlanta, taking active part in this throughout the 1970s and 1980s as a professor of social work at Temple University in Philadelphia, and I'm glad she did it. Time and again I recall her abruptly wrenching conversations in a direction that revealed to a forty-something pants-suit-clad white woman or sideburned white man the racist feelings underlying their seemingly innocent ideas. Sometimes she overdid it, I thought, but life isn't perfect; even if some of these people privately got a little tired of Mom, they also learned.

Where this mindset has become a problem is in combination with something else: Centuries of abasement and marginalization led African Americans to internalize the way they were perceived by the larger society, resulting in a postcolonial inferiority complex. After centuries of degradation, it would have been astounding if African Americans had *not* inherited one, and thinkers such as Frantz Fanon, Kenneth Clark, and Gordon Allport have eloquently testified to its tragic potency.

We do not want to think about this, or at least, I certainly don't. But one of countless ways it reveals itself immediately is in the battle cry "You're still black!" often hurled at African Americans who appear to question their membership in the group for one reason or another. The implausibility of a Jew telling an assimilated child or acquaintance "You're still Jewish!" points up the heart of "You're still black!" The statement implies that being black is in some fundamental way a stain, incommensurate with the hubris perceived in the addressee, and the fury in the delivery makes this even clearer. The black person who, for one reason or another, sheds cultural blackness is viewed with ire in the black community because it is automatically assumed that the person considers herself not simply different from, but *better than*, black people. The Jewish person who sheds cultural Jewishness, on the other hand, is not looked upon fondly by many more conservative Jews, but more out of fear of the disappearance of the race via intermarriage than out of a sense that the strayer might consider herself *better than* Jews.

Another indication that black America suffers a deep-reaching inferiority complex is the oft-heard defense of affirmative action in universities on the basis that children of alumni and white top-ranking athletes have always been let in under the bar. Five o'clock scholar legacy students and thick-tongued athletes like Moose in *Archie* comic books have always been held in distinctly bad odor. The comfort with which black admininstrators, professors, and students compare all-black student bodies to people who have always been a campus joke reveals a fundamentally low sense of self-esteem. Once again, note how difficult it is to imagine a rabbi defending affirmative action for Jewish students by drawing such a parallel, even seventy years ago when Jews were still an overtly persecuted group in this country.

Victimology stems from a lethal combination of this inherited inferiority complex with the privilege of dressing down the former oppressor. Encouraged to voice umbrage on one hand, and on the other hand haunted by the former oppressor's lie that black is bad, many African Americans have fallen into a holding pattern of wielding self-righteous indignation less as a spur to action than as a self-standing action in itself because it detracts attention from the inadequacies we perceive in ourselves by highlighting those of the other. An analogy, partial but useful, is the classroom tattle-tale. We all remember this kid, ostensibly committed to keeping everything on the straight and narrow, just as Victimologist blacks are ostensibly committed to rooting out injustice. However, we all knew that the tattle-tale was ultimately motivated less by a desire to improve student conduct than by personal insecurities, especially since the ills he pointed out were almost always minor ones that weren't hurting anybody ("Mrs. Montgomery, Jeffrey is licking the eraser again!"). The analogy with our Derrick Bells, depicting black American life as an apocalyptic nightmare when except for the quarter who are poor, it would, warts and all, be the envy of most people on the planet, is plain. What motivates people like this to keep screaming "Nooo" amidst such a glorious revolution is, at heart, insecurity.

My debt here to Shelby Steele's *The Content of Our Character* is obvious. Because Steele's ideas question the Victimologist mantra that racism is a significant barrier to black achievement, few blacks of any stripe have ever given them any serious thought. Yet they are absolutely key to understanding and getting beyond an America in which views like Derrick Bell's are accepted as a respectable point of view and taught to bright young African Americans as truth.

Steele tends to mostly "preach to the choir" partly because he seems to assume that the falsity of the Articles of Faith is too obvious to merit discussion, and perhaps also because of a sense one gets from his writings that blacks have nothing at all left to complain about. I in no way mean to imply that we need not sound the alarm, and loudly, at remaining strands of racism. However, when the whistle is frozen at a shrieking level while the conditions that set it off recede ever more each year, it becomes clear that what began as a response has become more of a tic, endlessly retracing the same cycle like a tripped-off car alarm. This cycle is driven not by the mythical America writers like Bell, Wiley, and Cose have created, but by a culturally based insecurity. Only insecurity could make a race downplay and detract attention from its victories, carefully shielding its children from the good in favor of the bad. Black America today is analogous to a wonderful person prevented by insecurity from seeing the good in themselves. Insecurity has sad, masochistic effects—the talented actor who abuses drugs and dies early; the bright, beautiful woman who finds herself only able to develop romantic attraction to heartless men; the brilliant first-time novelist who never manages a second novel out of fear of failure; the race driven by self-hate and fear to spend more time inventing reasons to cry "racism" than working to be the best that it can be. Victimology, in a word, is a disease.

## The Ironic Joys of Underdoggism

One thing showing that the apocalyptic vision of whites black Americans tend to maintain has lost its moorings in reality is its discrepancy with fact. Another indication is something so common that it is rarely remarked: the fact that many black people decrying their supposed victimhood do so with joy rather than the despair one would expect.

The Reverend Al Sharpton is a useful illustration. Here is an excerpt from *The New York Times* shortly after the murder of Amadou Diallo:

> Just before the evening news the other night, the parents of Amadou Diallo, the West African street vendor shot dead by plainclothes police officers last week, walked up to microphones to offer their first extended public remarks about the death of their son. The setting was a second-floor auditorium up a scuffed flight of steps in Harlem. And the host, wearing a crisp, gray three-piece suit and clearly enjoying this latest bustle at his Harlem headquarters, was the Rev. Al Sharpton.

But wait a minute. A man has just been killed and his bereaved parents just stepped up to the microphones. Why is Sharpton enjoying himself? The reporter was not a racist subtly slurring Sharpton—all of us are familiar with the air of exuberance about Sharpton each time something like this happens. The reason is that he *delights* in this kind of thing. Wouldn't a genuine response to victimhood be indignation? Wouldn't we expect especially a reverend to be consumed with remorse about such a tragic death? But no—Sharpton, as always, reveled in the cheap thrills of getting to stick it to whitey one more time by cloaking blacks as eternal victims and whites as the eternal oppressor.

We are so used to demeanors like Sharpton's that we forget that his is not the only way. For example, we did not see this swagger, this theatrical brightness of the eyes, in Martin Luther King. King was not having a good time, he was forging a revolution out of tragedy. Sharpton is having parties, and is, ironically, one more indication of how much better things have gotten. Before 1970, because there was so much achingly real work to be done, any Civil Rights leader without *gravitas* would have seemed too callow to even consider. Sharpton—a Civil Rights leader delighting in the murder of an innocent black man in cold blood—is possible *because* so much progress has been made that anyone who insists on pretending it's 1910 has to be a cartoon, to exaggerate, to spend years sporting James Brown's campy hairstyle—in other words, to be an actor. Significantly, you will look in vain for any cartoons like Sharpton among black leaders before 1970. Theatricality is one thing: Marcus Garvey had his outfits, Adam Clayton Powell liked to travel in style and was no stranger to twitting the white man for the fun of it. But these men had serious messages and concrete contributions to their credit; all Sharpton does is pose and scream.

Yet this pathologically misplaced joy goes far beyond politicians, percolating deep into the black community. I recall a decidedly Afrocentric schoolteacher describing to a group her life thus far as a litany of discrimination and marginalization because of her color. I cannot speak for the validity of her interpretations of all of these events. What I could not help noting, however, was that all of this was delivered with a beatific smile. One would naturally expect someone who had truly suffered to register pain and resentment—refugees from the Soviet Union and battered wives do not tell their stories with a grin. One does not delight in the noose around one's neck or the fire on one's skin. The only possible explanation for someone deriving pleasure from victimhood, besides outright sadomasochism, is if the victimhood addresses a lack inside of them. Because being the underdog confers a sense of moral absolution, we know what lack victimhood is addressing in people like this—it is serving as a balm for insecurity. What this woman reminded me of was not a Holocaust survivor but our classroom tattle-tale, who betrays that his motivation is less uplift than personal absolution by the glee with which he reports the torts of others.

Most important, though, a "victimhood" that one can smile through does not deserve the name. Black people do not grin as they narrate true suffering. A family driven from a new home by racist neighbors does not smile as they talk about it. A black woman denied partnership in a law firm after years of top-quality service because she never became "one of the boys" does not smile as she files a suit. The Cult of Victimology has forced people like this schoolteacher into wearing victimhood like a badge and reveling in it for the joys of underdoggism that it brings. There is a certain seductive charisma in this—this woman could definitely hold a crowd   but it has nothing to do with moving the race forward.

## Two Misconceptions About Victimology

It is not news for many people that a defeatist, paranoid attitude toward whites is not exactly the best recipe for moving the black race forward. However, Victimology is generally parochialized in one of two directions, under the impression that the problem is much less profound than it is.

### An Inner-City Pathology?

For example, many are under the impression that this is an inner-city affair, typified by students dropping out of high school under the assumption that they will not be accepted in the white world. To conceive of Victimology this way, however, misses not just some but most of what this thought pattern constitutes. Only one in five black people live in ghettos, while Victimology is just as prevalent among educated people with ample opportunities.

It's sad enough, for example, that in one poll 18 percent of black high-school graduates thought the U.S. government channeled drugs into poor black neighborhoods while 24 percent thought it might be true. But then 29 percent of black college graduates pegged it as true while 38 percent more thought it might be true—in other words, 67 percent of black college graduates consider Article of Faith Number Four "an issue." This would not surprise anyone with a modicum of experience with black college students, among whom an awareness of pseudofacts and cooked statistics of this kind—i.e., the Articles of Faith—is unofficially considered a vital part of a black person's higher education (*Higher*

*Learning* was the title of John Singleton's 1994 film about a race war on a college campus). Outright belief in such things is more typical of the uneducated, but most black college students consider such things at least up for discussion, making clear their sense of the health of racism in America.

Victimology is also a dominant strain of black academic work, far from the streets up in the Ivory Tower. For example, many of us might see Danny Glover's ubiquity in buddy pictures with white men as a sign of progress in race relations. But for Hazel Carby in *Race Men,* Glover's crossover signifies "the exploitative and oppressive nature" of Hollywood, where Glover is used to "expel the black presence" and is bound in a homoerotic relationship with Mel Gibson in their movies together. Carby is no marginal crank; her views of this sort have been rewarded with the chairship of Yale's African-American Studies Department. Yet obviously she could find racism in Glover's career no matter what kinds of films he made, because her central aim is less constructive thought than simply crying "racism" at all costs.

### *"Identity Politics"?*

The other parochialization of Victimology parses it as a political ploy cynically wielded by blacks in high positions to curry power. Shelby Steele's *The Content of Our Character* was a formative experience for me on the level that *The Autobiography of Malcolm X* has been for so many other blacks, articulately and bravely expressing feelings of mine that had been pent up since childhood. However, I depart from Steele's analysis of Victimology as a conscious manipulation strategy: I see it as a subconscious psychological gangrene. But Steele's view corresponds with that of many leftist intellectuals, some under the influence of thinkers like Michel Foucault, who see history as determined by power relations. Making use of the principle "the cultural becomes political," they often cheer on the likes of Al Sharpton and Maxine Waters. Their analysis of Victimology as utilitarian also alleviates the discomfort that illogical, underinformed Victimologist arguments cannot help stir up even in whites deeply committed to justice: "Deep down Derrick Bell must be exaggerating to make a point."

This makes Victimology analogous to the secession movement in Quebec, in which many Quebecers privately admit that they are only using the threat of secession as a way of currying power within the Canadian federation. There is some of this among blacks. Al Sharpton quite explicitly rouses the rabble with the intent of scaring the white man into concessions: "Confrontation works," as he admitted to Tamar Jacoby. But this is merely the tip of the iceberg. Drawing an analogy between black America and Quebec has two incorrect implications: 1) that Victimology is a conscious stunt, and (2) that Victimology is primarily limited to black people in power. But Victimology is not a spectator sport, it's a cultural tragedy.

## Subconscious Influence

For one, Victimology is not at all conscious. Instead, it leaves its prey unable to even conceive of ways of looking at race issues outside of the Victimologist box. Most such people are under the impression that they are open to a wide range of views, but in practice assume that a "new view" will present a new way of indicting whitey. To be sure, one hears calls for blacks to "help themselves," but almost never with concrete suggestions beyond calls for "community," and only as a backhanded slap at whitey, assumed to have no interest in helping blacks, despite welfare, affirmative action, and decades of enough federal aid to turn Zimbabwe into Brunei.

This dwelling upon a mere subset of possible views is not deliberate; black culture puts a mental block on even conceiving that other views might have any validity. The black person who takes issue with the basic assumption that white racism is omnipresent in all black lives is met with the torrid indignation rained elsewhere upon the Holocaust denier. The messenger is not seen as "out of the box"—because there is no "box" perceived—but out of their head.

Many blacks under the sway of this kind of thinking are outwardly "reasonable," but because Victimology infects the subconscious, it renders them incapable of being open to all sides, or even capable of perceiving most of the sides. A great many sufferers will admit, with a pause and a game swallow, that overall things are somewhat better for black people than they used to be. All too often, however, on this topic they are open even to civil dialogue only to a point. This point is passed the millisecond one suggests that it may no longer be appropriate to view white America as an enemy, at which time one is met with an incredulous scorn and summarily dismissed as evil incarnate. The tripwire alacrity of the transformation often reminds me of a friendly dog licking your hand one minute and then thirty seconds later growling when you pat him while he's eating. Like the dog's growling, Victimologist rancor is too deeply conditioned to reach or reason with. Some dogs can be trained not to growl when you pat them while they're eating, but the training only masks underlying reality; you can always tell the dog still wants to growl as it stops eating and tenses its shoulders. In the same way, there are some black people who make their best effort not to "go off" in discussions with someone who questions the going wisdom. However, there is always the glint in the eye, the tightened posture, the scornful facial tics, and finally the fact that after this conversation the person is closed to any further exchange beyond civil acknowledgment. Importantly, this response is too real to be a canny put-on.

More precisely, such opinions are considered so logically baseless that it is widely assumed that a black person could only espouse them out of opportunism. Put another way, such views are so utterly unimaginable to many blacks that it is simply beyond their conception that a black person could genuinely believe them, just as we would assume that a sane person insisting the sky was fuschia had an ulterior motive and was most likely being directed by someone else. Here, for example, is Christopher Edley, a black law professor at Harvard: "I could get an enormous amount of print from the *Wall Street Journal* or *The New Republic* if I decided to attack affirmative action and repudiate mainstream civil-rights positions, and I think there's no shortage of people who have been seduced by the glitter." Such a blithe dismissal of the legitimacy of differing opinions is unexpected from someone trained in the law—unless he is a black American, because Victimology blinds the sufferer to any perspective outside of the Victimologist box.

## Beyond the Corridors of Power

Edley, though, has one foot in politics, having served, for example, as top consultant to President Clinton's "Dialogue on Race." This brings us to the power issue. If Victimology were just politics, then presumably academics would chastise the likes of Edley or at least identify their behavior as a ruse. But listen to revered African-American historian John Hope Franklin on the same subject:

> You always have such people in any group . . . I suspect they may be Judases of a kind . . . betrayers, opportunists, immoral opportunists. It's very tempting, I suppose, for people of weak character to be co-opted by the majority that can use them. They are rewarded in one way or another. If not on the Supreme Court, then some other way. So many people have a

price, and it's not unusual, it's not surprising. Some blacks
have a price. It's just tragic when anyone sells themselves out.

With all due respect for Professor Franklin's legacy, this is vicious,
barely processible as coming from an academic, i.e., a high priest of
meticulously rational analysis. Imagine Arthur Schlesinger or Daniel
Boorstin casually deeming anyone a "Judas" for a sociopolitical opinion—except perhaps, notably, a Holocaust denier. Yet Franklin's life, that
of a low-key historian, has not been a quest for power. He holds these
views not out of a cynical attempt to hold whitey hostage, but because
he really believes them. In his mind as in so many, the persistence of
racism as an oppressive plague truly is as unequivocal as the Holocaust. This brings us back to the "reasonable" people who nevertheless
cannot hear anything but Victimology without shutting down—ex-
changes with people like this are as likely at a backyard barbecue as at
a Black Nationalist rally. Victimology infects our whole culture, not
just the power seekers.

Spike Lee neatly illustrates all of this in a scene from *Get on the Bus*
(1996). In a busful of black men on their way to the Million Man March,
Lee includes a wide range of views: One man's girlfriend chews him out
for attending a march that excludes women, two of the men are a gay couple, and one of them is even a Republican. However, Lee is ultimately
constrained by the Victimologist box. One small-time entrepreneur boards
and airs his view that black people simply need to pull themselves up by
their own bootstraps—in other words, he does not subscribe to Victimologist thinking. When I first saw the film, after he had said about four
lines I was waiting to see how long it was going to take for Lee to bodily
hurl this man off the bus, and that is just what happens. Talk about
stereotypes: Lee makes sure to make this "Shelbysteele" as repulsive a
character as possible. He is only attending the march because it will be a
captive crowd to sell his wares to; he is played by a plain, rather squat actor, contrasting with the good-looking ones playing the principal roles; he
expresses his views in a grandstanding, mocking manner that would make
any message offensive; and unlike most "black conservatives," he lacks
compassion for the minority of blacks who are truly suffering. Finally, he
is shown grinning maniacally as he is thrown from the bus—which shows
that anyone who has such beliefs must be a self-hating lunatic. As always,
Lee is brilliant (one of my three favorite directors), but Victimology suf-
fuses much of his work, with whites usually treated from a wary and dismissive us-vs.-them perspective. Nor does Lee express this view to gain
political leverage; his interviews make it clear that this is his genuine

worldview, not canny "operating." That scene in *Get on the Bus* reflects a strong current in black culture as a whole: the men throwing the apostate off the bus are not acting for Al Sharpton and Maxine Waters; they are acting from deeply felt personal feeling.

Indeed, Victimology is felt like religion. Hell hath no fury like an African American who has judged another one as co-opted by whitey, and I can affirm what I have heard from several young black Americans with a sincere interest in integration and getting past America's heritage of interracial warfare, which is that any antagonism encountered about once a year from whites on the basis of our color is vastly dwarfed by the white-hot, proudly unreasoning fury we must learn to cope with on a regular basis from African Americans of all walks of life in any discussion of race issues. If Victimology were simply a disease of politicians, university administrators, and other people courting power, this would be at the margins of our lives, not part of its fabric.

Thus to think of Victimology as only inner-city defeatism, as only Al Sharpton, even as only both, is like thinking of "sexuality" as only procreation, "cars" as only Nissan Sentras. Victimology is today nothing less than a keystone of cultural blackness.

## Passing On the Torch: Black and White

Part of the reason many associate Victimology with the inner city or with political chicanery is a natural supposition that such views must either have a concrete basis—genuine disenfranchisement—or at least a proactive motivation—cynical powermongering. Yet because it is a cultural keystone, Victimology, like religion or bigotry, is now passed from one generation to another regardless of external circumstances, and as we have seen, the vast majority of blacks have no stake in utilizing it as a political strategy.

Victimology is understandable, if still pernicious, in people who came of age in segregated America, even its later years. In 1997 a middle-aged black schoolteacher once told me to write one of my books "talking to us—because they only listen to us when they think they're eavesdropping." That assessment does not remotely reflect the world I live in, where whites are rather obsessed with listening to us, but then they most certainly were not before the late 1960s. It is only human to be imprinted permanently by formative experiences.

Not long ago, I contracted to perform two plays with a mainstream theater company. In the first play, I was cast in a dull, thankless, underwritten part, which I lacked the acting ability to flesh out. Although I usually get along well with theater people, even before rehearsals it became clear that I was not the director and stage manager's cup of tea, for reasons that had nothing to do with racism. The backstage cast chemistry was all but nil. Having to perform a dull part badly where I was not wanted night after night left me bitter, but I was stuck doing the next show. This one, however, was a joy: I had a dandy character role that fit me well enough that I did a decent job in it; I got to do a solo on the ocarina ("sweet potato") of all things; this show had a different stage manager I got along fine with; the cast was a lovefest. The only major thing the show had in common with the previous one was the director, but I had little contact with him after the run started.

Yet every night driving to the theater to do this second show, I had to fight back a primal tendency to curse the production company despite how much fun I was having. To this day I associate the company with marginalization and discomfort, and grumble internally a bit every time I drive by the theater. The first show was such a bad experience that even the wonderful weeks in the second one could not wash the bad taste out of my mouth. This human tendency is what led that teacher to say "They only listen when they think they're eavesdropping," and because he is elderly, it is also probably the source of John Hope Franklin's stance on racism.

But what are we to think of black *high schoolers* serenely convinced in the year 2000 that their lives are proscribed by racism, telling pollsters that they think the government sends drugs to Harlem and injects AIDS into black patients? Eighteen-year-olds in 2000 were born not in 1972 but 1982. They have only the haziest memories of Ronald Reagan's presidency, never saw one of the first three *Star Wars* movies in their first release, and think of *Cheers* as vintage television. They remember neither McDonald's food packed in Styrofoam nor *The Tonight Show* hosted by anyone but Jay Leno, and Atari is as antique to them as Pong is to us. By the time these children came of age, Colin Powell's tenure and the run of *The Cosby Show* were in the *past*, the statistics on pages 6 to 8 were already in effect, interracial couples were commonplace, and affirmative action was long established. I have stopped mentioning *Roots* when I lecture to undergraduates today, because they weren't born when it aired!

These children have never remotely known the world that spawned Victimology. Yet its clutches force them to conceive of themselves as victims regardless of their actual experiences. At Stanford University in the late 1980s, black undergraduates were surveyed as to whether they felt they were living on a racist campus. The survey was conducted in the wake of an incident in which two drunk white students living in the black theme house defaced a flyer for a talk on the possibility that Beethoven had black ancestry. They had made Beethoven's face on the flyer look black. Not the most gracious of pranks, but it was meant as a silly joke rather than a racist slur, and most of all, it was just one dopey little thing.

After this episode, though, most black students agreed that Stanford was a racist campus, but only 30 percent could report direct experience, and almost none of these could, or felt any need to, specify exactly what racist experiences they had had. Instead they reported that the racism was "subtle" and "hard to explain."

I was attending Stanford as a graduate student in the late 1980s and early 1990s. I participated in a lot of theater while there and sat in on a great many undergraduate classes, and so had years of extensive contact with undergraduates of all races. I can confidently report that the reason the black students polled had so much trouble quite "putting their finger" on the racism they had experienced was that they had experienced very little of it, in many cases none. Stanford students are absolutely marinated in racial sensitivity workshops and talks from the minute they hit campus, affirmative action is in full swing, and the "P.C." atmosphere typical of top universities heaps so much opprobrium upon any expression of any kind of "-ism" that only the very occasional jerk strays from the line. There is quite simply nothing more the university could do to work against racism on its campus; the Beethoven prank was an isolated but inevitable event, because Life Isn't Perfect.

If the systematic racism the black students sensed came from a perception that whites live in a separate world, this view was actively maintained less by the white community than the black, a great many of whom displayed a hostile wariness of white people. Most of the white students were baffled at the hostility of so many of the black students, but too censured by the P.C. climate to ever say so too loudly or allow themselves to think that they had done nothing to deserve it. Certainly some of the black students may have had the occasional passing experience in which racism played some part—I did once or twice, as I will discuss in Chapter 3. But to read these fleeting, isolated episodes as evidence that they were living in shackles—only somehow "subtle" shackles—is a massive and transparent exaggeration, stemming from a cultural virus having programmed them to come up with this output despite any input to the contrary.

Fear of this kind does not usually pass down the generations when its source disappears. Women who came of age before the Pill feared premarital sex because of unwanted pregnancy, but their children have naturally not inherited this fear. One thing that makes Victimology so easy to pass on is that the insecurity inherent in adolescence makes black teenagers particularly susceptible to a way of thinking that grants such easy absolution. Victimology *feels* good. In my teens and early twenties I espoused it wholeheartedly. When I was fifteen a high-school homeroom teacher made me sit separately from the other students because I had continued chatting with my friend in what I thought was a quiet voice despite her repeated requests that I stop. Embarrassed at having been singled out this way (in front of a girl I liked), I grumbled that she was putting me aside so that she could only see white faces in front of her—and worst of all addressed this sentiment to her daughter. It felt good at the time, but I still cringe thinking about it now. Racism had not a blessed thing to do with why she was trying to quiet my voice, which for better or for worse happens to be one of those that "carries," and the last thing that kind and enlightened teacher deserved was to be called a bigot. Victimology seduces young black people just like the crack trade seduces inner-city blacks, virtually irresistible in its offer of an easy road to self-esteem and some cheap thrills on the way.

Victimology is also kept alive, however, by whites, via a fashion of suspending intelligent disbelief in the face of rantings like Derrick Bell's, in favor of ascribing such melodramatic exaggeration to a vague "native wisdom." For example, every second month from 1989 to 1996 readers of the journal *The Progressive* were served up a column of Victimology *extraordinaire* by June Jordan, professor of African-American Studies at UC Berkeley. Most of these columns could only be described as festivals of hyperbole; here is a typical passage:

> Where I live now makes me wonder if Nazi Germany's night skies ever beheld a really big moon—a heavenly light that failed to dispel the cold and bitter winds tormenting the darkness of earth below.
>
> Where I live now there is just such a moon tonight—a useless, huge light above our perishing reasons for hope.

But otherwise, *The Progressive* is a bastion of carefully reasoned sociopolitical thought. Its editors published Jordan's melodramas because her, shall we say, creative approach to truth is considered "understandable" from a black writer.

The condescension in this approach is far more of an insult to black people than anything Jordan and others call insults. Some whites, consciously or unconsciously, classify black statements of this kind as being on some level "poetry," reminiscent of Derrick Bell couching his rantings as "stories." I recall this being one white undergraduate's entranced take on Jordan's contribution to a public forum on Ebonics, a truly brilliant fusion of Victimology, Separatism, and naked Anti-intellectualism in the name of educated insight. Jordan is in fact quite entertaining as a speaker, with an unerring instinct for trenchantly colorful illustrations and a ready chortle that somehow manages to be ingenuous and wise at the same time; much of this carries over into her writing. But blacks often complain that white America is only receptive to black people as entertainers and sports figures. There is an eerie parallel between this notion, obsolete Victimology though it is, and *The Progressive* printing Jordan's "understandable" temper tantrums in an otherwise serious journal.

Understandable indeed. There is a number in the musical *Chicago* when a woman who murdered her lover gives a transparently lame defense at a press conference. One of the reporters is an aunty, middle-aged female columnist known for sentimental defenses of the reviled, who like the rest of the press stands to profit from the notoriety of the sensational story. At one point the snappy, tightly choreographed number stops short for the reporter to glide stage center and sing "Understandable/Understandable/Yes, it's perfectly/Understandable, . . ." the song suddenly shifting to a parlor waltz tempo to underline the false sentiment at the heart of the message. Now joined by the murderess's cynical lawyer, she continues "Comprehensible/Comprehensible/Not a bit reprehensible/It's so defensible, . . ." the melody descending and the tempo slowing on the last line to evoke the "Poor babyyy! . . ." purse-lipped way we speak to a child or express mock sympathy. The depth of the reporter's insincerity is socked home when she turns out to be a female impersonator.

The way many whites today support black people in the fiction that persecution is their eternal fate always makes me think of this scene—even though most whites' patronization is neither as deliberate nor as bald as this reporter's. Every time a white person lifts her glass to a black person's Victimology, she is unwittingly contributing to the very interracial strife that she supposes herself to be against—because Victimology is not about change; it is all about nothing but itself.

Jordan, for instance, actually is a poet, and much of her work sets Victimology to verse. Her most recent collection, *Affirmative Acts,* includes a poem urging Berkeley students to rebel against the ban on affirmative action in admissions instituted as of 1998. Typical of Victimology, Jordan has since dared no rebellious acts to put her tenured position at risk, nor given anyone concrete directives as to how to accomplish such rebellion in her stead. Jordan wrote her poem and went out to dinner: the poem alone, underinformed, aimless complaint, was the sum and total of her "Affirmative Act." The above-quoted "Nazi Germany's night skies" passage from one of her columns was published in January 1995; yet in a column at the end of that very year she exulted, "Just now, I am awfully glad to live nowhere else but here: right here." How seriously, then, were we to take her "perishing reasons for hope" just eleven months before?

Business as usual. Victimology is neither about Acts nor even reality; it is, like a virus, about nothing but keeping itself alive. Whites have neither injected black people with AIDS nor injected the inner cities with crack, but in indulging Victimology out of a combination of guilt and thrill-seeking, white America is helping to spread a virus of a different kind among blacks in America.

## What's Wrong with Victimology?

In response to occasional "blacker-than-thou" charges that arise within the black community, it is often said that one need not display certain cultural traits to be "black"—one need not be a good dancer, wear dreadlocks, eat fried chicken, or even speak the dialect. Clearly, however, a black person culturally indistinguishable from a white person would indeed be considered "not black." What, then, is the essence of "black"? One sometime answer is "Being down with us," and that *down* is telling. A large part of being culturally black means operating under a fundamental assumption that all blacks are a persecuted race, still "down" at the bottom of Derrick Bell's well, forty years after the Civil Rights Act.

This is hardly to say that all black people are as strident and utterly impervious to reason as people like Bell, June Jordan, or leaders of the Nation of Islam. Victimology, like any virus, infects in degrees—it bypasses a few, leaves some bedridden, but leaves most with at least a persistent cough. The Nation of Islam's Louis Farrakhan, for instance, regularly plays to standing-room-only crowds when he speaks; in a Time/CNN poll, 70 percent of blacks said that Farrakhan has a message America should hear. But that message is the likes of "The God who taught me calls white men the skunks of the planet earth." Some say that most blacks only flock to Farrakhan as a sensationalist freak, rather like white teenagers going to concerts of bloodcurdling music by sociopathic rock stars. But the hundreds of thousands of men at the Million Man March did not give the impression of attending a side show, and Farrakhan's audiences regularly give full-throated ovations for his speeches, with no hint of the irony or heckling we would expect of people simply attracted to the fireworks. This man touches a chord even in very ordinary black people—the chord that encourages us to focus on and exaggerate victimhood.

Yet Victimology was not common coin among the black Americans who came before us, even experiencing an overt and omnipresent racism only the elderly remember today. Reading autobiographies and biographies of the Blacks in Wax, one is often struck by the lack of interest most of these people had in dwelling at any length upon their victimhood, despite being barred from hotels and restaurants, being called "boy" and "girl" by whites, and having most prestigious occupations all but closed to them outside of their own communities. Yet I doubt that anyone would accuse pioneer educator Mary MacLeod Bethune or inventor George Washington Carver of being oreos.

These people's low interest in airing grievance was partly because mainstream America was not yet interested in hearing it. It was also, however, because it was hopelessly clear that under conditions of true disenfranchisement and unclothed racism, to dwell upon victimhood rather than work against it would be defeatist, polluting spirits needed for concrete uplift. Adam Clayton Powell, Jr. (yes, he is my hero) and Martin Luther King did not pave the way for Derrick Bell and June Jordan's lives by merely standing around trying to outdo each other in articulate indignation. There is no logical reason why conditions today, so obviously so very much better than they were for our forebears, somehow call for Victimology where conditions for people two steps past slavery did not. Victimology is, ironically, *a luxury of widened opportunities;* if things were really as bad as we are so often told, natural human resilience would ensure that black people could not afford to caress and exaggerate victimhood—because real suffering would keep it from feeling good. Only when the victimhood one rails against is all but a phantom does one have the luxury of sitting back and enjoying the sweet balm of moral absolution undisturbed.

But in the end, one might ask, even if Victimology isn't the only way to be black, isn't it a good way? Even if things aren't as bad as they were in 1960, you can never watch your back too much, can you? Wouldn't Mary McLeod Bethune have been better off claiming that black students had been denied their due because they actually spoke an African language instead of English? Victimology is thought of as a kind of mental calisthenic in the black community, where "Know your history" is a mantra not directed at a quest for knowledge per se, but at knowing who did what to your ancestors and how badly, to make sure it doesn't happen again. In this light, isn't focusing on victimhood a matter of basic survival?

These are understandable questions, particularly from anyone under about forty-five. There is a theatrical rock concert thrill about Victimology that makes it addictive. However, all that glitters is not gold. The fact is that (1) Victimology would have *prevented* our forebears from turning the country upside down to make our lives possible, and (2) by nurturing Victimology today, Black America is shooting itself in the foot.

## Victimology Condones Weakness and Failure

First, a racewide preoccupation with an ever-receding victimhood, which generally entails exaggerating it, gives failure, lack of effort, and criminality a tacit stamp of approval.

Inner-city blacks resent Koreans for opening businesses in their neighborhoods—but what precisely has made it so impossible for inner-city blacks to open these businesses themselves? If they do not have the funds to do so, what—precisely—has prevented their representatives from formulating plans to pool their resources and provide start-up loans? After all, the government bends over backward to give small-business loans and contracts to minorities. Our tendency is to consider inner-city blacks somehow cosmically "beyond" this, but how clearly could anyone articulate a reason why, beyond appealing to unspecified "racism"? When is the last time Maxine Waters convened a group of thinkers and activists to work out a plan to spark entrepreneurship in South Central, or Charles Rangel in Harlem? If they have, why didn't they follow up on it? Part of the reason is a guiding sense among the legislators and their constituents alike that an undefined but mighty "racism" would hinder any such effort, such that only whites ever propose concrete solutions, such as the misbegotten but at least proactive enterprise zones. Instead, Waters chases a mythical CIA crack conspiracy like Ahab pursued Moby Dick while Rangel gradually warms to Al Sharpton. I do not intend to castigate inner-city residents with this point, but to argue that Victimology hinders black *leaders* from lending significant and creative energy to breaking cultural patterns that those born into them are largely powerless to change. Victimology, focusing attention on pointing fingers at whitey, blinds us to the potential for inner-city residents to take part in changing their lives, thus making failure look much more inevitable than it is.

Tupac Shakur grew up middle class in Brooklyn and Baltimore. No butler, no pool—but a child who had the advantage of attending not one but two performing arts schools cannot be said to have grown up "on the street." Yet Shakur lived a willfully violent life and died young in gang violence of his own instigation, having adopted a Victimologist "gangsta" attitude in both art and life. Shakur was by all accounts a uniquely charismatic soul with great potential, but he also lacked the instinctive recoil from criminality that, say, the child of a Korean shopkeeper in South Central would have. The reason we cannot imagine a Korean teenager choosing this path is that in black culture, Victimology subtly makes criminality seem excusable—and even "cool" as a fight against the onslaught supposedly endured daily by all black Americans.

It's one thing for inner-city teenagers who suffered the slings and arrows of the old-time LAPD to come out feeling this way. But for Shakur, growing up receiving formal training in performance in fine schools, "gangsta" was a choice, not a destiny; Victimology pulled a promising artist "down" indeed. Predictably he went out as an icon within the black community, while Victimology continues to process Shakur as on some level having been "another brother done in by The Man." "He was a thug, but that's what being a black man in America does to you," a rap journalist told us. That's good music, but being a thug is only virtually preordained for the sliver of black people who live in ghettos. Being a black man in an even humbler America than Shakur grew up in did not leave Will Smith a thug. Smith's wife, Jada Pinkett Smith, attended the New York High School of Performing Arts with Shakur, but she neither became nor married a thug; she grew up to be a successful, electrifying—and thoroughly black-identified—actress. It is Victimology that leads Shakur's fans to turn away from these simple contrasts and emulate his style.

Victimology has a way of deflecting inconvenient facts, like the fact that Shakur's death was self-imposed, with "There's some of that." But when it comes to the celebration of the "gangsta," the fact that there is *any* of that is more problematic than is often perceived. For example, rapper Lichelle Laws, who grew up in the "black Beverly Hills" Baldwin

Hills, has sung "trying to get to Watts, but I'm stuck in Baldwin Hills." A culture in which a message like that is at all valid, let alone heartily accepted and encouraged, is one that glorifies despair and stagnation. Successful Jews in New York in the first half of the twentieth century only sang paeans to the Lower East Side tenements they had escaped from in irony and not too often; there was no such thing as a Jewish man or woman standing on stage and singing seriously of how he was "trying to get down to Delancey and Essex but stuck in Murray Hill"; if one tried, he would have been booed, and no record company would have offered a contract.

In the 1980s, some of the most unpleasant experiences of New York City life were encounters with the "squeegee men" who would crowd the ends of exit ramps and wash your windshield with scummy water without your consent, and then require payment on the pain of damaging your car. Mayor Giuliani's crackdown cleared these men away. It turned out that most of them had homes. No matter how low a Chinatown immigrant sank, we all know we would never have seen one bopping up to our cars with a squeegee in one hand and a crowbar in the other. Yet the squeegee men were innocents in their way: The pall of Victimology over black culture made these men feel that this behavior was on some level pardonable for a black man.

Victimology means Maxine Waters on camera dancing joyously with South Central gang members—a federal official telling professional murderers and drug peddlers that they are okay. This is not the dream Martin Luther King had.

## Victimology Hampers Performance

Victimology also hampers any performance from the outset by focusing attention upon obstacles. There is nothing obscure about performance anxiety, a pan-human phenomenon. Asians suffer occasional discrimination on various levels, and yet no one would suggest that they would be better off thinking about these remnants of discrimination constantly, because it would do nothing to eradicate the discrimination, and would hamper the only thing that can, performance. The middle-class black person in the year 2000 is no different. Many blacks suppose that one must know what one is going to "face," but this feeling is couched in the Articles of Faith. What most black people "face" today is not decisive enough in their life trajectories to merit this kind of obsession.

## Victimology Keeps Racism Alive

Many white college students have told me that they left college with warier and more negative feelings about black people than when they arrived. This is because even as people who revile racism and sincerely want to get to know people of other races and learn from them, for four years black professors and students delight in telling them what racist pigs they are without even feeling the need to specify why. When I was an undergraduate at Rutgers in 1983, most of the students demonstrating and sleeping in front of the student center several nights a week in protest of the university's investments in South African companies were white. Yet at the same time the consensus among black students and administrators was that Rutgers was a "racist campus," despite an affirmative action policy that was soon revealed to be among the least nuanced, most bluntly quantitative in the country; the expected battery of minority-oriented services, workshops, counseling; and a social atmosphere in which any overt racism was tantamount to asserting that women should go back to the kitchen.

This was one more demonstration of how yelling "racism" has now much too often lost its connection to reality and become a kind of sport. This ultimately traces to understandable insecurity. But as black Americans get ever closer to the mountaintop, the lack of fit between Victimologist rhetoric and reality is ever widening, and increasing numbers of white people are becoming impatient with suspending their disbelief, and even pitching in to help, only to get kicked in the teeth for their efforts.

The late black performance artist and filmmaker Marlon Riggs was invited to give a presentation at a Queer Studies forum at Stanford in the early 1990s. One of the organizers told me that Riggs casually fired a number of potshots at the audience implying quite directly that they were racists, despite the fact that they had invited, lodged, and paid him, were all politically leftist sorts deeply committed to identity group causes, and were even mostly gay.

It was one thing for a black activist to pull this sort of thing in 1971, the year *All in the Family* premiered, in front of a group of whites most of whom had barely ever conversed with a black person, would have been uneasy to have him in their home, and would have been horrified if one of their daughters had married him. That is "understandable."

But the group Riggs was dissing were those white people's children, many with black intimates and lovers, many active in race-related causes, none who would even have a bigot in their homes. Surely one does not invite a performance artist to be soothing: None of these people would have had any problem with Riggs exploring the nature of white racism; indeed, this was most likely what he had been invited to do, and most of the audience would have welcomed being made aware of residual racism in themselves. But in the 1990s, did this particular audience deserve to be designated outright as bigots after spending hundreds of dollars from their tiny budget to sit at Riggs's feet, and did this designation serve any purpose? If we consider it unreasonable for young black people to resist feeling deep, inconsolable offense at the slightest hint of racial bias, then how reasonably can we expect young white people not to take offense at being called racists despite their most earnest efforts to transcend their ancestors' mistakes? If some of the people who had paid this man to come enlighten them only to be treated this way started to wonder whether reaching out to black people was worth it, Victimology will say that it is proof that racism never went away. But in the meantime, the bottom of the well will remain that much closer to our feet.

## Victimology Is an Affront to Civil Rights Heroes

I have saved this point for last because it is less practical than simply moral. Insisting that black Americans still lead lives of tragedy forty years after the Civil Rights Movement is a desecration of brave and noble black Americans who gave their lives for us. Martin Luther King did not sit in those jail cells so that black professors could make speeches about the hell they live in and then drive to their $200,000 homes in Lexuses and plan their summer vacations to Antigua. "Why won't they accept me as a human being?" Ellis Cose asks—but it would be interesting to see how disincluded from American society such people would feel after spending about three days in the America our Civil Rights leaders fought to pull down.

As Ralph Ellison put it, "For us to remain in one narrow groove while ranting about 'freedom' strikes me as an affront to those who endured and sacrificed to enable us to become better prepared for our continuing role in the struggle for freedom." Every time a black person outside of a ghetto calls herself oppressed because of scattered inconveniences, as opposed to the brute horrors that our ancestors lived with daily, she is saying that Thurgood Marshall and Martin Luther King didn't accomplish anything but get some signs taken off some water fountains and allow us to sit where we want to on the bus. That, if you ask me, is sacrilege.

\*   \*   \*

There is a flutter of awareness in the black community that crying about victimhood is not exactly the best way to go about solving it. On the late, great comedy variety show *In Living Color,* Damon Wayans's Homey the Clown was a Victimologist *par excellence,* endlessly blaming his lowly job as a clown on a hopelessly exaggerated conception of racist oppression, and in one classic sketch grudgingly taking a job as a busboy at a restaurant called Chez Whitey.

Yet Homey addressed only Victimology this naked; few blacks were aware that these sketches were touching upon a disease that permeates the entire community. For example, I once heard a black stand-up comedian joking that white people try to slip the word *nigger* into conversation without black people hearing, as in saying the name of Arnold Schwarzenegger. The audience was screaming, but then look what happened to David Howard in Washington a few years later. The comedy routine quite literally came to life.

For the record, the *niggardly* episode was no flash in the pan. Soon afterward, an English professor at the University of Wisconsin used the word when discussing *The Canterbury Tales.* A black student approached the teacher about it after class and he explained what the word meant, informing the student that it had no racist connotation. In the next class, he explained its meaning to the class and asked if any students had comments. This time the black student bolted from the class crying because the teacher had repeated the word, and reported him to the faculty senate. She was not just an isolated hothead; just as black talk radio in D.C. supported Anthony Williams in firing David Howard, when this student made her case at a faculty senate meeting on the campus speech code, she was heartily applauded by the black students in the audience. On top of all this, the Wisconsin episode was not part of a "rising tide" after the D.C. episode—*this student had not even heard about what had happened in Washington.*

This student will surely take away from this incident that she encountered racism during her college years, despite the professor having gone as far as to address the class about the issue and try to foster a discussion. But this student could not be satisfied, because the Victimology virus cursed her to seek the cheap thrills of moral indignation regardless of actual circumstances. Importantly, this woman was neither a disaffected inner-city casualty nor a politician seeking power. She was a modern middle-class black woman, and her actions demonstrated that one need neither grow up in South Central nor attend Nation of Islam rallies to fall under the sway of Victimology. One need only grow up with black parents and black friends. Victimology today pulses through the very bloodstream of African-American identity.

Ralph Wiley will smugly shake his head and sneer that this is merely the armchair musings of an "intellectual" who would change his tune if he spent some time "out there" seeing "what's really goin' down". But what people like this consider themselves to "know" that people like me do not is (1) the first six Articles of Faith, which are all myths, and (2) what can be summed up as "Rodney King," the idea that police brutality means that white America still hates black people. That is one possible interpretation, but it is not supported by facts. Police departments continually improve, and the obvious gains blacks have made throughout society show that police brutality is a final hurdle, not business as usual.

Along those lines, I can guarantee that if I spent a year living in a housing project, teaching in a hopeless school down the street, and was beaten senseless by the police for asking a question during a stop-and-frisk, I would think of myself as having lived with and taught representatives of one fifth of the black population rather than "black America" in general, and as I fingered my head bandages would think of myself as having caught the vicious tail end of a racism on the wane, not on the march. I would maintain that the black American community as a whole, especially the four-fifths I had spent that year away from, is mentally hobbled by celebrating victimhood instead of addressing it.

The Civil Rights leaders' rabble-rousing, then, is a by-product of a culture-wide disease. They are not posing: They are simply manifesting an inherited black cultural trait in one of many possible ways. In short, today, black *is* Victimology, and this is a grave detour from the path to the mountaintop. Condemned by Victimology to wink and let failure pass, to choke in performance, and recreate racism where it was receding, we will never savor the freedom Ralph Wiley finds so elusive. In the name of the paradoxical high of underdoggism, we have replaced the shackles whites hobbled us with for centuries with new ones of our own.

The direst news is that, like AIDS constantly spawns new strains of itself, Victimology births new viruses. We will meet the next one in Chapter 2.

# 2

## THE CULT OF SEPARATISM

Lost-found Asiatic Black people are, in fact, not members of that union or nation styled the United States of America.
—ERNIE SMITH, *The Historical Development of African American Language: The Islamic Black Nationalist Theory,* 1994

Several years ago, an episode of the television crime drama *Jake and the Fat Man* focused on a black female detective played by Nell Carter, as a test run for a possible series. Watching that show was not usually how I chose to utilize my evening time, but I make sure to watch anything Nell Carter appears in. At one point the plot required Carter and her assistant to examine some antique Russian jewelry, and upon catching sight of it the Carter character was enthralled, whispering as the soundtrack welled up, "I love Russian history!" and proceeding to give an account of some obscure monarchical events in Czarist Russia.

It struck me as a false moment, and I wondered whether the script had originally been written with a white actress in mind. I couldn't help thinking of how very few black people I have ever met who were so passionately interested in a subject that had nothing to do with being black. I felt guilty for even having the thought, and considered it progressive of the writers, if they did write the script with Carter in mind, to portray a black woman as having such an arcane interest without making a point of it. But I also found myself thinking that if the writers actually supposed that such an interest was common among black people although unremarked by the media, they were in fact mistaken—they were less filling in a gap than pushing the envelope.

This was just ten seconds of a little TV show, of course, but the thoughts it stirred up stemmed from something much larger, a mighty current of Separatism in black American culture. Separatism is a direct product of Victimology. The sense that whites are an eternally hostile presence has encouraged a conception of black America as a sovereign entity. It would be one thing if within this entity blacks attempted to set up a kind of alternate, but equivalent, universe (as they often did in the first half of the twentieth century). However, because the detachment is a response to perceived victimhood, the mindset of this sovereign world is refracted through the prism of Victimology, conditioning a restriction of cultural taste, a narrowing of intellectual inquiry, and most importantly, studied dilution of moral judgment.

Separatism may appear to be a simple matter of self-protection, but in practice it narrows horizons, holding blacks back from being the best that they can be. Briefly stated, Separatism both concretely and metaphorically keeps black people in the ghetto.

The Cult of Separatism is manifested primarily in three ways.

## The Three Fruits of Separatism

### Mainstream Culture as "White" Culture

Under the Cult of Separatism, expressions of mainstream culture considered "default" by most Americans of all colors are processed by many if not most blacks not as common coin, but as "white." This alienates many black people from some of the most well-wrought, emotionally stirring art and ideas that humans have produced, miring the race in a parochialism that clips its spiritual wings.

On a lunch date with a young black woman some time ago, I happened to be carrying a copy of *Jane Eyre*. For whatever it's worth, at any given time I am as likely to be reading Alice Walker or Gloria Naylor as Charlotte Brontë or Henry James; I read Tolstoy not out of a self-hating fascination with white people, but because the man wrote a crackling good and highly affecting story. (*Anna Karenina* so grabbed me that one day when I was reading it in Washington Square, the woman next to me said, "Oh, look, there are Anna and Vronsky over there" and I looked up fully expecting to see them gliding by the skateboarders and drug dealers in their bourgeois finery, so real had they become to me.) However, for my black friend, *Jane Eyre* was not a book, it was a "white book." "Oh, I'd never read something like that," she said, quite casually. She preferred to read only books written by and about her own people. That includes a lot of great literature, but the person who can immerse himself in the richness of James Baldwin but never experiences Tolstoy is like someone who thrills to a Haydn string quartet but refuses to hear one note of a Beethoven symphony. This person never tastes the whole meal.

Yet as I have already said so often, Life Isn't Perfect, and in terms of the world in general, none of us ever gets the *whole* meal. This woman will live a full life despite missing out on "white" novels. But often this perspective ends up selling out black Americans.

For example, there is a magnificent complete three-CD recording of the original score of the musical *Show Boat*. It is marred at the beginning, however, when what is supposed to be a black chorus of stevedores sing stiffly with slightly British accents. This was a last-minute emergency measure. *Show Boat* was the first American musical to substantially address the tragedy of race relations, and includes a black chorus and a white chorus. Fittingly, a black American chorus was hired for the recording, but walked out upon being required to sing the original lyrics of the opening chorus "Niggers all work on the Mississippi." The recording was made in London, and while using American performers, had recruited a British white chorus. On such short notice, the producers had no choice but to have them step in to sing the black choruses as well. The accent difference is not a serious problem in the passages for the white chorus, but it naturally stands out much more when these Britishers are supposed to be deep Southern blacks.

Over the years, the lyric in question has indeed been increasingly watered down for new productions in line with increasing racial sensitivity: "Darkies all work . . . ," "Colored folks work . . . ," and finally, "Here we all work . . ." by the 1960s. This made sense, but by 1988, with *nigger* safely quarantined as one of the most socially inappropriate words in the English language to use in real life, the producers thought that singing the original lyric could be perceived as historical in intent, and furthermore, the original line had a true-to-life power that none of the substitutions have. The "Niggers all work on the Mississippi . . ." line is sung not by a happy shuffling gang of minstrels, but by grim, overworked black laborers bitterly quoting whites' opinions of them; it is also an accurate depiction of the tendency for blacks to use *nigger* among themselves. Whether one calls this a therapeutic defusing of an epithet via appropriation, or evidence of underlying self-hatred (it is in truth both), the fact is that this use of *nigger* is undeniably *real*.

It is difficult to believe that anyone who actually watches a production of *Show Boat,* seeing how openly and sympathetically it treats the black condition, could fail to understand that the blacks singing this opening chorus "Niggers all work on the Mississippi" are eloquently protesting racism, not underlining it. This opening chorus portrays blacks giving vent to their frustration at their victimhood, surely something these protesters would champion. The only possible reason someone would misunderstand this lyric is, quite simply, not having had occasion to listen to a recording, see a production, or rent a video. One suspects that these singers were only glancingly familiar with *Show Boat,* out of a sense that it is a "white musical"—"Oh, I'd never go see anything like that." As a result, they passed up an opportunity to lend one of black American culture's most precious legacies, the unique timbre and precision of our choral singing, to this monumental recording, instead leaving our ancestors portrayed by British whites unable to render the material in the authentic style.

This sense of mainstream culture as alien extends into academia as well. Manning Marable has explicitly urged black scholars to restrict their research to black issues, thereby explicitly deeming intellectual curiosity for its own sake to be inappropriate to black American people. Under this rubric, the black scholar is to study slavery, Africa, and social welfare, but never Russian history, *Jane Eyre,* or mainstream theater history. Many will see Marable as "concerned," a "serious brother," or "cool," but obviously it is a short step from Marable to "Oh, I'd never read that" and the *Show Boat* walkout.

Separatism also has a tendency to close black people off to foreign cultures other than black ones. I once met an aspiring black linguist who had spent two years in China without learning Chinese beyond what he needed to buy food at the market. Most people who spend two years in a foreign country come back speaking the language, and this is especially true of linguists, for whom the experience often serves as a basis for a career's work. This was the only linguist I have ever met who spent two years abroad without becoming bilingual, and it is not likely to be accidental that he was black. Separatism has a way of discouraging black Americans from learning foreign languages other than French and Spanish, spoken by many Caribbeans and Africans, and Swahili. In my lifetime, I have known only one black person who studied German (it was a required course), one (a Black Muslim) who took Arabic, and not one who took Russian, Chinese, or Japanese. Certainly there must have been some who studied the latter three (e.g., Condoleezza Rice speaks Russian). Nevertheless, it is significant that in a thirty-four-year language-centered life, I personally have never met any. What makes black people shy away from these languages—even in elite universities—is a sense that they are not "black" things. This particular branch of Separatist orientation has roots in segregation, of course, and was crystallized in the sixties as Separatism expanded into a general coping strategy. Now, however, this wariness of nonblack culture is too often a barrier sealing the black community off from enriching influences. This linguist wanted to go on to do academic study of the Chinese sound system, but he will never be competitive—almost every other linguist studying Chinese has learned to speak the language.

## The Ghettoization of Academic Work

As the spawn of Victimology, Separatism shares with its progenitor a tendency to be allowed to trump truth in cases that require choosing between them. In this vein, a considerable amount of black academic work downplays logical argument and factual evidence in the service of filling in an idealized vision of the black past and present, which is founded not upon intellectual curiosity but upon raising in-group self-esteem.

### Mother Egypt

"Afrocentric History," for example, is primarily founded upon a fragile assemblage of misreadings of classical texts to construct a scenario under which Ancient Egypt was a "black" civilization (was Anwar Sadat a "brother"?), raped by the Ancient Greeks, who therefore owed all notable in their culture to them. Professional classicists easily point out the errors in these claims, only to have their proponents dismiss them as "racists" for having even questioned them, neglecting in the process to provide actual answers. Indeed, to insist upon facts—or apparently, to master the complex classical languages in which the original documents were written—is "inauthentic." The goal here is not to weigh evidence carefully in order to unearth the truth, but to construct interpretations of evidence that bolster a pre-conceived "truth," like "Creation Scientists" whose objectivity is decisively crippled by a fundamental conviction that God must be the driver of the universe. Uninterested in any information inapplicable to the construction of the Afrocentric myth and closed to constructive engagement, these people may be many wonderful things, but one thing they are not is scholars. Yet they are respectfully addressed as "Professor" by gullible students, and one eminent black undergraduate profiled in *Ebony* cited a volume of this kind of history as the most important book she had read that year.

Ideally, an Afrocentric academia is conceivable in which people simply apply the tools of mainstream academia to illuminating black concerns. This is the vision most defenses of Afrocentric work are based on. However, in practice, the centrality of victimhood in the black cultural identity subverts this ideal. All too often, black scholarship is devoted not to general scholarly inquiry about black people, but a subset of this: chronicling black victimhood past and present, and to remedy that victimhood, celebration and legitimization of black people past and present. Because black people are no more perfect than anyone else and life past and present is complex, this abridged conception of academic inquiry inherently conflicts with the commitment of mainstream academia to striving for assessment as unbiased as possible. In this conflict between Victimology and truth, Victimology is naturally allowed the upper hand.

The result is a sovereign entity where the outward forms of academia—articles, books, conferences, symposia—are harnessed to a local set of rules: a Separatist conception of academia. In "black" academia, as often as not, comment is preferred over question, folk wisdom is often allowed to trump rigorous argumentation, and sociopolitical intent is weighted more heavily than the empirical soundness of one's conclusions. There are certainly quite a few excellent black scholars, but overall, Separatist academic standards are pervasive enough to make black conferences quite often perceptibly less rigorous than mainstream ones.

Many mainstream scholars would be, or have been, surprised at the sparseness of serious, constructive debate at many black conferences, unaware that because of the grips of Victimology and Separatism, this kind of debate would be superfluous to the proceedings, and even unwelcome. After four decades, many black academics have spent their entire careers in this alternate realm, and as such, have never been required to assess the full range of facts applying to a case, to construct rigorous arguments, or to address anything but the very politest and most superficial of criticism. Here is the beginning of notions at the center of "Afrocentric History" such as that Cleopatra was "black," that Aristotle stole books from an Egyptian library that wasn't even built until twenty-five years after he died, etc. Moderate black academics are more likely to say of the most egregious Afrocentric work that "more work needs to be done" than to actually pin it as nonsense, which makes complete sense when we realize that the fundamental commitment of much black academic work is not assessment of facts and testing of theories, but chronicling victimhood and reinforcing community self-esteem.

*Ask Me No Questions . . .*

This problem is by no means limited just to the collection of people committed to "Afrocentric History"; it is seldom far from the surface in any scholarly setting in the realm of "Blackademia." At a conference on black performance in 1999, a black scholar from England argued that whites' tendency to adopt black American popular cultural forms is evidence not of an identification with black people, nor of a desire for cross-cultural harmony or understanding, but of a desire to eliminate the black presence via co-opting what makes them unique.

Interesting idea, but hardly as obvious or incontrovertible as the operations of gravity. Does the white teen who likes Snoop Doggy Dogg want to eliminate niggers, or does he simply like the beat and vibrate in tune with the antiestablishment attitude that has enthralled young Westerners since Goethe's Young Werther? Did whites stir the blues and jazz into their marches and jigs to create rock music because they were racists, or because blues and jazz are among the most sublimely intoxicating aesthetic creations humanity has ever known? Here in the Bay Area, I have noticed that white females of ages roughly ten to fourteen are fond of imitating black women's "sassy" "Uh-UHH! . . ." accompanied by the pushing forward of an admonishing second finger pointed upwards, and waved back and forth in opposition to corresponding "sassy swivel" neck movements (tough to describe on paper—think of Aretha Franklin in *The Blues Brothers*). Perhaps I lack some exotic brand of insight, but I simply do not see subliminated hate in these little girls—on the contrary, they are expressing a joyous admiration of black women's trademark strength; it's the melting pot in all of its glory. Similarly, among the white male high schoolers and undergraduates I see who perform hip-hop, imitating "ghetto" gestures and intonation as closely as they can, what I see is a sincere admiration of a massively compelling art form. A lot of these kids will even say "Sometimes I wish I *was* black"—and I do not think that what they wish is that they could become black while real black people disappeared; what they wish—regardless of the fact that this would of course be more complicated than a fantasy dwells upon—is to *join* black people.

Some might disagree with me, but just as many would not, and the point is that there are obviously issues to be discussed here. Yet the scholar at this conference simply put forth his declaration that this kind of imitation masks racist hatred without a shred of support. To be sure, his point was rendered especially seductive by the densely elegant jargon in which academics in the humanities are trained to couch their thoughts. Furthermore, this was all delivered in a gorgeous Oxonian accent which, in all of its calfskin suave, also betrayed that he is extremely unlikely to have experienced any of the particular slings and arrows of a black American inner-city, or even middle-class, life. In general, there was not a hint of anything but Sir Alec Guinness in his demeanor, and thus his statement cannot have been informed by any personal discomfort with seeing "his" culture "co-opted." Indeed, put aside his references to "mimesis" and "negation," and all this guy was saying was "The only reason they imitate us is because they hate us." Preface the statement with "Yo," and its content remains exactly the same. Yet if "Imitation is the sincerest form of flattery" has any value as a general aphorism, his was in essence an extremely underargued thesis. Mainstream conferences are devoted not to tossing out colorful accusations, but to sifting and evaluating the ideas proposed by the participants. Yet despite this man's having presented no evidence or argument whatsoever to support his claim, he was heartily applauded several times, and was one of the hits of the conference—he could barely get out of the auditorium for coffee, so besieged was he by people lauding him for telling it like it is. (No, I was not jealous—I was just attending the conference, not speaking at it!) Because this was a black conference, making an argument was less important than reaffirming common wisdom, and to hear common wisdom dressed up in arcane words and an Alistair Cooke accent is even better, in lending it the air of scholarly authority. The *substance* of scholarly authority, however, was a distinctly lesser concern.

What was significant about this was that for anyone to ask this man to supply evidence for his point would have been as shockingly inappropriate as pulling out a tuba and blowing on it. His point was simply assumed to be true, or at least, by the more exploratorily inclined, "a valid point of view." But what this meant was that this was not a forum devoted to presenting findings or evaluating conflicting interpretations of data or events—i.e., properly speaking it was not an academic exercise at all. It was a rally, designed to reinforce the emotionally based sentiments the audience and participants came in with. After all, even if the man was right, mainstream academia is not inclined to convene conferences with the purpose of proclaiming what is already known. Political science conferences do not feature various speakers presenting nimble variations upon the point that "war is bad"; biologists do not convene to urgently remind one another that all forms of life are based on DNA. The Separatist current makes this kind of thing seem natural to conveners of many black conferences, out of a sense that actual academic debate is somehow "beside the point" for African Americans since our status as eternal victims makes our regularly proclaiming this, as it would be for villagers in Chechnya, a more pressing concern.

And make no mistake—the same priorities reign even without plummy accents and Judith Butler jargon. I once attended a conference where a black woman gave a paper taking issue with an article which, by her reading, denied that black female speech had any unique patterns. After criticizing the author, with the unspoken implication that this writer was one more oppressor trying to deny black people their identity, the professor presented a few features of black female speech. In the question session afterwards, a white woman very politely pointed out that the author of the article in question was quite aware of the uniqueness and richness of black female speech, and that the professor's interpretation was based on a misreading of the author's phrasing.

Ordinarily in academia, the presenter would defend herself by making specific reference to the article and its argumentation. Here, however, was a conflict between the tenets of mainstream academia and the very different ones of black academia. The professor's sole answer was, "Well, I read it as denying the uniqueness of black female speech, and that was my interpretation." Period. It did not appear to even occur to her that an actual address of the issue might be germane. Unlike mainstream academics who come to a conference prepared to field criticism during question sessions, she considered herself to have done her job in simply presenting the list of black female speech traits—and at a black conference, she had.

Indeed, her presentation was constructed not as a reasoned demonstration but as a backyard "calling-out" of the author in the name of injured pride. She opened by reading a passage from the author's paper and then repeating it in a challenging intonation of mock disbelief, with friends in the audience assigned to shout back the phrase in the same tone of voice to evoke the black church's call-and-response tradition; she then did this with two more phrases. This was cute, but couching an academic paper as the prelude to a ghetto catfight renders one's presentation inherently immune to constructive discussion. To criticize it in any way, even politely, is to question not the lines of an argument, but an expression of cultural identity—and thus the person themselves. Indeed, the professor's set jaw at being questioned made it painfully clear that any further dwelling upon the point would be processed as a slight against her and her race, and the questioner was hip enough to intuit the conflict in traditions here and dutifully sit down.

Furthermore, the misreading was not due to the writing of the scholar under fire, quite clear by any standard, but was of a sort suggesting that this professor was not particularly well attuned to the basic nuances of nonfiction prose. The author she was criticizing is in fact a vocal and passionate advocate of minority rights and even is a minority herself; the article, for example, was based on an extended study of how language was used to foil Anita Hill. The unavoidable impression one got from such a stark misreading of an actually rather simple article is that this professor was simply not much of a reader—at least of nonfiction and scholarly writing. This seemingly ironic combination of a doctorate with an ambivalent relationship to the printed page was not an accident: Chronicling victimhood requires less of a passion for the book than chronicling a whole picture, and one does not need to master as vast a literature to chart a victory as to formulate and test a theory.

One could see the Separatist academic tradition being passed on at the same conference when a student went up to the microphone and introduced himself as a "doctorial" student. We need not make light of the mispronunciation in itself—we all mispronounce the occasional word (I pronounced *albeit* as "all-BITE" until I was about twenty-eight). However, this particular mispronunciation was symbolic—the graduate student who says "doctorial" reveals himself as unimmersed in academia as a whole. The mechanic does not come home from the garage saying "curburetor," because being surrounded all day by people saying *carburetor* would get him on track after about an hour. In the same way, a graduate student in daily interaction with professors well-ensconced in the academic world, and immersed in books and articles tailored to scholars, is inevitably and unconsciously taught out of saying something like "doctorial." Predictably, this student was in a highly Afrocentric language and education program founded upon a conception of Black English as an African language with English words. This conception has no scholarly foundation and can only be imparted via personal tutelage by a small number of adherents or via a few unpublished pamphlets written by a Black Nationalist medical school teacher (quoted at the opening of the chapter). Yet the student was piqued that the conference attenders were giving this school of thought short shrift, either unaware that solid scholarship is backed by published work or convinced that racism has kept these ideas off the presses. One can only laud his aim of helping inner-city black students, but it is obvious that he will become one more black professor granted a Ph.D. with no conception of the meaning of scholarly assessment and debate. I would not be surprised to see him several years from now giving a paper and being offended at serious questions.

## Hollywood's Depiction of Black People

Few topics reveal the Separatist conception of academia more vividly and regularly than popular entertainment, whose "academic" discussion in African-American settings regularly centers upon a self-generating, circular indignation over the television and film industry supposedly refusing to portray black people as anything but, to use film scholar Donald Bogle's terms from his book title, Toms, Coons, Mulattoes, Mammies, and Bucks. Obviously this was true in the past. However, it remains a truism in most black American thought despite the fact that it has not been true for fifteen years at the very least, and most significantly, to the extent that this change is acknowledged, it is regularly assailed as denying black people their individuality.

At one conference I remember a black professor complaining that in black-white "buddy" pictures, the white man always learns by taking on traits of the black man ("loosening up," etc.) while the black man never learns from the white man, the idea being that this showed whites' resistance to allowing blacks to fully take part in mainstream culture. Yet if in *48 Hours,* Eddie Murphy had learned a certain amount of social reserve and shed some of his comfort with Black English, then by now there would be several academic papers in the journals and anthologies decrying how Hollywood is determined to strip African Americans of their culture, "neutering" poor Eddie Murphy in the name of a racist hegemony. Once again, the purpose of accusations like this is not constructive discussion, but reinforcement of reflexive, aimless bitterness. Sadly, it always works—when the professor made this point, the blacks in the audience spontaneously erupted with a chorus of "Mm-hmm"s, finger snaps, and "All right?!"s. To question the logic of what the professor said would have been processed not as intellectual engagement, but as an unwelcome gaffe (while it was at this same conference that the young woman I mentioned in the last chapter had presented her long, profane rap unrelated to the topic of discussion to enthusiastic applause).

But how could the black people in the audience help it when, as well educated as many of them were, they are fed this line about American entertainment year after year by educated black leaders and scholars regardless of what is actually being produced? A few weeks later a superb black actor said of Hollywood in a newspaper interview that "When we see a mainstream work, and a black actor enters, he is the representative of the black guy. It's so absurd." Mm-hmm!, All right?!—but no; when people used to say this when I was little in the 1970s it was true, but today it simply isn't anymore. Morgan Freeman as the president of the United States in *Deep Impact* (1998), with his race never so much as mentioned, was not "the black guy," nor was Wesley Snipes, married to Chinese Ming-Na Wen, romancing Nastassja Kinski and best friend to

Kyle Maclachlan, again with his race immaterial to the proceedings, a "black man" in *One Night Stand* (1997), nor was Halle Berry's temptress character in *The Flintstones* (1994) ever designated "black." These were all major releases shown across the country, sold on video by the millions, rerun endlessly on myriad cable stations, and dubbed into several foreign languages to be shown around the world; Samuel L. Jackson and Angela Bassett also play an increasing number of race-neutral parts. Yet all of us black and white are encouraged to either pretend that these films were never made, or to decry them for denying black people their "essence."

Recall that Hazel Carby sees sublimated homoeroticism and coded racism in the *Lethal Weapon* series' depiction of the friendship between Mel Gibson and Danny Glover as one between individual human beings, rather than between a White Man and a Black Man. In that same vein, I would not be the least bit surprised to find that somewhere someone has written, or said at a conference, that Berry's character in *The Flintstones* was "white people encoding deep-seated primitivization of the African into the farthest possible reaches of their history to reinforce the preservation of the racist impulse in the present." And yet if Halle Berry had played a buttoned-up next-door neighbor in the movie while, say, Michelle Pfeiffer had been the sexpot, then Hollywood would be guilty of "suppressing the sexuality of a beautiful black woman in the indelible tradition of negating the fundamental humanity and fertility of African peoples out of the deep-seated antimiscegenationist impulse born of fear and self-doubt."

The tragic thing is that it is never even considered that the logic here is hopelessly circular, such that there is nothing whatsoever Hollywood could do that would meet with the satisfaction of the African Americans considered to be "telling it like it is." This is because the aim is not reason but Victimology-based indignation, and as such, a great deal of black academic work on popular culture—an arena in which we have made some of our richest and most profoundly influential contributions—does not qualify as intellectual investigation or exploration. This work, "Afrocentric History," and its ilk, elevating attitude over analysis, fruitlessly mischannel our mental energies and thus debilitate the race from within.

## Black People Can Do No Wrong

The most crippling symptom of Separatist thought is a conviction, sometimes explicit and sometimes tacit, that because black people endure such victimhood at every turn, they cannot be held responsible for immoral or destructive actions, these being "understandable" responses to frustration and pain. Victimology channels through Separatism to create a sentiment that black people are still so mired in oppression that to express any real criticism of them is to kick them while they're down, like castigating a person bleeding on the ground for using foul language when he cries out in pain.

This began as romantic Black Power rhetoric, which made somewhat more sense when a larger proportion of the black population was still figuratively in chains. An example is Eldridge Cleaver in *Soul on Ice*, widely read in the 1960s and 1970s by young blacks, saying that black prisoners are "the victims of a vicious, dog-eat-dog social system that is so heinous as to cancel the prisoners' own malefactions." Cleaver was talking about the poor, but today this idea has expanded to a sense of moral absolution for anyone with black skin.

Nothing demonstrated this more conclusively than the O.J. Simpson trial, followed closely by most black Americans. The evidence of Simpson's guilt was absolutely crushing. It is widely believed in the black community that the drops of Simpson's blood at the scene were planted by the LAPD. They cannot have been, but this is not the place to dwell on that; for our purposes, there was a mountain of other evidence that made the chance that Simpson was not a murderer extremely small—and the facts would be thus even if the murder had taken place in Birmingham with Bull Connor heading the police force. Simpson's dog didn't bark when Nicole Simpson was killed, suggesting that he knew the killer. Fibers matching the carpet in Simpson's Ford Bronco were found at the scene, fibers from Simpson's shirt and hairs from his head were found on Ronald Goldman, Mrs. Simpson's friend who was killed with her. A bloody shoe print at the scene is from a rare shoe, sold in only forty stores during two years, during which time Simpson was a regular customer at one of the stores; Simpson denied he had any such "ugly ass" shoes but turned out to be wearing them in several photos. Simpson had nasty cuts and scrapes on his left hand which he never gave the same explanation for twice; a blood trail at the murder scene was from a left hand. Simpson never accounted for where he had been at the time of the murder; a limousine driver waiting to take him to the airport at that time got no answer at his house; Simpson was sweating during the limousine drive despite air-conditioning. Simpson never asked about his children when informed of his wife's death. Simpson claimed that he would try to find the real killer, but refused the LAPD's offer to help him in this search, and has made no such search since his acquittal.

I listed these things, which are only about a quarter of the total case against Simpson, to make clear how minuscule the possibility was that Simpson was innocent. A legacy of violent confrontation with abusive police forces led the jury, composed largely of blacks with little education, as well as many other less educated blacks, to insist that Simpson was innocent. Black people with more education and less alienation from whites, however, are often aware that despite the real problem of police brutality, this particular evidence was too damning to indicate anything but guilt. Nevertheless, despite the cold-hearted brutal double murder that this evidence suggests, to this day, very few black people of any level of education could bring themselves to simply say that Simpson was guilty. There are those who can utter it, but only by immediately following it with *but,* and then saying that "what we really need to talk about is why the media pays so much attention to scandals involving black public figures" (JonBenet Ramsey? Joey Buttafuoco?) or, as was common at the time, "I'm tired of the whole thing" (in contrast, we are urged to keep the Tawana Brawley case as a communal memory). For most African Americans, to say out loud with no qualifications or deflections that O.J. Simpson murdered two people would be as uncomfortable as admitting out loud that one has a favorite child.

This demonstrates the pervasiveness of the Separatist sense of morality: what Simpson did is processed as having been on a different plane than a white man having done the same thing because blackness is seen as absolving one from real guilt. Tupac Shakur is absolved from judgment despite having sought, rather than been born in, pathology; conversely, Simpson is absolved despite having been born in but having long left behind the kind of lifestyle that makes committing murder a virtual destiny. Simpson had done nothing for black causes, had left his first wife for a young blond white one, and thereafter rejected black romantic company ("I don't shovel coal" is how he is reported to have put it). Yet even those who see that he was probably guilty withhold him from criticism, even despite the extreme edginess of the interracial dating issue among many blacks. Like Victimology, Separatism trumps truth: a decorated football hero with a lavish lifestyle, beautiful (white) women at his disposal, and the LAPD in his pocket is nevertheless processed as so much a victim of racism that if he kills two people in cold blood, it is thought cruel to explicitly hold him accountable for it or even to say it too loud. Maya Angelou urged whites to let blacks "take care of" Simpson, with the implication that in our arms he would be lovingly shown the error of his ways, rather than treated as the murderer he probably was.

For many, the issue is perhaps less protecting Simpson than protecting the black community: we are not to say out loud that Simpson was guilty because we are not to call attention to the fact that black people in general are fallible. But this leads us right back to appearing dim, because "protecting" the black community in this way requires that one abstain from grappling with the simple logic of the Simpson case, and thus appear congenitally incapable of doing so.

Indeed, this kind of reflexive absolution goes far beyond the barbershop, extending even into academia. To take the Simpson example again, a black professor at Berkeley I had yet to meet once e-mailed me to ask if I would come speak to his class about how language use in the media had affected the controversy over the Simpson case. I responded that I would be glad to, but that he might want to know in advance that I thought Simpson was guilty and that Johnnie Cochran was no hero of mine.

I never heard from the man again, and when I later happened to meet him he was distinctly cool toward me, obviously having decided that I was no hero of his. His feeling this way only makes sense when we view it as an index of Separatist morality: Whatever the formal logic of thinking that Simpson was guilty, to this man, for a black professor to intend to say so before a predominantly black class was a faux pas. My opinion as a linguist on the Simpson issue was not what he was really seeking. In an institution devoted to the free exchange of ideas, presumably my stance would not be assumed beforehand, and the value of my thoughts would be in training students how to come to their own conclusions about important issues. What this man was seeking was for me to explain how the media's use of language during the controversy indicated how deeply racism pervades society, all delivered with a coded wink to the black students in the class. Therefore, my opinion made me not simply someone with an opinion that differed from his, but someone unfit to speak before his class, and, more to the point, a jerk.

This episode was a demonstration of how black academics are required to shade and edit their statements about current affairs according to Separatist tribal norms. People like this mild-mannered and genial professor, not given to extremes of ideology, would not recognize themselves as part of the Separatist problem, identifying it instead with extremists like the leaders of the Nation of Islam. However, Louis Farrakhan and his ilk are mere extremes of a phenomenon of which people like this professor are nothing less than the heart.

Like Victimology, Separatism is not formal or conscious much beyond the temples of the Nation of Islam and Al Sharpton's office. Just as you

barely notice the orchestra playing for a musical unless a player makes a mistake, the Separatist requirement only becomes obvious when flouted. It had surely never even occurred to this professor that I might not share his and most black people's opinion. Although he would not overtly put it this way, there was only one opinion that a "brother" could have. This man will sit at commencements and symposia supposing himself to be committed to giving students a liberal arts education. However, he has also been inculcated into the Separatist mindset, sadly at odds with the goals of liberal arts education, which allows a wide range of conclusions about an issue as long as each is supported by fact and coherent argument. Separatism, on the other hand, requires a bedrock assumption that because all black people are eternally victims, they are exempt from censure.

It follows naturally that at heart, this professor considers his job to be to teach black students not how to carefully assess an issue, but something much more specific, much easier, and ultimately limiting—how to resist any interpretation of any racial issue not founded upon the notion that blackness in America is a fundamentally tragic condition absolving one from serious judgment. If a black person is accused of doing something wrong, deny it unless the evidence is far more watertight than what you would require in deciding whether a white person did something wrong. If he turns out to have done it anyway, then remember that it's okay if he grew up in the ghetto. If he didn't grow up in the ghetto or hasn't lived there for decades, then think less about the person than the fact that the media called attention to him at all. Etc., etc. The unspoken consensus among many blacks in the academy is that this kind of narrow distortion of what it means to be educated is the most important benefit a young black person gains from higher education aside from increased earning power.

The roots of this Separatist morality in Victimology showed themselves in the alacrity of the professor's dismissal of me, reminiscent of the abrupt indignation with which one is rejected by many blacks for questioning that racism cripples all black lives. After my response, nothing—no questions as to what led to my opinion, no dialogue, not even a token excuse. Having revealed that I did not adhere to the party line, I was immediately and unequivocally *persona non grata* and cut dead. The black academic who is unable to suspend intellectual engagement is sharply rejected as "against us," "not one of us"—indeed, because today, exempting all blacks from general standards of evaluation is a defining thread of what it has become to be "culturally black"; like Victimology it affects individuals to varying degrees but is rarely completely absent.

One also encounters compromised standards of evaluation in the writings of many black academics. I once saw a black professor on a talk show discussing his new biography of Elijah Muhammad, one of the founders of the Nation of Islam. Muhammad may well have "done some good things," as is often said in the black community. However, he tortured and killed, even extending this savagery to having Malcolm X assassinated.

Yet this professor, calm and eloquent as he was, sitting coiffed in his smart suit and sipping a cup of tea, conveyed with his every inflection, with his quiet "cool cat" smile, and with an ever-so-subtle smug drop of the eyelids, that he considered this man certainly no saint, but fundamentally "okay," a "brother," whose deeds were justified by his membership in an oppressed race. For example, he made sure to have the interviewer show photos from the book of Southern lynchings of the sort Muhammad had seen in his childhood. A quiet but powerful subtext of this man's message was ultimately "Okay, I have the fancy degree but don't sweat it, I'm down with y'all." Okay in itself, but isn't it sad, then, that immersion in black culture in this case meant a lack of serious engagement with the moral issues inherent to any scholarly assessment of an Elijah Muhammad?

After all, we must ask—to respect this professor as a thinking person—did even seeing lynched black men as a child justify having Malcolm X gunned down in cold blood? It's one thing for uneducated inner-city teenagers to worship criminality and ignorance—we all would if we grew up as they do. But how noble is it for a college professor with a doctorate to write a book about Elijah Muhammad whose main approach to the man—even if dutifully criticizing this or that—is one of respect, who gives an interview about Muhammad where, if one hadn't caught the name of the subject, one might suppose he was talking about Medgar Evers or Bayard Rustin?

Of course, one can write a biography of a rascal and still come out admiring the subject; it has even been said that a good biographer must on some level like his subject. One comes to the end of many a biography of a person who slept around, stole money, and abused people feeling that his flaws were balanced by just as many good points, that his imperfections were inevitable by-products of what was at heart the kind of elemental élan that moves the world forward and makes life worth living. Adam Clayton Powell exemplifies this for me—he was a self-glorifying, opportunistic philanderer, but he also laid the groundwork for the Civil Rights Movement, playing a vital part in creating the world we know to-

day, and was a walking good time in the bargain; I wish I had known him. One senses an irresistible life force, a charisma, pulsing through the man, and anyone who knew him corroborates this.

But Elijah Muhammad? The racism is "understandable"; I personally would be a racist too if I had been born before 1960. But meanwhile, the man claimed to be a paragon of Islamic faith in direct communion with Allah while womanizing shamelessly, giving the excuse that he was reliving the sins of the prophets in order to recapitulate their journeys toward redemption. He ordered or condoned the savage beatings of any member of the church who went against the party line; Malcolm X's assassination was only the culmination of business as usual. He scorned the Civil Rights Movement, considered Martin Luther King a "fool," scoffed at young blacks participating in sit-ins, and played no part in paving the way for blacks' successes today. And as for the Nation of Islam, they have indeed "done some good things," but last time I checked, the ghettos were still thriving, and none of the gains blacks in America have made since the founding of the great Nation trace to their efforts. And on top of all of this, one does not even sense the infectious charisma in Muhammad that draws one irresistibly to the likes of an Adam Clayton Powell or even a Richard Nixon. This is a hero? Can't we do better than this? Haven't we?

To be sure, the author is no hagiographer. His book is a massively researched and carefully reasoned piece of scholarship. He quite openly and at length chronicles Muhammad's myriad and glaring flaws, and has little respect for the uncritical deification of Muhammad from some quarters, including previous biographies. I learned most of the bad things I know about Muhammad from his book, for example. Thus I intend no criticism of his scholarly abilities of any kind; it's the implications he draws from the material that I find indicative. In the end, he sums Muhammad up as "misunderstood," and it is clear that at heart, he thinks Muhammad was a chill brother because he founded the Nation of Islam.

The tragedy is that somehow we don't find this surprising in a black college professor—somehow it's "understandable." But imagine an Italian-American college professor writing a book about Al Capone as a hero, justifying his actions on the basis of the oppression of immigrants from Southern Europe in the early twentieth century (which was often as virulent as that against blacks)? The professor might well occasionally pause to praise Capone's intelligence, observe the personal charisma that allowed him to rule men, or marvel at the intricately configured operations of his Mafia squads, but we would expect that the fundamental stance of anyone treating Capone would be that the man was a thug, someone the world would have been better off without. We will see no scholarly works on Al Capone judging him in the afterword as "misunderstood." Those commisioned to do society's highest-level thinking do not sing paeans to the worst of human nature.

Yet we can be sure this black professor will hear no such thing from black colleagues. So powerful are the Victimologist and Separatist strains in black American culture that the black professor with a "black identity" cannot help but fall into moral lapses like winking and letting Elijah Muhammad pass. Suspending moral judgment in the name of racial solidarity is an integral part of being culturally black in America today.

One also encounters this sense of blacks as morally pristine among students. I once found a class of black students good-naturedly but steadfastly reluctant to accept that most slaves were sold to Europeans by other Africans, with only a small portion captured directly by Europeans with lassos as is shown, for obvious dramatic reasons, in *Roots* and *Amistad*. The students had no trouble processing the evil of the whites, but simply could not imagine that black people could be so cruel as to sell one another into servitude. Even after I presented them a week later with more detailed information and figures, much of which my personal work has brought me into direct contact with, a few of them were still skeptical. One student even explicitly told me that she was disappointed that whites did not carry the whole of the guilt.

At another time, the one nonblack woman in a class I was teaching said that she was offended by the misogyny in "gangsta" rap music lyrics. One of the women in the class—who for the record had grown up nowhere near a ghetto—snapped that she had no right to criticize what she hadn't grown up in, and was joined by a few other students. The nonblack woman (actually Bolivian) tried to defend herself but quickly elicited responses sharp enough to leave her in tears. So deeply runs the sense that no black person can do wrong that this woman had to be put in her place, in front-stoop tones otherwise all but unheard of in a college classroom.

Black students are immersed in this kind of sentiment in the four years of college, often coming out with a Separatist bent they did not have as freshmen. A friend of mine's niece came back after four years at Howard University with a leaning toward Black Nationalism, as well as the feeling that it was "possible" that whites had created AIDS. "Don't you feel oppressed?" she asked me—being carefully taught that one is a victim, and that the white world ought be conceived as one apart, is often a signal experience for a black undergraduate. The feeling runs so deep—from Stanford through Rutgers down to the humblest community college—that rejecting that message often requires dissociation from the campus black community.

This absolution is extended beyond reconstructable, long past, or artistically rendered murder into concrete maiming and killing. After the Rodney King verdict, Damian Williams and three other young black men crushed innocent white truck driver Reginald Denny's jaw up into his sinuses with a brick, smashed a bottle in a Japanese man's face leaving him half-deaf and partially paralyzed, and robbed and beat a Latino man and painted his testicles black while he lay unconscious. Yet Williams and his "crew" were considered nothing less than heroes in the Los Angeles black community and beyond, under the idea that their actions were justifiable rebellion against racism. The Nation of Islam, doing one of their "good things," I suppose, set up a defense fund, and the roots of Separatist morality in Victimology showed with unusual explicitness in Williams defending himself on the basis of having been abandoned by his father.

This episode also showed that we cannot sweep Separatist morality under the rug as a mere "understandable" reluctance to air dirty laundry, in the vein of the ambivalence toward openly discussing O.J. Simpson as what he is. In cases where the crime is too obvious to talk around, Separatist morality drives eminent blacks to send the dirty laundry on tour and call it our Sunday best.

Maxine Waters framed the ensuing trial as "revenge" for the Rodney King verdict and said "If we don't get justice, we're going to have a civil war." But what kind of "justice"? Apparently a "black" justice: Williams's lawyers even argued that individual guilt is a tool of the white establishment. That argument tied into a frequently encountered attempt to defend negative black behavior by claiming that it is conventional "white" behavior that is deviant. This emerged alongside the white counterculture's indictment of middle-class American mores, and was summed up by eminent black sociologist Kenneth Clark, who said in 1965 that blacks should "reject notions which demand that the Negro change himself and accept the requirement that society itself must change." It wasn't long before the African-American Teachers Association in New York declared that disruptive black students were "high-spirited nonconformists" resisting the repression of middle-class white values.

That may sound a bit forced thirty years later, when it would be difficult to tell a teacher that the student pulling a knife on her in class is merely "expressing himself." But echoes of such statements strongly determine black community attitudes toward black people's behavior, be the perpetrator an inner city thug or a religious leader. Cultural blackness may not necessarily be hair, dancing, dialect, or KFC, but one thing it is is a sense that the black person is an eternal innocent, who deserves at most a slap on the hand by a fellow black (Maya Angelou "taking care of" O.J. Simpson), but no criticism more sustained or serious than this, and certainly never society-wide condemnation.

## Aiding and Abetting: Whites and Separatism

Whites today nurture Separatism in line with political and ideological goals of their own. Often under the impression that they are working on behalf of the oppressed, they fail to realize that they are feeding hatred against themselves, which also in turn discourages blacks from helping themselves to be helped, by infecting them with the idea that they are hunkered behind a barracks against a barrage of outrageous racism.

Nothing exemplifies this better than welfare. We naturally tend to think today that open-ended and generous welfare was an emergency measure instituted to help people in the spreading inner cities of the late 1960s. In fact, black employment was growing in New York City when welfare was expanded there. However, an influential cadre of white leftist activist intellectuals became convinced that to expect blacks to work their way out of poverty was reminiscent of debt peonage in the South and thus unethical. White guilt fed directly into Separatist sentiments already sanctioned in the black community by Kenneth Clark and Eldridge Cleaver. Today's black welfare clients in New York do not know that their grandparents were often carefully ushered into welfare, often urged to give up jobs and get on the rolls.

Certainly our country needs a welfare program of some kind to assist those helpless, down on their luck, or disabled. Furthermore, it must also be granted that Frances Fox Piven, Richard Cloward, Edward Sparer, and Richard Elman's position was based not on an outright sense that black people must be exempt from hard work, but on a contention that blacks in America were caught in a special sociohistorical bind. They argued that the fast rise of automation justified a special exemption for blacks from working upwards on the social scale themselves, since so many blacks were hobbled by the poor educations they had gotten in the segregated South. But there are two problems here. First, their assessment turns out to have underestimated black strength. Today we are faced with the uncomfortable juxtaposition of third-generation black welfare cases left culturally unable to adjust to working for a living on the one hand, and on the other, new immigrants, many not even comfortable in the English language, providing their children with the wherewithal for middle-class lives amidst much more automation. And many of these immigrants are black Caribbeans and Africans.

Second and most importantly, whatever the theoretical or even sympathetic basis of these intellectuals' original intent, it is now lost to history. The present-tense result of their efforts thirty years later is a three-generations-deep culture of black (and Latino) people who have known nothing but handouts, such that self-support and personal responsibility may be seen on television but are virtually unknown among family and friends. Yes, for a long time there were more whites on welfare nationwide, but the problem has been the greater *proportion* of people *within the black community* who have been shuttled into this existence, despite simple cross-racial headcounts. The people locked into this existence have had no way of knowing the arcane facts of political history that played a major part in ensuring their fates in New York City. What they know is what they grew up in, and that is a world where a great many of the black people they know work rarely, if at all. No one disputes the importance of role models. Most of us, growing up seeing most adults working, develop a natural, even subconscious, prototype of the adult life as including work. Deprived of role models who work, welfare children cannot help but develop a much less strong sense of work as central to adult existence. Here is the rub. More specifically, what the black child sees is the black adults around him not working while white ones around him do. Result: a Separatist sense that work is an option rather than a given when it comes to black people.

Thus Piven and Cloward, with their good intentions, ended up feeding the Separatist morality of a great many black Americans.

We cannot file away Piven and the other Columbia radicals as extremists spawned by the heat of the countercultural revolution. There is a direct line from them to what is now called Critical Race Theory, typical of which is Richard Delgado urging blacks to conceive of themselves as victims not based on the "rigid" structures of objective truth, but as inextricable parts of a "broad story of dashed hopes and centuries-long mistreatment that afflicts an entire people and forms the historical and cultural background of your complaint." This is the product of a predictable synergy between the leftist leaning among academics and the idea fashionable among them that there is no objective truth, and people like Delgado, like the Columbia radicals, are ultimately motivated by sympathy. But the detriment to the black community far outweighs the satisfaction of intellectualized good intentions. It is a short step from a "broad story of dashed hopes" to Separatist standards of moral evaluation in the black community: Tawana Brawley ten years after her fabrication of being raped by white police officers declaring to a black audience that "something happened to me" without specifying what and getting a standing ovation; a black jury openly ignoring DNA evidence and letting O.J. Simpson free on the basis of "payback justice." If Richard Delgado and his ilk think that this kind of crippling paranoia, and the often violent reverse racism that goes with it, are good things, then we must question the wisdom of their being allowed to inflict such humble expectations of life upon the rest of us.

## Black Culture Versus Separatist Culture

Like Victimology, Separatism—the sense that to be black is to restrict one's full commitment to black-oriented culture and to be subject to different rules of argumentation and morality—is today so deeply rooted in the black American consciousness that many might find it difficult to imagine that anyone could be culturally black without situating herself within this sovereign universe, which is felt to be nothing less than "black culture" itself. To be sure, if asked "Do you believe that black people are subject to a different morality?" few blacks would answer yes. In practice, however, the culturally black person is from birth subtlely inculcated with the idea that the black person—*any* black person—is not to be judged "cold," but considered in light of the acknowledgment that black people have suffered. As uncomfortable with such a description as many blacks might be, the stark split on the O.J. Simpson verdict was eloquent testimony to its reality.

June Jordan once hammered through a poem of hers on National Public Radio, where she is assured frequent appearances as a mediagenic proponent of Victimology. In the poem she accused Clarence Thomas of being "not a proper black man"—i.e., the person who believes that eternal set-asides are ultimately harmful to a race has not an alternate opinion but one disqualifying him from sanction as "black" at all. To be meaningfully "black," it is assumed that a black person will spontaneously filter all of his opinions through in-group Separatism, which focuses on victimhood. This is not a conscious phenomenon. No one is taken into a corner and told what he "must" say like a Serbian reporter; black academics and journalists do not sit in their studies yearning to assess a case objectively but "forced" to "follow the party line." Separatist morality, despite the temptation that certain academic theories offer to analyze it this way, is not a strategy wielded deliberately to amass resources or shape thought or gain power. It is a cultural thought pattern: the culturally black person does not need to be told or taught what to say any more than a child has to be taught to swallow; the black academics and journalists who dwell in Separatism do not know any other way to think, and indeed are appalled to encounter black people who do not think like them. Because Separatism is so much more psychologically deep-seated than a mere political pose, it is that much more difficult to imagine being culturally "black" without.

Because a third generation of blacks is now coming of age steeped from birth in Separatist ideology, it is easy to miss today how unusually narrow the boundaries of "blackness" have become in the name of distance from "whiteness" and the absolution conditioned by victimhood. There is a scene in the Marx Brothers movie *Animal Crackers* (1930) where the brothers "out" a snobbish art critic as having begun as "Abie the Fishman," news the man is none too comfortable to have shouted gleefully through the mansionful of aristos. A man named Abie who sold fish during the first two decades of the twentieth century in New York was a Lower East Side Jew, but the Jewish Marx Brothers are needling the man not for any perceived incompatibility between Jewishness and status, but simply for the man's general class pretensions. Their mockery is not based on a sense that a Jew who is successful has stepped outside of his "proper realm." In contrast, sixty years later in the comedy *Strictly Business* (1991), when black street cat Tommy Davidson mocks straight-backed businessman Joseph C. Phillips (perhaps best known as Denise's husband on *The Cosby Show*), he is riding him for not being "black" enough; predictably he has a light-skinned, proper-talking wife who is bad in bed. Jewishness, despite the hideous suffering that Jews have endured throughout history, has always been much less restrictive in terms of speech, body language, dress style, and politics than blackness is, and indeed there is no tighter in-group definition in America today than blackness.

People like June Jordan, then, pose a question that is entirely reasonable when we peel away the rhetoric: Can a person who reads *Jane Eyre* as well as *Native Son,* considers Molefi Kete Asante a charlatan, and thinks of O.J. Simpson as a murderer be culturally black? I am not, as it may well appear, narrowing the focus to myself; quite a few black people fit this profile: We just don't get to hear from them very often.

A trip to the past helps us answer this question. Will Marion Cook was a black theater composer most prominent around the turn of the twentieth century. He could barely be in the same room with fellow black theater composer Bob Cole, because of their different positions on how blacks should contribute to popular culture. Cole, with his partners John Rosamond Johnson and James Weldon Johnson, wrote theater music only minorly distinguishable in style from that of his white contemporaries', and toured singing European vocal pieces onstage in tails as John accompanied him on piano (they would close with a medley of their stage hits). Cole, then, was the "sell-out" by modern standards, and Will Marion Cook would have agreed, infusing his theater music with black church harmonies, syncopated rhythms, and training black choruses to sing it with the particular sonorous robustness that only a black chorus can capture.

Yet there were other things about Cook that translate less easily into modern black consciousness. His musical abilities did not spring from a black musical tradition; he did not play church organ, nor was his the Scott Joplin/Jelly Roll Morton story of coming up through the world of brothels playing honky-tonk piano. On the contrary, he was a virtuoso violinist, who had been classically trained in Europe and studied composition with none other than Antonin Dvorak. His music was "black" by the standards of the era, but it was based in thoroughly European conceptions of harmony and structure and had none of the "groove" that we associate with black church and pop music today. He was a gratingly proud man, sporting a dandyish mustache and tailored clothes. He was so offended by being billed as the world's best black violinist that he left the classical music world, unsatisfied unless he could be considered the best violinist, period.

Cook, then, combined a dedication to his roots with an insistence on being judged according to mainstream standards, with an impatience for the demotion inherent in being designated the best *black* anything. We must remember that he felt this way just two generations past slavery—from our perspective, as if Emancipation had been in the mid-1960s and captured on film, with most blacks over fifty having grown up slaves. He was not unique in his time. If we could bring the blacks living in America in 1900 to spend a week in the year 2000, many of them would casually reveal beliefs that most blacks today would find tricky to square with the post–Civil Rights conception of "blackness." In the last chapter we saw that modern blacks would be surprised to find the blacks from 1900 rather reluctant to join them in dwelling at length on victimhood. This is also true of Separatism: particularly in the stable working class and above, blacks in 1900 had not been taught that, as Marion Barry would put it eighty years later, "There's a black culture and a white culture; there's a black psychology, and there's a white psychology."

Specifically, Paul Laurence Dunbar or Frederick Douglass, slightly dazed from their resurrection and watching CNN, would be surprised and disappointed by the middle-class black people who hold mainstream culture at arm's length and consider sociohistorical misfortunes as justification for lowered bars of evaluation. In contrast to the black linguist who spent two years in China without learning Chinese, for example, Paul Robeson was proficient in several "white" languages out of simple personal interest, and came back from his years in Russia speaking Russian. Separatism now has it that it is difficult to imagine a black leader having such an interest today (*pace* political adviser Condoleezza Rice), and yet Robeson was no Uncle Tom. As for morality, if all evidence suggested that Robeson, who had been a star football player at Rutgers before his performing career, had killed his wife, then despite how much more open and impregnable police brutality was in the 1930s, the black community would have considered him an embarrassment, not a hero. If the Scottsboro boys had turned out to be guilty, Adam Clayton Powell would not have pardoned them as "rebels" and danced with them in the newsreels.

Of course most of these people would also have had a pronounced ambivalence toward lower-class art forms like rap, and an outright aversion to being associated with African "savages," which would strike us today as rather blinkered and snobbish. Perhaps they could have learned something from us. But their embrace of the mainstream while preserving their heritage, and their insistence that being judged by the same standards as everyone else was the only way to achieve equality regardless of the handicaps to be overcome, are not in themselves so unthinkable for us. Such things even seem rather attractive on paper. In real life, however, they are no longer the way *we* do things.

Few of us would feel that Cook was an oreo for cherishing classical music and insisting on being the best at it. Few would call Louis Armstrong an oreo for not yearning to return to the cutthroat black quarters of New Orleans he grew up in as Lichelle Laws longs for Watts from her bedroom in Baldwin Hills. We do not think of a calendar of historical black heroes as an Oreo Calendar, despite how baffled almost all of those people gazing stolidly into the camera would be by the Separatist current in modern black American thought. W.E.B. Du Bois did not fight to give four of his descendants, young black men who went on a rampage after the Rodney King verdict, the right to be feted by black public officials as "The L.A. Four" after beating an innocent Hispanic man and leaving his testicles painted black. Yet if the Blacks in Wax aren't meaningfully "black," then I don't know who is—it was just a different way of being black.

## What's Wrong with Separatism?

Yet some might ask whether the Blacks in Wax would have indeed been better off reinforcing their self-esteem via constructing a separate but equal conception of blackness as modern blacks have. Isn't Separatism a matter of, as many academics might have it, the "construction of an identity"? Isn't Separatism a healthy example of "the cultural becomes political"?

The problem with the modern "separate but equal" black identity is that, like the low-quality segregated schools that this phrase was used by racist whites to justify, the Separatist world is not equal to the mainstream one. On the contrary, Separatism, in the name of protection, has taught generations of blacks to settle for less. Not just for less integration—I know that less integration would be considered a blessing by most blacks at this point. I mean settling for less as human beings. Separatism makes us small.

### Separatism Reinforces the Dumb Black Myth

For one, teaching black people, even passively rather than actively, to allow tribalism to trump logic reinforces the myth of black mental inferiority—a myth that drives the very racism that Separatism responds to.

When even the most eminent black thinkers and public figures insist in the face of overwhelming evidence that O.J. Simpson was probably innocent, or any variation upon this such as the oft-heard one that "He probably knows who did it," the black race looks, quite simply, stupid. Justifications in the name of police brutality ring hollow in this case, because Simpson had been nothing less than coddled by the LAPD in being allowed to regularly beat his wife without punishment. Defenses in this vein are fine fodder for the media and academic discussions, but in

the real world the black community's steadfastness on this almost hopelessly obvious case of murder gives the appearance that black people are
incapable of drawing logical conclusions based on simple facts.

When black linguists and education experts look television cameras
in the eye and agree that Black English is an African language with
English words and that inner-city black students ought be treated as
bilinguals, or wink and let pass this idea by refusing to utter anything
but support for a school board that says so, black people once again
look like imbeciles. During the Christmas holidays of 1996–97, Americans heard black kids chatting along in what is obviously English every
day and came home to watch black people with Ph.D.s on the television news declaring the urgency that we address the "linguistic needs of
African-American children." As the country laughed in understandable
disbelief, black academics in linguistics and education shook their
heads ruing the persistence of racism and hunkered down even more
firmly into Separatist logic, when in fact what America was laughing at
was what justly appeared to be stupidity.

In 1987, fifteen-year-old Tawana Brawley constructed a lie about having been raped by white policemen to cover for having stayed away from
home to escape the wrath of a severe mother and stepfather. Her story
was so transparently false that even those who feel, as Ralph Wiley does,
fire on their skin tended to suspect something amiss about the story.
Brawley claimed to have been left in the winter cold unconscious for
days but showed no symptoms of exposure; there were no physical signs
of rape; patches of fiber found on her person matched the filling of
Brawley's sneakers found sliced open in the apartment she had been
staying in, she having obviously intended the fibers to look like white
men's hair; and these were just a few in a numbingly long procession of
similar facts. When Al Sharpton and his lieutenants insist on defending
lies as transparent as Brawley's, anyone who followed the case at the time
cannot help wondering whether in the end, Sharpton and his ilk are simply incapable of reason. It is no accident that a *New York Times* article described Sharpton as "developing an articulate public presence," with
former mayor Edward Koch noting that Sharpton is "smart." Harmless
enough on the surface, but when is the last time you read Bill Clinton described as "articulate" or "smart," despite the fact that he is obviously
both? It is simply assumed that white people who have achieved positions
of authority and power are "articulate" and "smart," just as we assume
that they bathe daily and wear clothes. The fact that such things have to
be explicitly said about Sharpton reveals an underlying question as to

whether they are true of him. This is no surprise: Sharpton is the king of
Separatist logic, and Separatism forces black people to sacrifice mental
acuity in favor of the balm of tribal identity. The very reason Sharpton's
open racism rarely attracts much comment is that the man is not considered bright enough to know any better.

Only occasionally will particularly intrepid and antisocial whites, such
as Charles Murray and Richard Herrnstein in *The Bell Curve,* actually
say such things out loud. But Gloria Naylor nicely shows how such
things are said without being said in my favorite novel, *Mama Day,* describing an academic trying to get to the bottom of what the flexible colloquial expression "18 and 23" means to a community of black people in
the isolated Sea Islands near South Carolina:

> He done . . . made it to the conclusion that 18 & 23 wasn't 18
> & 23 at all—was really 81 & 32, which just so happened to be
> the lines of longitude and latitude marking off where Willow
> Springs sits on the map. And we were just so damned dumb
> that we turned the whole thing around.
>
> Not that he called it being dumb, mind you, called it "as-
> serting our cultural identity," "inverting hostile social and po-
> litical parameters." 'Cause, see, being we was brought here as
> slaves, we had no choice but to look at everything upside-
> down. And then being that we was isolated off here on this is-
> land, everybody else in the country went on learning good
> English and calling things what they really was—in the dictio-
> nary and all that—while we kept calling things ass-backwards.
> And he thought that was just so wonderful and marvelous,
> etcetera, etcetera.

When blacks hate whites after seeing the Rodney King tape, they are
exhibiting a human tendency to generalize. When whites watch blacks
regularly indulging in Separatist logic, they exhibit a human tendency to
generalize. But in their case the result is a black Columbia Law School
graduate described as "a bright, energetic and intellectually curious student who participated vigorously in class discussions and did well with
legal intricacies." Picture that said about a Jewish law student—it would
only be said about a white *child,* never an adult. Praising a law student
for "doing well with legal intricacies" is like praising a surgeon in training for knowing their anatomy; this description unwittingly reveals a
sense that for a black person to reason closely is unexpected, a special
case. Of course, whites started this, charging blacks as stupid long be-

fore giving them any chance to prove otherwise. But is it any wonder the stereotype continues today when the black community is taught to absolve O.J. Simpson because "If the glove don't fit, you must acquit"?

Many blacks might say "Well, who cares if they think we're dumb?" so deeply has Separatism penetrated modern black consciousness. Of course, for one thing, nurturing that attitude is not the best strategy for integration, or, if one could do without that, even basic harmony. A country where whites (as well as immigrants, as they become acculturated and watch blacks engaging in Separatist logic) quietly consider blacks mentally inferior will forever be one where blacks are condescended to, sowing resentment which leads to the perception of condescension even where there is none, and on and on. It may feel good to say "Who cares if they think we're dumb?" but deep down, we all know that we care, because if we didn't, knowing they think we're dumb wouldn't hurt so much.

## Separatism Is a Drag on Hiring and Career Advancement

For some, even here the answer might be, "Well, we *shouldn't* care if they think we're dumb." That's a rich point, but it is more important for our purposes that Separatism sabotages black people in a more urgent way.

The black person who processes all whites as surrogates for the policemen who beat Rodney King is often capable of interacting with whites only on a utilitarian, guarded basis. The comfort and vindication he feels is outweighed by the fact that this social distance can interfere with his being employed or promoted by those who will all too often be his interviewers and superiors—and almost all of whom want to go out of their way to avoid hurting him and don't like the LAPD any more than he does.

During my first year of graduate school at Stanford I lived in a law school dormitory, where I got to know most of the black law students. In the spring, every law student, backed by his or her Stanford credentials, got a cushy summer internship at a leading law firm, with a few highly indicative exceptions. Two black students did not have jobs close to the end of the year; one got one at the last minute while the other was given a consolation job by a relative. They naturally considered this evidence that racism marches on. But the fact was that all the other black students got jobs as quickly as the white students. It was not an accident that it was these two students who were quite explicit in black company about not liking white people, and their guarded, thanks-but-no-thanks demeanors around whites made their sentiments clear. Law firms have to choose from dozens of interviewees for summer positions, and if a white person interviewing one of these men decided that she would rather hire the white guy she interviewed that morning because he laughed at her jokes, seemed like he would be more fun to have around, and in general did not give the impression of hating her, this does not make her a racist, it makes her human. This is especially the case given that often these law firms hired the *black* student who had been able to at least meet them halfway. It was highly indicative that the only two white students who did not get jobs were both quite awkward socially. The two black students were snubbed not because of racist bias, but because of their immersion in a Separatist sense of whites as malevolent aliens.

I once met a black freshman, son of a college professor, who was "black-identified" by his own explicit acknowledgment, and already processing UC Berkeley as a "racist school" after a few months on campus. At our table sat three women, one white, one Asian, and one black. While readily engaging the black woman, this fellow would only give polite answers to the attempts by the two other women to speak to him, and it was clear that for him they essentially did not exist. Twice he drew blanks on casual references they made to campus traditions and landmarks—spiritually he had ensconced himself in "black Berkeley," living on a black dormitory floor and majoring in African-American Studies. Many people would see this student as "nurturing his cultural identity," or as having "inherited the fears of his ancestors." Perhaps—but so determinedly reserving his sincere and open engagement for interactions with blacks only, he, too, is likely to have some trouble getting internships and jobs, and will be warmly supported by his friends in attributing this to racism. However, a white manager can be an outright Negrophile and be chary of hiring someone who gives all appearances of not liking him. If he refrains from hiring this guy because his guarded demeanor makes him seem less pleasant to be around than the equally qualified woman he hires instead, he is not necessarily a racist (especially since the woman he interviewed may herself have been black). This manager is human—people black, white, yellow, and brown would rather not spend time with people who have something against them. The kind of inbred and permanent wariness of whites that this student had is natural in someone who grew up in segregated America, north or south. It is also "understandable" in an inner-city teen today. But in an eighteen-year-old who grew up comfortable in an integrated suburb, this wariness has outlived its usefulness and become a hindrance toward success.

## Separatism Makes Us Inferiors

The most damning way in which Separatism forces black Americans into self-sabotage is in identifying cultural blackness with pardoning and even glorifying immoral behavior. This is for the simple reason that the person who cannot be taken to account is not an equal.

In an America where polite discourse requires us to think of a black murderer as a victim, a black lazy person as a nonconformist, and a black person who refuses to reason from A to Z as a storyteller, we have resurrected the Founding Fathers' reprehensible classification of the black American as three-fifths of a person. The positive reception of the O.J. Simpson verdict by educated blacks, the uproar over the restriction of welfare benefits to five years, and the calls to treat Tawana Brawley's callow lie as a "communal truth" are among the issues that keep all of us from being able to imagine even a prosperous black corporate manager living in Palo Alto as a representative "American."

The sovereign world so many black Americans have been driven to hide in by the lethal combination of freedom with insecurity is historically "understandable." In our time, however, this response has spun out of control. The sad fact is that there is not a people in human history who have made any lasting mark in the world—or even been happy— closing themselves off to influence from other cultures, discouraging even their best and brightest from unfettered curiosity and close reasoning, and aggressively pardoning moral lapses and murder. Black America can do better than this, because any humans can, and most have, from the metropolises of Japan to the Congolese rain forest. To do so, however, we must cover our ears to the Victimologist siren song which encourages us, decade after decade, to settle for less and teach our children to do the same.

Few things make this dilemma clearer than the performance of African Americans in school, which is directly traceable to Separatist pollution of the black American soul.

# 3

## THE CULT OF ANTI-INTELLECTUALISM

We're afraid that black students who perform at that high a level aren't going to be concerned with nurturing an African-American presence at Berkeley.

— Undergraduate black student recruiter, spring 1998

The reader may have detected by now that I watch a lot of television. Another stray moment I remember was an episode of *The Facts of Life* where a black girl (not Kim Fields's Tootie, but a one-shot character) was depicted as being obsessed with Latin. Every now and then she would get up and passionately declaim some Latin phrase to emphasize a point.

It was another moment that struck me as so false that I still remember it almost twenty years later. Latin is harder than French or Spanish, and because it's dead, you don't learn it to express yourself or talk to anyone, but to read mostly formal things written by extremely dead people about a world quite different from ours. In other words, learning Latin is very much an intellectual exercise, which one engages in out of curiosity about a different time and place, and ideas of a universal nature. The little girl in this *Facts of Life* episode struck me as so otherworldly because I had met only one black person in my life who had ever taken Latin; twenty years later I have met one more.

There is a popular motivational book for black people called *Success Runs in Our Race*. In some ways, it does, but that thirty seconds on *The Facts of Life* is a reminder that one area where everyone would have to agree that Success Does Not Run in Our Race is school. Almost forty years after the Civil Rights Act, African-American students on the average are the weakest in the United States, at all ages, in all subjects, and regardless of class level.

The Cult of Victimology insures that this problem is viewed as the result of black suffering. Victimology plays its first hand in infusing almost all discussions of the issue with the tacit assumption that "black" means "poor," when in fact only a portion of black children are poor. From here, it becomes even more natural to attribute this lag in black scholarly performance to inequities in school resources, teachers' racist biases, and chaotic home lives.

We are given this message so steadily and with so little variation that these assumptions can appear unassailable. However, in reality, school funding, racist bias, and quality of home life have the same relationship to why most black students do so badly in school as a weakened immune system has to whether or not one gets a cold. A virus causes the common cold. Various factors make people more susceptible to that virus, but if the virus is not present, not even all of those factors together will cause a cold. In this light, it is important, and insufficiently considered, that (1) the very factors considered to preordain black students to mediocrity do not thwart a great many minority groups from scholarly achievement, and (2) black students as often as not continue to perform below standard level even in plush, enlightened settings where all efforts are being made to help them.

As the common cold is caused by the rhinovirus, black students do so poorly in school decade after decade not because of racism, funding, class, parental education, etc., but because of a virus of Anti-intellectualism that infects the black community. This Anti-intellectual strain is inherited from whites having denied education to blacks for centuries, and has been concentrated by the Separatist trend, which in rejecting the "white" cannot help but cast school and books as suspicious and alien, not to be embraced by the authentically "black" person.

That this attitude is a problem in inner-city communities is not unknown, but it also permeates the whole of black culture, all the way up to the upper class. Certain components of cultural identity are felt more subconsciously than consciously, and often become apparent only upon travel elsewhere, such as the American commitment to the individual over the collective. In this vein, the African-American "cultural disconnect," as a black teacher friend of mine calls it, from the realm of books and learning operates covertly as much as overtly. Yet its pervasive power in either guise renders it, like Victimology and Separatism, a defining feature of cultural blackness today.

Nevertheless, the conviction that black children are barred from doing well in school, rather than culturally disinclined to, is fiercely held, because the reign of Victimology in the media as well as much black American thought makes it so difficult to believe that a race issue might break down in any other way. The problem is that this leads us to aim solutions to black school failure at black victimhood rather than at an unfortunate aspect of the culture. Because these solutions are misaimed, they either stall or fail outright. The media emphasizes the onset, and later the defense, of such programs rather than their actual results. Yet it is a fact that after the institution of affirmative action, Head Start, campus minority counseling programs, and African-American Studies curricula, black school performance has risen a couple of notches and then plateaued.

This corresponds neatly to the minor extent to which black victimhood contributes to the problem; the rest of it is the culture—just as if all Americans' immune systems were normal, the common cold would be a bit less rampant but would still be around. But Victimology ensures that the failure of educational strategies to make more than a dent in the problem is traced to the eternity of racism, and that the plateau is either attributed to racist "backlash," or more often, simply ignored.

Because of this ideological holding pattern, in our America it is difficult not to feel that black students do poorly in school because the System does them in. The problem is in fact one of modern black American social psychology, and will yield only to solutions that squarely face this uncomfortable but decisive cultural trait.

Many of the things in this chapter were difficult to write about; some may feel, as many black women did during the Anita Hill–Clarence Thomas controversy, that I am unjustly airing the community's "dirty laundry." Yet I feel compelled to do so because there are times when airing dirty laundry is the only way to help. Only by taking a deep breath and devoting as much attention to these problems as we currently do to victimhood can we really start black students on the path to doing as well in school as anyone else.

It is important to realize when reading this chapter that it is not intended simply as a survey of unpleasant facts about black students' performance in school. My aim is to carefully build a specific argument—that the appearance that black students do poorly in school because the System does them in is an illusion that denies these students' basic humanity, and that the actual determining factor is a culture-internal legacy. The argument will consist of three parts.

The first part will attempt to undo a natural tendency to associate the black scholarly lag with poor people, and show that it cuts deeply across the culture as a whole. It must be understood that this is the *sole* goal of this upcoming section. I will address the Anti-intellectualism issue *itself* later; however, I cannot productively discuss this until it is clear that the black scholarly lag extends far beyond crumbling schools and violent neighborhoods. It is only this that I am arguing in the following section.

## Black Student Performance: The Realities

### SAT Scores

Black students' notoriously poor performance on Scholastic Achievement Tests is widely discussed, but few are aware of the breadth between black students and others, and even fewer that the gap has no correlation with income level. Even on the broad level, the numbers are disheartening: From 1981 to 1995, among students at a sample of twenty-eight selective universities, William G. Bowen and Derek Bok found that almost three-quarters of white students taking the SAT nationwide scored over 1200 out of 1600, but little more than one-quarter of black students did. This lag had the effect that, for example, the black students entering Berkeley with the best SAT scores in 1988 clustered in the lowest quarter of scores for all students at the school.

Through the "black is poor" lens that race issues are almost always filtered through in American discourse, statistics like this tend to be attributed to the fact that a greater proportion of blacks are poor than whites. But poverty is only a subsidiary factor in overall black SAT performance: for one, we must consider how few poor black students even take the SAT.

More to the point, in 1995, the mean SAT score for black students nationwide from families making $50,000 or more was a mere 849 out of 1600. This must be compared with the mean score in 1995 for white students from families earning $10,000 or less—i.e., really, no money—869. Money isn't everything, but even when we take parents' education into account the facts are the same. In 1995, the mean for black students whose parents had graduate, not just undergraduate, degrees was 844, even lower than the overall middle-class black mean. Statistics can deceive, but here even headcounts tell the story: In 1995, exactly 184 black students in the United States scored over 700 on the verbal portion of the SAT—not even enough to fill a passenger plane. In the math portion, 616 scored over 700. This was 2 percent and 6 percent of the black test takers, whereas five times and almost ten times, respectively, that proportion of white test-takers scored above 700. Many people addressing this issue point to the tricky relationship between income and class; I will discuss this issue later. Few of us, however, could honestly say that so many black people are "poor" financially or culturally that we would expect the entire group of black students in the United States doing better than 700 on the verbal portion of the SAT in an entire year to not even be able to fill one floor of a movie theater. Clearly poverty is not the issue here.

In their pro–affirmative action study *The Shape of the River,* William Bowen and Derek Bok note that most blacks' SAT scores at top schools are above the national white average and that blacks' average scores are better than the national average in 1951, which for everyone was lower. These points distract us from the crucial questions. Even if blacks' average SAT scores at top schools are higher than the national white average, why are they still the lowest in the schools overall? Even if blacks score better on the SAT than Archie Andrews and Henry Aldrich would have in 1951, the important issue is that today's black students' scores are still closer than anyone else's to the lower averages of yesteryear.

## What Does a Black Kid Know About Skiing? The Validity of the Tests

A standard answer to this question is that the tests do not measure black students' competence. It is casually assumed in most discussions of black school performance that whatever their SAT scores, black students go on to perform as well in college as other students. At one of many symposia on the demise of affirmative action at UC Berkeley, one particularly vocal (Latino) professor who advocates racial preferences in admissions bellowed to a round of applause "We hear these abstruse philosphical discussions—'I got a higher SAT score than you, it's not "fair"'—let's know what SAT scores *mean!*" But there are figures on what they mean, and black students' lower SAT scores mean that they make lower grades in college.

First, SAT tests have been shown to correlate rather well with student performance: There is a tendency for SAT scores to correlate with college grade point average over four years for both whites and blacks. The correlation is nowhere near a lockstep, but neither is there all but no correlation, as is assumed by many. Here, for example, are William G. Bowen and Derek Bok who, although avid advocates of affirmative action, note after tabulating extensive data from twenty-eight selective universities and subjecting it to statistical analysis:

> The simple association between SAT scores and grades is clear-cut. As one would have expected, class rank varies directly with SAT scores. Among both black and white students, those in the highest SAT interval had an appreciably higher average rank in class. . . . Moreover, the positive relationship between students' SAT scores and their rank in class . . . remains

after we control for gender, high school grades, socioeconomic
status, school selectivity, and major, as well as for race.

Bowen and Bok also found that in the class of 1989, white students'
average class rank was in the 53rd percentile, but black students' was in
only the 23rd—the bottom quarter. Even after adjustment for factors
like SATs, high-school grades, income, major, and others, black students
rose only to about the 37th percentile—the lower second quarter. This is
only one of many studies, all done by people concerned about black education, confirming the same discrepancy and disproving the commonly
believed yet counterintuitive idea that college regularly sparks mediocre
high-school performers into high scholarly achievement.

Indeed, studies have shown that SAT scores if anything *overpredict*
black students' performance. In other words, the slippage between the
score and future performance leans backwards—black students tend to
make worse grades in college than white ones with the same SAT scores.

These solid demonstrations of the correlation between SAT scores
and performance are a contradiction to the commonly heard assertion
that "SATs don't mean anything anyway." Nor is it surprising. Few of us
could name students with excellent SAT scores who found themselves at
sea in university-level work, unless, of course, there was some extenuating psychological or social factor—the SAT is not, in itself, simply a
meaningless hoop students are made to jump through that has no relation to college performance. If it were, then students who made *abysmal*
SAT scores would often sail through college with top grades with little
effort—yet how many students like this have any of us ever met? No
matter what the societal reason, statistics show that there is a meaningful correlation between SAT scores and school performance.

Many will counter that there are plenty of students who do poorly or
only okay on standardized tests but do well in school. Yet this does not
signify that the SATs are meaningless, because again, the fact remains
that students who do well on them almost *always* do well in school. It
does mean that the SAT's predictability wanes somewhat in the middle
range. So we have two facts. One is that not only statistics, but common
sense show that it is reasonable to use the SAT as *one* indicator of how
well a student is likely to do in school—for the simple reason that a high
SAT score virtually guarantees strong performance in college.

The second is that, contrary to the going wisdom, the black-white
SAT lag does signify that the proportion of black high-schoolers who
will do well in school is lower than among other groups. It follows from

simple math. For white and Asian students, the proportion who will do well is composed of the ones who do well on SATs *plus* those who do not, but will excel in school anyway. Among black students, however, almost all of those who excel in school are from the second category rather than from a combination of both—which means that *the fraction of black students overall who will excel constitute a lesser fraction than that in other groups.* There might be a temptation to suppose that the fraction is not smaller, and that instead, the proportion of potentially excellent black students is the same as in other groups but that for some reason almost none of them do well on standardized tests. However, this idea forces one to claim that there is something inherent in black psychological makeup that prevents the expression of scholarly aptitude via tests, and our response to that must be, as one hears around nowadays, "Don't *go* there! . . ."

Many these days do go there, of course, charging the SAT as inappropriate for minorities in "testing only one kind of intelligence," what psychologist Howard Gardner calls "linguistic" and "logical-mathematical" intelligence. Gardner urges that teachers take into account spatial, interpersonal, intrapersonal, existential, musical, and other intelligences as well in communicating ideas. There is much value in this, but until by chance such teaching techniques by chance become established nationwide, "linguistic" and "logical-mathematical" intelligence will remain the most applicable to college material and how it is taught—reading critically, writing coherent papers, doing problem sets. In any case, almost every other group in the country manages to develop its "linguistic" and "logical-mathematical" intelligences and post regular averages or above on the SAT, so once again, our question is why black students are so uncomfortable taking a test that requires these kinds of intelligence. Separatism encourages some to essentialize blacks as having a "black intelligence" separate from wonky "logical-mathematicality," but let's be careful—that assertion is ironically reminiscent of some highly unsavory arguments. An America where black students are encouraged to nurture their artistic and spatial intelligence out of respect for their culture is an America where black people are our house entertainers and athletes. Last time I checked we were trying to get past that—isn't this what *The Bell Curve* told blacks they should sit back and be satisfied with?

Meanwhile, one often hears that high-school grades ought be the central focus in admissions rather than SATs, out of a belief that performance on standardized tests is unrelated to how students are doing in their actual schoolwork. Yet Lawrence Steinberg and his researchers have found that in nine high schools in California and Wisconsin, including both predominantly white suburban schools as well as inner-city minority-dominated ones, black (and Latino) students made the lowest grades *regardless of family income*, with low-income Asians regularly outperforming middle-class black ones by a wide margin. Along the same lines, black students in the class admitted to Berkeley had an overall average of B+ while the whites students had straight-A averages.

Finally, the idea that SAT scores are culturally biased is an anachronism. The formulators of standardized tests are now dedicated almost to the point of obsession to eliminating all possible instances of cultural bias: How many of us have ever heard a black student complaining that the SAT she took assumed that students knew which wine goes with chicken? In any case, the rare examples of this type that used to elicit complaint only applied to the few poor black students who took the SAT (a classic example being references to skiing, a sport alien to an inner-city resident).

The performance gap continues in postgraduate school. There were 420 black students in the 27,000 who entered the top 18 law schools in 1991, but only 24 of them would have been admitted without racial preference policies. In New York in 1992, 63 percent of black takers of the bar exam failed while only 18 percent of the whites did. In 1988, 51.1 percent of blacks, but just 12.3 percent of whites, failed the first part of the National Board of Medical Examiners exam.

Thus all of the relevant evidence confirms that black students tend strongly to underperform in college, and most important, this is regardless of class or parental income. The figures are not simply drawn down by those contributed by poor students, then; we are faced with a culture-wide problem.

So far, of course, all I have given is numbers. But the numbers reflect concrete experience. At Berkeley, I have had occasion to teach large numbers of both black and other students. I spent a long time resisting acknowledging something that ultimately became too consistent and obvious to ignore, which was that black undergraduates at Berkeley tended to be among the worst students on campus, by any estimation. I tried my very best to chalk up each experience I had to local factors and personalities, but as one episode piled upon another, it got to the point where pretending that there was not a connection among them all would have required a suspension of disbelief beyond my capacity.

What sort of episodes do I mean?

\* \* \*

A black student intended to write a senior honors thesis under my supervision transforming episodes of her family history into fiction. At the beginning of the semester she submitted a three-page selection she had written for a previous class. As the semester passed, while my white senior honors students were engaged in research for their papers and consulting with me weekly or biweekly, this student came by only twice, regaling me with tales of her family history and promising written work "soon." I let her know that she would have to submit some kind of written material to me before the end of the semester so that I could grade her for her semester's "work." Even that was generous, of course, but I got nothing from her until just before Christmas break, and what she handed me was, quite simply, her family tree, drawn in pencil on a piece of notebook paper. I never saw her again.

That same year another black student writing an honors thesis under me managed to turn in a brief progress report before Christmas, but had obviously only looked at one book. She was diligent enough to report to my office every two weeks, but while by the second semester my white students were turning in chapters, she would always come empty-handed, with vague plans for traveling to do research. In the end she handed in an eleven-page thesis, in contrast to the thirty-page average of the others, and it was obviously a last-minute job based more on impressionistic reflection at her desk than on research.

A black student in one of my classes turned in a midterm so poor that it was difficult to believe that he had actually been physically present in the class, and after this disappeared for five weeks. Most students if they miss more than one class tend to call, leave a note, or send an e-mail explaining why, but sadly, black students often do not. He finally reappeared saying that he had been very sick and that he would get notes from the previous classes and attend regularly from then on, resisting my gentle suggestion that he drop the class. Nevertheless, his attendance thereafter was spotty, his final was predictably even worse than the midterm and made it clear that he had never gotten notes for the classes he missed, and he did not submit a final paper. I could not help but flunk him, but a few months later he came to my office hoping I would retract the F because it would interfere with his continuing to get the scholarship paying his tuition.

Another black student joined one of my linguistics classes. He had not taken linguistics before, but the nature of the subject was such that this was not as important as it is in many other linguistics classes, and I assured him that I would help him through any rough spots he encountered. He was very good in class at giving dramatic speeches about discrimination when race issues happened to come up. But his homework showed that he was not taking in the ideas that I was teaching, and he did not improve even after I had more than once tutored him in my office. Shortly before the final, he vanished, and I did not hear from him again until months later, when he said he had simply frozen at the thought of taking the final.

Within reason, I try to give black students as much slack as possible. I used to do it out of a conventional vague sense that black students were "victims" on some level, but lately I have come to do it out of a sense that most of them are caught in a cultural holding pattern they cannot help. In any case, I made an arrangement with this student to take another of my classes, an African-American Studies course assuming no linguistics background, where he could use his grade to cancel out the F I had had to give him in the previous course.

Yet in that class, the story was the same: an almost strangely clueless first midterm, spotty attendance, and one day he even showed up at the end of a class eating a plate of food from the campus eatery, having come by just to pick up a handout (as well as another one for his friend, who had simply not shown up at all). He disappeared before the second midterm, later explaining that a relative had died. When he came back, because it would have been easy for him to get answers to the midterm by talking to the students who had already taken it (and also because I could not imagine it not being a disaster anyway), I made up a few extra credit research questions for him to take home and answer. I based the questions entirely upon class material and was extremely explicit about the kinds of answers I wanted.

What he gave me back had obviously involved effort, but what he had done was go to the library and look up new information, having learned so little from the class that he did not perceive the connection between the questions I gave him and the material I had been covering. Furthermore, the material he presented was largely undigested paraphrasing of his sources and had only diagonal connection to the questions I asked. Later on, this student came to my office hoping I could raise the C I gave him, as well as write him a recommendation for law school.

A student came to not one but both of my African-American Studies classes six weeks into the semester to enroll. She seemed strangely casual about joining classes when so much material had already been covered, but said that she had been having trouble with the administration, and desperately needed my classes for credit. She claimed to be a good reader and seemed mature and sure of herself, so I took a chance. I let her know that in one of the classes, there was no textbook and that class notes were essential, such that to prepare for the upcoming midterm she would need to borrow someone's notes. Yet two days before the midterm, I asked her how her studying was going and she told me she had only been going through the course reader, which contained only about 10 percent of the information I was going to test the students on. I arranged for her to borrow notes from one of the better students in the class. Unsurprisingly, she did very badly on the midterm, but then most of us would in a class where we had only seen most of the material as someone else's notes and only heard a few of the professor's lectures.

In the other class, there were two midterms and then a final, and the student had joined that class right after the first midterm. On my way to the classroom to give out the second one, I ran into her on her way to my office to tell me that she just "couldn't" take the midterm. She couldn't give a reason why, and therefore I insisted that she come along with me and take it and do her best, since she had been present in all of the classes that the midterm covered, and to give her a dispensation would be unfair to the other students. She did very poorly, to an extent which again left me wondering how she could have been present in the class and taken in so little.

Shortly before the end of the term she disappeared from both classes with no explanation. In the other class, the students were assigned to write final papers about some aspect of Black Musical Theater. I gave them free rein on topics, with the exception that they were not to write biographies of performers, since it would be too easy to merely paraphrase a couple of books. I said this often and had written it in the syllabus. In the middle of the summer, I found a paper from this student under my office door, marked "I didn't write this for a grade, just the credit." That message was not only rather enigmatic, but sad, because I still wondered whether something terrible happened to her, or whether she had been overwhelmed by university work; to this day I don't know. But what was even sadder was that her paper was a biographical sketch of a black performer, derived entirely from one book.

In a large class that I taught not long ago, one black student attended class only rarely. Each student was enrolled in a section run by a teaching assistant, and in an assigned debate on a societal issue, this student argued for her position based only on folk wisdom I had carefully shown the errors in and even told the class not to resort to in the debates. Another black student failed the midterm, telling the teaching assistant that he had not been able to study because his car broke down. However, he hadn't been doing well in previous assignments either, and the fact is that a car breakdown does not prevent a diligent student from studying. By hook or by crook, diligent students study—or let the professor know that they have had an unusual problem and make arrangements to take tests the next day, etc. Yet I frequently get inadequate excuses from black students—when I get any excuse at all.

These stories go on and on; for each one, I could tell another two. One student's answer to an essay question was two literally incomprehensible sentences, and she handed in the test with a jolly, salutory smile. There was one student who kept not showing up to class on days when I had seen him socializing on campus; one day I asked him what was up and he said that he had been in a car accident not long ago that had sent him into a depression which led him to come to campus but not go to classes. (To his credit, he at least admitted that this was not right.)

The reader might justifiably wonder whether there is something intimidating about my classes that elicits these reactions. I can only say that in my years of teaching, I have never had a student disappear without explanation, or turn in a test that made me wonder how she could have attended class and done so badly, who was not African American. The reader might also wonder whether the problem lies in my making these students uncomfortable personally. I should first note that I have never shared any of the kinds of views I am putting forth in this book in these classes, none of which have been on sociological or political topics. Morever, I can only say that on the personal level, many of these students tend to be my favorites. Despite the against-the-grain sociopolitical opinions I am sharing here, there is a special comfort I feel with black students, and I would venture to say that most of them found me more accessible than most of their professors, partly because of my relative youth (this, for example, partly explains why so many of them ask me for recommendations and favors). I *liked* most of these students as people and most of them (at least, perhaps, until they got their grades) liked me, and that is much of why it pains me to write this section, or to even re-read it as I edit it.

In any case, however, something I cannot stress enough about all of the students I have mentioned is that not a single one of them grew up in the ghetto or has ever known poverty or anything close (this was part of why I chose them to write about). Opinions differ on what "middle class" means, but none of these students would even strike most of us as "working class"—all of them are more *The Preacher's Wife* than 227. We must resist a possible tendency to envision me as a stand-in for Jaime Escalante in *Stand and Deliver,* facing surly students fresh off violent streets slouched in their chairs with knives in their pockets, complaining that school is for "chumps." Black Berkeley undergraduates are almost all upwardly mobile, bright-eyed young people, many with cars, none of whom would be uncomfortable in a nice restaurant and many of whom probably do know what wine goes with chicken.

Thus these students' behavior has nothing to do with the 'hood. Many might respond to these stories by pointing out that there are bad white students as well. Of course this is true; I have my stories of white (and even Asian) slackers, too. Importantly, however, despite the fact that white and Asian students vastly outnumber black ones, I encounter episodes like this with white and Asian students perhaps once or twice a year. More to the point, sad as it is to say this, I have gradually had to admit that this sort of thing has been the *norm* for black students I have taught.

None of this is to say that there are not excellent black students—I have had those, too. In the same large class I recently taught that the two unfortunate cases I described not long ago were in, another black student was one of the best out of 180. In particular, my impression, albeit limited, has been that black students at the very best schools perform more or less at the same level as others; the handful of black students I encountered during the year I taught at Cornell were nothing less than exemplary, and I have reason to suppose that the facts are similar at other top schools. But the existence of these people does not belie my sad point about the culture as a whole, because as the very cream of the crop, they are *exceptions,* not the rule. At Berkeley, I have found it impossible to avoid nothing less than fearing that a black student in my class is likely to be a problem case. We are trained to say at this point that I am "stereotyping," but I have come to expect this for the simple reason that it has been true, class after class, year after year. A few white professors I have spoken to reluctantly admit that they have had the same experience over their careers.

And finally, we must remember that I am writing about UC Berkeley—these students are among the best black scholars in the state of California.

It is not fun to write this; I would rather just let these crummy episodes fade into history. It might be useful to restate here that I am recording these stories not to criticize, but to build a point—that the black scholarly lag is not merely due to a drag exerted by inner-city casualties, nor is it a mysterious statistical point that has no reflection on the ground in real life. On the contrary, what stories like these show is that black students of all classes exhibit a strong tendency to dedicate themselves less to schoolwork than do other students, regardless of life history or present conditions.

Facing this without turning away is, in my view, so important that I feel compelled to address it a bit further. The urge is very strong to frame each of these black students as individuals and not "stereotype," or to resort to "There's some of that" (which essentially translates as "The real problem is racism"). This is how I myself tried to deal with the issue for years at Berkeley, but besides my and others' anecdotal experience about individual students, another factor made it painfully clear to me that something much larger than isolated "cases" is involved. At Berkeley, I have had occasion to teach first nearly all-white and then nearly all-black versions of two classes on completely distinct topics. The contrast between the white and black versions of these classes as a whole was too stark and too consistent to be explainable as anything but a general factor, and that factor was not the 'hood.

One of the classes was a course on the history of black musical theater. One year most of the students were white or Asian; the next time I taught it almost all of the students were black. The white version of the class was, if I may, a success. The students loved the material, many of them wrote great papers, and some of them kept in touch afterward. I looked forward to teaching it again, but the black version was another world.

The white students had enjoyed the historical material, such as anecdotes about bygone creators and performers, old recordings, and weird old film clips. However, presenting the same material to the black students, I might as well have been reading out of the phone book. The glazed eyes and aggressive doodling (during class one student even read a comic book) were things I had never encountered in a classroom. Two white students from the Linguistics Department who had enjoyed a class they had taken with me sat in for fun, and were also struck by how different the atmosphere was from that of our other class together. Attendance was terrible; after the first couple of weeks I was lucky to have half of the class in the room on the same day, and some came so seldom that

I assumed they had dropped the class, only to see them turn up for the midterm (something not unknown in large classes, but rare in classes of twenty or so like this one).

The reader is right to wonder whether the problem was my teaching, but it is important to remember that the other class had eaten up the same lectures and material, and a class about singing and dancing that includes listening to tapes and watching movies is not exactly the hardest to make interesting. It was clear that the material simply did not interest most of the black students. When Todd Duncan, the original Porgy in *Porgy and Bess,* died during the semester, I did a little tribute to him where I talked about his life, dimmed the lights as a gesture of deliberately stagey yet also sincere gravity, and played one of his recordings. A couple of weeks later, we got to *Porgy and Bess,* and I mentioned him again and even showed a video interview with him made shortly before his death. On the midterm, one question was "Name one of the principal performers in the original production of *Porgy and Bess.*" Exactly two people out of about twenty wrote "Todd Duncan"; one person wrote "John Bubbles," who played Sportin' Life; the rest of the class either wrote "Paul Robeson" (who I had explicitly told the class never sang Porgy) or left it blank. In general, most of the class did very badly on the midterm, and I had to curve way up to avoid flunking most of them. One student politely expressed surprise that I had expected the students to memorize data; yet I had deliberately avoided making the course an exercise in trivia, only giving names that were important and only requiring students to be able to place a musical within a decade rather than the exact year. I asked him what he was expecting to be on the test, and he wasn't sure.

I couldn't help noticing a particular contrast. In the white class, interest waned a bit as we passed into the 1970s and beyond. The students got a kick out of the vintage stuff; for most of them, *The Wiz* and *Once on This Island* were more recognizable and thus less interesting. The black students, on the other hand, perked up a bit just as we got to the 70s—the official moment was when a few of them boogied a bit in their seats when I played "Ease on Down the Road" from *The Wiz.* They were happy when we got to what they already knew and had a personal relationship to, but the older material, less familiar and requiring more active engagement, was a turn-off, despite all the artists being black. Notably, throughout the semester I could count on a bit of a "click" when I talked about the discrimination people had encountered—they were open to being reinforced in Victimologist ideology. Indeed, many may have wished that had been the foundation of the whole course, as it was for a black musicals class I sat in on at Stanford years ago. But they were not interested in learning anything new.

I have also taught a course on pidgin and creole languages, Euro-African hybrid languages like Haitian Creole, Jamaican patois, and Papiamentu, to white and black classes, the black one for African-American Studies and assuming no linguistics background. One of the three black versions I taught over the years was especially instructive. There were two white students and seven black. The black students mostly quickly lapsed into spotty attendance, one of them even going as far as not showing up for a midterm, giving no explanation, and coming to the following class casually expecting to be allowed to take it home (I had to dismiss her from the class). One day I gave a lecture on the two main creole languages of Surinam, quite different from one another, with very different histories, and spoken by very different people. Two weeks later before a midterm, two of the black students sought some last-minute clarifications before I gave out the test. I am not generally averse to this kind of thing within reason, but their clarifications included wanting to know what the names of the two creoles were, how they were different, and whether "Surinam" was the name of a country or a language—and one of these students was the only one in the class who had taken linguistics courses. After several weeks of this kind of thing (including the botched extra credit assignment for the student I mentioned earlier), even I began wondering whether I wasn't communicating clearly. But the problem was that the two white students, neither of whom had had any linguistics background, were doing very well, listening to me say the exact same things and watching me put the exact same things on the board. One of them, for instance, was diligent about coming to my office hours for help, while not a single black student ever came.

The difference between black and white here was too obvious to explain away as a matter of isolated characters, and the most striking thing was that the black students were mostly blithe about all of this. Of course, there was a gray zone: One black student did far better than the other black ones. Pointedly, he had been one of the only black students in the white version of the musical theater course, and thus knew my "style." There was also another one who, quite unusually among Berkeley students, had actually had the underprivileged upbringing mythically attributed to all black students. He did not do well, but he was trying as hard as he could, I gave him a lot of extra attention, and I graded him taking his circumstances into account. But the contrast between the two white students dutifully taking notes and asking thoughtful questions and most of the other black students, including two who regularly whispered in the back like junior high schoolers, was telling.

When I finally realized that there was an unmistakable pattern in the classroom behavior of black students at Berkeley year after year, I began to recall that I had been seeing this pattern at other schools throughout my life. When I was a graduate student at Stanford, I took a course on pidgins and creoles that remains the best I ever had; it was where I chose my career focus. The class mixed undergraduates and graduates, and was a lively, stimulating group, with almost all of the twenty-odd people speaking and commenting often. The one exception was the two black undergraduates, who generally sat politely waiting for the class to be over, with their facial expressions making their lack of interest plain. Both of them later told me that they found the subject ultimately rather pointless. Like most academic subjects, pidgin and creole studies indeed only occasionally has direct application to life as we live it in the United States, where few such languages are spoken natively, but the other students in the class enjoyed the material simply because it was interesting—these two, however, did not. Later I lived with a white engineering graduate student who told me that as much as he hated to say it, he had noticed as a teaching assistant that black students tended strongly not to work as hard and to give up more easily when encountering difficulty.

The two in the pidgins and creoles class reminded me of two other black undergraduates in a strange class I took in Romance languages at Rutgers in 1984. They were relatively interested in the big, familiar languages like Spanish, but as the professor got to the obscure Romance languages like Romanian, Catalan, and languages spoken in Swiss and Italian mountains that few of us will ever hear spoken, their attention waned, and they ended up spending most of the semester passing notes. When I entered a private middle school, my best friend was a black guy from a middle-class, racially mixed neighborhood. He gave no indication of being unintelligent except his silence in the classroom—and the problem was not racial discomfort because our class was taught by a black woman who, actually, had a way of subtly giving special attention to him, me, and the other two black kids in our classroom. Yet the following fall my friend wasn't back; it turned out he had flunked summer school, extremely rare at this school. As I will discuss further in a different context, two years later at the same school I watched several black students leave after ninth grade, the year schoolwork became much more challenging than it had been in middle school. In fifth grade, a group of black students in my elementary school turned away from schoolwork and, as "cool" kids, gradually dragged a couple of other black students' performance down with theirs. One of my best friends in second grade, a black student, had one problem: not being committed to doing schoolwork. Throughout my life, I have seen that Anti-intellectualism is a central component of black identity. Like a virus, it sets in early, it has no regard for status in society, and once settled, it almost never lets go.

Of course, in the best of all possible worlds, one would base conclusions about black American student performance upon having taught both white and black students in colleges and universities all over the country. Along those lines, one might ask "How can he make these broad claims based on his experiences at one school?" For one, however, since within one lifetime no one person could teach at more than a few schools long enough to see any general trends, to make this objection is to claim that no nationwide generalization about black students' orientation to school is possible at all from one person. In that light, however, we must note that if I were instead saying that my impression was that black students are done in by racism, then not a soul would object that I had no grounds for saying such a thing based upon my experiences at one school!

More to the point, any argument that conclusions based upon experiences at UC Berkeley are somehow not representative is incomplete without an explanation as to what makes Berkeley so different. What precisely would it be about UC Berkeley that would make black student performance there so anomalous compared to black student bodies in the rest of the country? Moreover, while I have used Berkeley as my main source of illustrations, I have also argued based upon my life experiences in Philadelphia, New Jersey, and Palo Alto, which leads to the question as to whether there is some particular element in the water supplies of Berkeley; Palo Alto; Philadelphia; New Brunswick, New Jersey; and Lawnside, New Jersey, that presented me with skewed data unparalleled in Houston, Trenton, Baltimore, or Los Angeles. During the writing of this book I have more than once been told things like "You'd find a lot less of that in the Northeast" or once even (my favorite): "California is not exactly the center of progressive black thought, nor is Philadelphia." Yet never has anyone explained just *why* black people in Cleveland, St. Louis, and Atlanta are apparently so different in their thinking than are those in any of the particular places I happen to have lived, nor why life seems to have so consistently shuttled me, and just me, into one supposedly backwards locale after another.

In any case, I have only presented my observations as illustrations of national trends in grades and test scores charted in the hard numbers I began this chapter with, and these nationwide data show that my experiences, as most of us would suspect, reflect general tendencies, not California *bizarrerie*.

My point is that there is a misconception that the black scholarly lag is essentially a matter of poverty, and that outside of that context, black students do as well in school as anyone else regardless of their SAT scores. It would be much easier for all of us if this were true, but it isn't. Not only black students' SAT scores, but their high-school and college grades lag behind those of all other groups, and this is not simply because professors grade them down out of racist bias, as many black observers of the issue privately suppose. The sad but simple fact is that while there are some excellent black students, on the average, black students do not try as hard as other students.

The reason they do not try as hard is not because they are inherently lazy, nor is it because they are stupid. Furthermore, while many of these students are quite obviously disinclined to dedicate themselves meaningfully to school, just as many give their best efforts, but are unaware that white and Asian students' best efforts come from a level and depth of commitment beyond theirs. The reason black students so rarely hit that particular bar, while such a disproportionate number are disinclined to even try, is that all of these students belong to a culture infected with an Anti-intellectual strain, which subtly but decisively teaches them from birth not to embrace schoolwork too wholeheartedly.

In today's climate, this statement will naturally be processed as naive at best, traitorous fighting words at worst—and usually the latter. I make the statement not out of any preconceived political bent, nor to contribute to anyone's agenda except my own, which is to forge effective solutions to the problem of the education of black students—a problem urgent in *all* classes. I have arrived at my conclusions based on what I see as empirical evidence.

The typical counterarguments against this view, however, are not based on empirical evidence. Instead, they are perspectives based on the filtering and distortion of the empirical evidence through the treacherous lenses of Victimology and Separatism. Let's take a look at these arguments.

## Black Student Performance: The Myths

### Class

Victimology ensures that most discussions of black scholarly performance center upon the obvious and well-known barriers to learning in inner-city neighborhoods; "black" is tacitly assumed to be shorthand for "poor." When the fact that these problems persist among middle-class blacks occasionally comes up, it is usually only engaged long enough to be dismissed as due to the fact that a rise in income does not guarantee a rise in class profile. It is widely assumed that the black family considered "middle-class" financially is generally "working-class" or lower culturally, and that their children's poor school performance is traceable to their parents' lack of advanced degrees, the scarcity of books and magazines in their homes, the fact that conversations over dinner do not center upon the issues of the day, etc. The Latino affirmative action advocate who dismissed the value of SATs later touched briefly upon this issue by saying "We hear about 'middle class'—but most of these people are from struggling blue-collar families," "struggling blue-collar" being a phrase that comes up with almost uncanny consistency in this context.

The first problem here is that this speaker had no evidence to back up his characterization of "most" minority students at Berkeley, and in general, the proposition that "most" blacks and Latinos at schools like Berkeley are of "struggling blue-collar" parentage is extremely questionable. Very few of the black students I have met at Berkeley have parents who work for UPS or drive buses; most of their parents are managers, school principals, and even doctors and lawyers. This speaker, who has taught at Berkeley for years, cannot have missed this in itself. Victimology, trumping truth, forces him to maintain a sense that "black" (or Latino) means the ghetto (or barrio) or just a few steps beyond it, and Separatism reinforces this, in creating an uneasy sense that upward mobility threatens "authenticity."

The conflict with truth here reveals itself in the fact that for every Berkeley minority student's parent readily classifiable as "a working person," that this man might meet, another would be quite uncomfortable being designated "working-class" as he glides in his Nissan Altima every day to his job as a middle manager at Pacific Bell. It is also interesting to imagine Ross Perot, or even Daniel Moynihan, making a speech declaring that "regardless of income level or educational achievement, the black American remains blue collar." There would be an indignant barrage in response, furiously pointing to the millions of black families living in plush suburban homes, financially defining "middle class" as far downward as possible, and decrying the eternal racism at the heart of Perot's or Moynihan's statements. The fact that once education comes up all black Americans are the Honeymooners is a trick that Victimology and Separatism play on the mind.

How black America would respond to the " 'black' means 'struggling' " idea outside of education need not be guessed at. For example, upscale car companies have been reported to have a policy against selling advertising time to black and Hispanic radio stations even when their listeners are shown to include people of the financial demographic they target. These companies have decided that whatever proportion of affluent minorities is among the listeners would not justify the payments to the stations—in other words, that generally speaking, black and Latino people are salt-of-the-earth. This has been processed as evidence of the same old racist story by minority movers and shakers: "This report's findings are bleak and shameful but they come as no surprise," said Carolyn Cheeks Kilpatrick, Democratic member of Congress from Michigan.

But when the black scholarly lag is discussed, if anyone points to the burgeoning black middle class, then academics white and black carefully note things such as that blacks with middle-class incomes have less aggregate wealth than other groups in terms of savings, stocks, etc., all dedicated to showing that black success is a marginal phenomenon dwarfed in importance by a fundamental and pervasive lag—i.e., that by and large, black is poor or just getting by and that we'd better not forget it, and that to focus on occasional successes is callous and elitist.

So which is it? If white people agree with that assessment and refrain from paying black stations to run ads for BMWs, then they are racists. If black people say it, then they are "telling it like it is." Or: Whether or not black is poor depends on whether it will get us something. If saying so will get us into top schools or get us breaks on business loans, then black is poor. If saying so denies us radio advertisements, however, then suddenly attention must be paid to the black middle-class success story.

When it comes to education, we are told that what I am supposedly missing is that there is a slippage between income and class, and that someone with the income to buy a BMW may still not have the cultural background to create a mindset and environment designed to make one's children good students. But the link between class and school performance is vastly exaggerated when black students are discussed. We have no trouble imagining the Chinese immigrant family who run two restaurants, smiling in front of their new Volvo, sending their children to fine

THE CULT OF ANTI-INTELLECTUALISM **103**

universities. These parents are unlikely to discuss politics over dinner and do not subscribe to *The Economist,* but we do not see their children as cursed by "working-class culture" to make SAT scores under 1000 and only the occasional A. In the 1930s, the Jewish couple in Queens smiling in front of their new Studebaker often produced children who went on to become intellectuals, and no one wondered how they pulled this off, despite their having suffered overt discrimination worse than any black person encounters today, with their own parents often having been tailors, peddlers, and washerwomen on the Lower East Side.

Yet we are told that it is unreasonable to expect the children of the black family smiling in front of their new Lexus to do any better than average in school because their parents grew up working class. But why, precisely, do we consider black people different, and how often have we ever heard anyone even consider it germane to address that question? The idea that a student is only likely to do well in school if she comes from a home with book-lined living rooms, magazines on the coffee table, and lively discussions of current affairs over dinner is a myth, constructed especially to explain black underperformance. This is shown by the millions of people who have gone on to success in school without this, with no one even considering it to merit comment.

My point here is not to simply make a useless and critical charge along the lines of "Heck, why can't they do as well as everybody else—a white kid doesn't have to grow up in Beverly Hills to do well in school." My aim is to show that while there *is* a reason beyond laziness or mental unfitness that the black kids in front of the Lexus are unlikely to be stars in school, that reason is not class. We have expectations of blacks so different from those we have of other groups for a reason: because of something specific to black culture.

## Racism

Another truism about black education is that the burdens of societal racism hinder all but a lucky few black children of all classes from doing well in school. This apparently sympathetic notion has transmogrified into nothing less than an infantilization of black people.

Often in this book so far I have noted that racism is not dead, and the proof is not only isolated hate crimes, police brutality, or the (increasingly marginal) unvarnished bigot. Being a middle-class black person in America does involve becoming accustomed to coping with being subtly classified as a second-rung being in all manner of interactions and activities. This is only rarely a matter of "endemic hostility," as our Ralph Wileys and Derrick Bells would have it; most of it entails unconscious acts and biases on the part of people who would be quite surprised to realize the residual racism inside of them. To compare any of this to what it would have been like to be black in 1950 is like calling a puddle an ocean. Yet the residues of racism can be wearing.

To understand why racism is not a significant factor in black underperformance in school, it helps to take a detour and look at the kinds of racism that the typical middle-class black person encounters in America in the year 2000. This will serve two purposes. First, I hope it will alleviate any reader's sense that my views might stem from an inability to perceive racism where it does exist. Second, the detour will serve as an explicit base upon which I will make my point that these things, unfortunate though they are, do not doom a child to a C+ average.

### My Experiences with Racism

When I was a teenager I often took the commuter train between Philadelphia and Southern New Jersey. At rush hour, quite consistently the seat next to me was one of the last to fill up, despite the fact that with my head down reading a book, I cannot have given the appearance of being a hoodlum.

I once applied for a summer job at a food stand in a mall, and as I asked the manager when I might hear whether or not I got the job, I could sense that he was never going to call me. By chance, a woman who worked there was later hired by the company I did get a job with that summer, and she told me that the man had a policy of not hiring blacks (this was 1986 in New Jersey).

I once lived a few doors down from an older (white) couple whose son visited them often and tended to sit outside. He drank a lot, and when one night he had been screaming invective at his girlfriend from 1:00 to 2:00 A.M., I asked him if he could be a little more quiet so I could sleep. He picked an argument and finally I just went in; as I expected, before I shut the door he growled "Just a fuckin' nigger anyway." The man was ordinarily quite the Goodtime Charlie—but it wasn't exactly surprising to find that epithet under the surface of a very parochial, semi-employed, working-class man, especially one drunk and angry.

At the beginning of a semester at Rutgers, I walked into a German class only to have the teacher, a German woman, quickly and irritatedly say that she was afraid I was in the wrong class. There was no reason whatsoever for her to assume this other than my color. What was even more surprising was that throughout the semester she made it quite clear that she couldn't stand me, despite the fact that not only was I a quiet student (in that class, at least), but because language is the thing I happen to be hard-wired for, I was the best one. Her naked bias against me became the running joke of the class; she was casually hostile to such a point that I decided to stay in the class just to experience such open racism for the sensationalist thrill of it, like dropping acid or slowing down to check out a grisly car wreck—each class felt like a trip in a time machine. I am not usually one for sadomasochism, but this racism was ultimately harmless—either you get the sentence right or you don't, I fully intended to drag her to the highest court in the land if she tried to give me anything but an A+, her being foreign exoticized and deflected the sting of her racism somewhat, and its openness frankly made me feel superior to her rather than inferior (a sentiment I often wish more African Americans could internalize). But racism it was, and it was about nothing whatsoever but the color of my skin.

Some racism is subtler but no less of a nuisance. In a graduate school history class at New York University, I once made a suggestion (which had nothing to do with race) about the era being discussed, based on a book I had read years ago by eminent historian Daniel Boorstin. The professor said "Well, if you ask me, John, that's just bullshit, because . . ." The class (all white) sucked in their breath, and the teacher apologized, saying that she got the sense from my personal sense of humor that she could say that without me interpreting it as an insult. I could go along with her to a certain point: I did often try to use a little bit of humor in getting a point across. Yet she was a very buttoned-up sort of lady; it was odd to hear speaking that way in a classroom; I had in no sense been the class clown, nor had I even spoken that much; she had never before responded to anything anyone else had said in such a tone; nor did she even have the excuse of having let fly a spontaneous eruption in the rising heat of a lively discussion—it had been, as always, a very calm, quiet class. Today I encourage a fairly jolly discussion atmosphere in my classes, and occasionally tease a student a bit who I sense can take it in the spirit in which it is intended, but never, ever would I tell somebody that what he had said was "bullshit" (even if it was). This woman is unlikely to have burned any crosses on anyone's lawn; she probably supports affirmative action and disapproves of the change in welfare laws a few years ago. Also, contrary to "racism forever" hounds, people in the class came up to me afterward and asked if I was okay, and the professor apologized again after class. But what she did came from subconscious racism—an automatic denigration (word chosen on purpose) of a black person's ideas. I recently heard her on National Public Radio discussing her latest book on women's history, and I could not help noticing the contrast between her heightened sensitivity to slights against women and how easily she had let that "bullshit" slip from her mouth that night in New York.

My sister, if I may, was one of the most beautiful women in her predominantly white high-school class by any estimation, and yet was asked out on dates barely at all. During those years, she also noticed a certain tendency regarding just which white classmates did ask her out. We all remember the pecking order that develops in middle school and high school on the basis of superficial attributes like looks and clothes. One of the cruelest things about this is the sense that a given person is "out of one's league" to pursue romantically because she is better-looking, or "cooler" in terms of general acceptance. Of course, as we all know, this "pecking order" goes on to become a sad aspect of adult life as well, but never is it as explicitly wielded as in the teen years. One white guy with a weight problem who was generally ostracized was particularly persistent in his attentions to my sister. On one level, we should all take as a compliment that anyone finds us attractive. However, it is also true that this guy was not pursuing the white girls considered the best-looking, because he knew that the vicious "pecking order" would have made success unlikely. As such, we must ask: What made this boy comfortable pursuing my sister? As sweet as he was, my sister said that she couldn't help sensing that underlying his concentrating on her was "I'm fat but you're black." I know many black people who have noticed a similar tendency, and what it signals is an unconscious sense that "black" means lower on the social pecking order. When my sister went to all-black Spelman College, she was immediately pursued by the best-looking and most socially fluent guys—i.e., those at the top of the "pecking order." My sister, for the record, is not one to choose a mate based on where he falls in this cruel hierarchy—but the contrast between her experience in high school and in college is highly significant nevertheless.

I perform on stage as a hobby, and years ago at Stanford, an outside production company staged a workshop performance of a musical. I'm certainly not holding my breath for a call from the Metropolitan Opera anytime soon, but I have been cast in my share of lead singing roles in the Bay Area, and am happy to often be asked to sing solos on the piano bar circuit. Yet this company quickly put me in the chorus while some of the people cast in the male leads were only adequate singers or actors.

This sort of selection process is hardly alien to any black performer, but the bias behind decisions like these raised its head again, and even higher, soon thereafter.

One of the male leads dropped out early in rehearsals. The character was a bass; I am a bass. The character was middle-aged; something about my demeanor almost always gets me cast as middle-aged (I was often told as a kid that I was "born fifty"). The character was sarcastic; sarcastic I definitely am. Yet there was no thought of even letting me read for the part. The company scoured the campus performing community for a replacement, aggressively courting even one actor whose singing voice was barely suitable for the part. With no takers and limited time, they finally asked me to do it, obviously considering the decision a last-ditch compromise.

I am no more likely to ever get a call from the Royal Shakespeare Company than the Met. Sometimes, however, there is a special fit between an actor and a part, and for me, this was that part. After our workshop performance, the company staged a larger, full-dress production in the area with local professionals, and the workshop performers were invited to the after-show reception. No fewer than three people came up to me independently and said that they had seen both productions, and that the only thing they had missed in the larger one was my performance.

I mention this not to toot my own horn; I'm sure nobody even remembers that I was in it today (in fact, recently I worked with the choreographer in another production, and it took him six weeks to recall that we had ever met!). However, we must ask: Had it really been so inconceivable for the producer and director and their aides to see that there might have been *some* reason to give me the part in the first place, or especially after the first actor dropped out? What kept them from considering me was not "racism" per se; in general, they were wonderful people I recall fondly. The producer later even got me a job as music assistant with a regional theater company, without my even asking. What was at work was a different grade of racial bias, what another black Bay Area actor I know calls "lack of imagination." There is a deep-seated sense that "black" is in inherent conflict with parts written as "white" regardless of the performer's ability or even personality type—shades of the "un-American" black corporate manager.

One sees subtle examples of racism throughout American life. On the subject of the performing arts, for instance, too often for it to be accidental, black characters on television shows are given no personalities to portray, their being black alone being seen as their "character." In the brilliant ensemble comedy *Night Court,* for example, what would we say Charlie Robinson's Mac character was "like"? He had no actual character—his job was to stand around being alternately amazed or frightened at the other characters' clever, eccentric high jinks. Being constantly flabbergasted is not a "character"—how many white characters can we think of in a modern sitcom whose entire personality consists of pacing around saying "Oh my God!"? Victoria Dillard's secretary Janelle on *Spin City* didn't even get this much; while the other characters were given fully fleshed-out personas, her job was simply to blandly set up opportunities for other characters to say funny things. Again, there is no white character so faceless in any sitcom; Janelle's "character" was thought to be "brown skin." How would you have described Gloria Reuben's Jeanie on the first seasons of *ER*? She was HIV-positive, but this is a medical condition, not a personality trait. Her job was to take mechanical part in plot developments propelling other characters to the cover of *TV Guide,* and otherwise to be black and pretty.

It was also extremely telling that in the film *The Pelican Brief* (1993), costars Julia Roberts and Denzel Washington did not become romantically involved. "How come every movie has to have sex in it?" Point taken—but let's face it: if Julia Roberts had been costarred with absolutely any attractive white male working in Hollywood, a romantic angle would have been assumed, you name him—Brad Pitt, Harrison Ford, Mel Gibson, Clint Eastwood (even though he was a sexagenarian at the time), heck, even Matthew Perry, God, Neil Patrick Harris! If there was no such romance in the book, it would have been considered financial suicide not to write one in for the movie. Yet there was America's black matinée idol, who drives black females in movie audiences to unabashed squeals of admiration, on screen with lovely Julia Roberts with her dreamy eyes over that marvelous smudge of a mouth, and the two of them are "friends"—maybe a little "sexual tension" there but that's it. We've come a long way—black-white romances are no longer *causes célèbres* in films or on TV; *Primary Colors* (1998) tossed one in between Adrian Lester and Maura Tierney with no fanfare whatsoever, to note one of many examples. But we are still at a transitional point. When it comes to a blockbuster adaptation of a Grisham novel (as opposed to a background subplot, some indie film, or a TV show at sweeps time), Denzel Washington can be a lead (unthinkable even fifteen years before its premiere—imagine a major release starring a young black man and young white woman in 1978)—but he still has to keep his hands to himself.

On the subject of *TV Guide*, they once did a spread in which one capsule praised Queen Latifah's "grace and style" in her performance on the late, great sitcom *Living Single*. But would Calista Flockhart ever be praised for her obvious "grace and style" in portraying Ally McBeal? No, because it is assumed that attractive young women on television have "grace and style" just as we assume that a barber has scissors. This comment about Queen Latifah unwittingly revealed a sense that "grace and style" are special traits, rather than the norm, for even an attractive, charismatic young black woman. In the same vein, a woman on a talk show once announced the guest appearance of Cuba Gooding, Jr., the next day by mentioning that "He's a nice gentleman—so tune in!" Again, if Keanu Reeves, Brad Pitt, or even a decidedly ungentlemanly young white actor like Sean Penn were slated to appear, he would never be billed as "a nice gentleman." The implication here is that a young black man being a "nice gentleman" rather than a thug is news, an accomplishment.

### A *Time of Transition*

Thus black students, even middle-class ones, certainly experience racism in their lives and see symptoms of it around them. I certainly have and do.

However, the question is: Would we reasonably expect these things to prevent a person from doing well in school—and the answer here, contrary to popular belief, is no.

For one, there is the all-important issue of degree. In 1950, I would have had to sit in the back of that commuter train if I had lived south of the Mason-Dixon line; northwards, even ten years later than 1950 and even in New Jersey, the seat next to me would sometimes have *stayed* empty even in a full car. In 1950 I would have been barred from *most* summer jobs I applied for by my color, rather than meeting one anachronistic racist holdout. I would have been called "nigger" a lot more than once, by sober people, and to my face. I would have been all but barred from white universities, and if admitted to one would have had to live separately from white students, and also would have encountered teachers like the German one on a regular basis, and not filtered through a foreign accent. Being accepted into a graduate program would have been a major hurdle, and I could not have expected to find a teaching job outside of an underfunded, obscure black school. I would have been lucky to get cast even in the chorus of any musical, and if a lead dropped out, they would have cast the prop man in a lead role before even considering me. Mac on *Night Court* was a cipher, but black Marsha Warfield was dripping with personality and walked away with the show; black Michael Boatman's Carter on *Spin City*, a sharp-tongued, "straight acting" but activist homosexual, was one of freshest characters on television; one of the main purposes Jeanie on *ER* served was as a romantic interest for black Eriq LaSalle's Peter Benton, whose brooding, self-centered yet committed character is another one of the richest black presences in television history.

The often-heard claim that black characters on television and in movies are disproportionately cast as criminals has not been true for at least twenty years: Blacks, 13 percent of the population, commit about 10 percent of the violent crimes on the television shows they appear in today, and in films are regularly cast in roles of status whose real-life models are white, such as Morgan Freeman as president of the United States in *Deep Impact* (also surrounded by many black staff members, unlike current reality at the White House) and Courtney Vance as the sonar operator in *The Hunt for Red October*, in the novel version of which the character had been white.

In other words, we are in a time of transition, and we are a lot closer to the mountaintop than we are to 1950. There comes a point when we must ask not simply *whether* we are dealing with racism—of course we are—but how *much*. A quick glance through a newspaper at interethnic situations around the world sets in a certain perspective the claim that the increasingly occasional and almost always subtle and unintended instances of racism a modern black student usually experiences is enough to crush the inquisitive spirit and make excellent grades and test scores all but an impossibility. The reason for the black scholarly lag lies elsewhere.

I could be accused of lacking empathy here, but perhaps a thought experiment will show how the lenses through which we are trained to reflexively view black people work.

### Obstacles and Performance: A Thought Experiment

Imagine a white female student who is considerably overweight. On a day-to-day basis she leads a peaceful, comfortable existence, with a number of friends and recognition of her talents and abilities. But she cannot help but notice that some teachers expect less from her out of a general sense that obesity is due to sloth or weakness; she is never the first one called upon, and has never been singled out for grooming for special scholarships, as opposed to shiny happy skinny kids. She is al-

ways chosen last for sports teams at school; she has gone through high
school never having been asked on a date; the lockerroom after gym is a
quiet ordeal; and she has in general been quietly but decisively excluded
from the heady explorations of romance and sexuality that consume
most of the kids around her. Over the years she has built an emotional
shield against the taunts and catcalls she can expect from groups of men
she passes while walking down a street, although it never stops hurting;
she shops for clothes alone and as often as not cannot find what strikes
her fancy in her size. Self-image is clearly imperiled here. Yet—do we expect this person to be unable to achieve a GPA above 3.0 or an SAT
above 950? Surely not. We'd see such an assumption—despite all she
suffers—as condescending.

Now let's try a black person. This eighteen-year-old comes from a two-
parent suburban home; his mother is a social work professor and his father is a public university administrator. He goes to good private schools,
and on a day-to-day level leads a peaceful, comfortable existence, including a number of white friends and the same basic acknowledgment
of his achievements as available to whites. Once in his life he has been
called "nigger." He was once explicitly denied a summer job because of
race. Once he entered a store only to meet an expression of anxiety on
the proprietor's face, and was then followed. He can remember perhaps
a few teachers over the years who, while superficially well-intentioned,
obviously had rather lower expectations of him than they had of other
students. In innumerable ways this person is now and then aware of being perceived, despite superficial and sometimes even excessive respect,
as on an inherently lower rung than whites, being a sort of party trick
rather than a person.

Do we spontaneously expect this person's experiences to prevent him
from achieving a GPA higher than 3.0 or an SAT score above 950? Is this
the sort of thing that makes a twenty-year-old student turn in a family
tree drawn in pencil on notebook paper as three months' work on an
honor's thesis? Can we truly say that it is things like this that render
most of a class unable to name a creative figure who has been discussed
at length and even been shown on video just a couple of weeks before
the test? (A black figure at that—I wasn't asking them to identify Ethel
Merman.) Why, exactly, do we expect so little of the black person but not
the white one? Precisely what about the fact that the black kids' great-
great-great grandparents were slaves, or that his grandfather grew up in
a segregated Southern town, makes his case so profoundly different from
that of the overweight white woman, especially when, for example, if she

is Jewish, her grandfather was severely restricted in where he could work, and even she has probably at least once or twice in her life experienced some form of subtle anti-Semitism? The trickiness of coming up with an explanation is due to how deeply ingrained our association of blackness with victimhood—i.e., weakness and pitiability—has become.

I personally know that the black student should not be expected to phone in his schoolwork, because as you may have already noticed, this person is me at eighteen, and I shudder to imagine my mother's response if I had dared to claim that there was only so much that could have been expected of me in school because of these occasional episodes—and my mother had participated in sit-ins, was deeply aware of racism in American society, and taught a course on the subject at Temple University for years.

And even if I had gone to a public school instead of a private one, and had been stopped and arrested by a surly officer at a shopping mall because he thought I had stolen the shirt I was wearing, does it make that much of a difference? We are underestimating black people. Frankly it insults me. Jews can survive centuries of persecution and the Holocaust and have their children be expected to reach for any bar; Chinese in San Francisco in the early 1900s can be tortured on the streets and barred from employment anywhere but in laundries, sweatshops, and restaurants and have their children be expected to reach for any bar. But pull a well-fed suburban black kid over for a drug check one afternoon and subject him to a couple of teachers who don't call on him as often as other students and he's forever subject to lower expectations.

### Victimologist Portraits of Racism on Campus

The Victimologist party line claims that the typical black student encounters racism much more overt than this on a regular basis, but these portraits are more theater than reportage. This view is eloquently laid forth in Beverly Daniel Tatum's *Why Are All the Black Kids Sitting Together in the Cafeteria?* Here is Tatum's characterization of the typical black experience in college:

> Whether it is the loneliness of being routinely overlooked as a lab partner in science courses, the irritation of being continually asked by curious classmates about Black hairstyles, the discomfort of being singled out by a professor to give the "Black perspective" in class discussion, the pain of racist graffiti scrawled on dormitory room doors, the insult of racist jokes circulated through campus e-mail, or the injury inflicted by racist

epithets (and sometimes beer bottles) hurled from a passing car, Black students on predominantly White college campuses must cope with ongoing affronts to their racial identity.

Some of this is overblown. Why is being asked about one's hair a "racist" imposition? And wouldn't Tatum be the first person to complain that black students felt "invisible" and "marginalized" if they *weren't* asked about their "perspective" in class? (One can imagine: "After centuries of persecution, the Black American finds a gaping lack of interest in his heritage or his thoughts, such that one form of dehumanization has replaced another . . .") The openly racist episodes happen, but once again, degree is important, and they are very rare, especially at top universities where such things are so generally deplored. Tatum has gathered isolated anecdotes from various campuses over decades' time into one picture frame and presented it as representative of a black student's daily life, like a natural history diorama that for the sake of convenience depicts dinosaurs that lived in different eras all browsing and hunting around one lake. I have spent over half of my life as a black person on white campuses since the early 1980s, and the implication that white guys yelling "nigger" out of passing cars or that anything of the sort is just a typical occurrence for the black undergraduate, or even that something like this happens to that undergraduate even once in a typical *year*, is nonsense, pure and simple. Descriptions like John Hope Franklin's in *The Color Line* that "Under the banner of racial neutrality, white students have been encouraged to intimidate, terrorize, and make life miserable for African-American students at many of our institutions of higher learning" are good theater, but they simply do not correspond with the reality I have richly experienced on several campuses. Why is it so easy for us to say that a black student cannot be expected to perform at whites' level because the very occasional idiot acts up in the dorm across campus? Only Victimology makes black thinkers so ominously comfortable portraying their own people as the weakest, least resilient human beings in the history of the species. Note that Tatum writes smiling from the dustcover of a book she couldn't have gotten a major publisher for just thirty years ago.

In this vein, black students often claim that white people on campus throw them "looks"—such as at UC Berkeley where white students and professors are up in arms about the ban on affirmative action, interracial couples are so common as to not even attract notice, and there is both an Ethnic Studies *and* an African-American Studies program (the latter even having recently been expanded, like Ethnic Studies, into a doctoral program). In my twelve years as a university student, never once did I detect a "look" randomly thrown my way by a white student, and the idea that white undergraduates are truly walking around in the year 2000 grimacing at black passers-by is a scenario few of us could accept, as well as a disservice to the black people who really did suffer such treatment on college campuses in the immediate wake of *Brown v. Board of Education* in the 1950s. I do know that people's faces can fall into any number of expressions as they walk along, depending on sunlight, weather, and whatever is on their mind, and that if one was *looking* for it, a white person who glanced up randomly without happening to smile could possibly be misinterpreted as throwing a "look." Students referring to these "looks" have been *taught* by Victimology to consider themselves victims—an easy and comfortable lesson for any human being (witness the new "victimhood" of white males, or Asian students up in arms at the "affront" of being assumed to be smart).

### Teacher Bias?

Racism is also commonly thought to hinder black students in the form of white teachers grading them too harshly or disciplining them disproportionately in the classroom. Surely this phenomenon exists—for example, it is not difficult to imagine that the teacher who called my ideas "bullshit" would be likely to grade a paper by me a notch lower than she would grade the same paper written by someone else, probably white. Our question, though, is whether this would have a *significant* effect: i.e., whether a bit of this kind of bias here and there would restrict the number of black students who turn in stellar SATs to some few hundreds a year, and make it impossible to have a representative number of minorities on a top university campus without lowered standards, even when taking grades as well as SATs into account, etc. Lawrence Steinberg, for example, has found not only that complaints of racist bias from teachers were rare in his extensive survey of twenty thousand teenagers and their families, but that Latinos and Asians registered the same levels of such complaints—*and yet Asians manage to do excellently.* Thus while this kind of biased treatment is certainly unacceptable, the decisive factor in black school failure lies elsewhere. To imply otherwise is to leave us to wonder how a race could survive three hundred years of brutal oppression and yet is left unable to read for comprehension or do higher math simply because the occasional schoolteacher sends black kids into the hall a little more readily than white kids or is more likely to decorate white students' grades with plusses.

The teacher bias argument also falls down when we consider that black students generally do not perform appreciably better in schools where they are taught by mostly or all black teachers (except in the few special small all-minority schools geared toward addressing black students' performance directly and sustainedly with particularly intense teaching strategies). Studies have found only fitful correlation between black teachers and high performance among black students, with the class of the teacher as important as race (apparently both white and black teachers of higher socioeconomic status get better results), and with the results varying significantly by subject. A friend of mine is now teaching in a functioning public school in a big city with a mix of working-class and middle-class black children. He has found himself facing the same basic lack of commitment to school that we hear about so often and which I have described at Berkeley—and yet all of the teachers are black.

The weakness of all of the variants on the racism explanation is decisively revealed in the fact that children of black African and Caribbean immigrants do not underperform in school as black Americans do. Anyone who wants to claim that Caribbeans (with the same legacy of slavery as black Americans) and Africans are not subject to the degree of racism that American blacks are ought to consult Abner Louima (Haitian) or the parents of Amadou Diallo (Guinean), and yet repeatedly I have noticed in my classes that Caribbean and African students usually perform at the same level as whites, something also supported by studies. The traditional wisdom that "racism" extinguishes the intellectual spirit simply does not hold up. For example, a high-school sophomore of Boston born in Cape Verde once said about affirmative action: "I don't believe they gave me some slack on the test. I'd rather not think about that because it would really bring down my self-esteem and how I rate myself as a student." It is sobering to realize how unusual that would sound coming from a black American student today; typically, black American students furiously defend being given the "slack" of affirmative action, and I have never once seen one at all concerned about its impact on self-esteem. This reflects a devaluing of education local to *black American* culture, not the operations of societal racism.

## Confidence

In a widely publicized study in 1992, Claude Steele showed that black students at Stanford did better on various SAT-like verbal aptitude test samples when they were not required to indicate their race or when the test was not presented as measuring racial ability. Less well-known is that these were only one part of the experiment, much of which showed that even when the students were neither required to indicate their race nor presented with the tests as measures of racial ability, they performed less well when the tests were presented as measuring intellectual ability than when it was simply presented as examining "the psychological factors involved in solving verbal problems."

What these experiments suggest is that black students' school performance is hindered by self-doubts brought on by the stereotype of black mental inferiority, and it quickly became accepted in many quarters that "Stereotype Threat" was a major factor in black students' lagging school performance, particularly those performing at relatively higher levels. Predictably, this study has been marshaled to bolster the wisdom that black children are *kept* from doing well in school rather than *disinclined* to, and that what must be addressed in order to make black students do better in school is the societal racism behind the stereotype.

Claude Steele's experiments rather clearly show that black students do less well in contexts where the stereotype of black mental inferiority looms. However, we can be sure that any human being's performance would suffer under equivalent conditions, as has been shown to be the case for women—and even for white men when given tests billed as measuring their abilities against Asians' (another part of Claude Steele's study). Our question, then, is how *important* this factor might be in black students' performance *here in the real world*—where they are never required to indicate their race on their schoolwork, and are only rarely threatened so explicitly with racial stereotypes in the course of being assigned schoolwork.

Of course, Claude Steele's point is that the overall impact of the stereotype "in the air" interferes with black performance. Here one might again ask why this isn't thought to be so crippling for women, but then the answer could be that the stereotype of mental weakness regarding black students is stronger and more deeply entrenched than the one regarding women. There is an argument there. But this is not the only difference between (white and Asian) female students and black ones. Namely, there is a certain smugness and insouciance about many black students' lack of engagement in school (at private schools, Berkeley, and sometimes Stanford, not just in Harlem or South Central) which one does not often encounter in, for example, white women, and which strikes me less as fear than as active dismissal. It is much easier on the soul to return always to racism to explain black underperformance. I tried to for years, because we would all prefer not to criticize a culture that has suffered so much for so long. But I suspect that many of those who are indignant upon hearing explanations that stray too far from victimhood would see things differently if they could spend just a few days watching the expression on many black students' faces when finding out that they are expected to internalize new ways of thinking for a class rather than simply memorize concrete facts—a slightly amused, quietly disbelieving smirk. I have watched this smirk all of my life, come to realize its meaning and rootedness in black identity itself as I got older, and can richly attest that it is as likely from a doctor's daughter as from a UPS deliveryman's son.

It is tempting to surmise that the smirk is a defense mechanism masking frustration, but where, then, is that smirk on other children's faces? I have almost never seen that smirk on a white or Asian student's face, even when their confidence problems were quite clear. Confidence problems create a look of trepidation. A cultural hallmark creates a smile.

Thus the traditional approach to this issue that Claude Steele's study reflects, that black students want to learn but are thwarted from doing so, is not the usual case. When students cannot remember someone's name or career highlight two weeks after the person has been singled out for a ten-minute eulogy and then discussed, illustrated, and shown on video, when a university student writes me a biographical book report after I have said innumerable times that biographies would not be acceptable, when a student writes two incoherent sentences as the answer to an essay question and hands her test in with a smile, the problem is not confidence. There is an obvious fundamental detachment from learning itself.

Tracing the black scholarly lag to a lack of confidence is also another example of a tendency to suppose that black students are the only ones on earth who can be expected to excel only under ideal conditions. Without denying that "Stereotype Threat" has some effect (I have felt it on occasion), we must ask why we suppose that black students are incapable of rising above this whereas students of various other backgrounds rise above obstacles much more concrete. It would be nothing less than unusual if, for example, a fourteen-year-old Vietnamese immigrant did not feel some trepidation in an American school when he was still learning the language, not at home in the surrounding culture, physically smaller than the average American his age, and even found himself teased and harassed by American kids. Imagine going to high school in

Vietnam, with little hope of ever returning to the United States, and thus with one's fortunes in future life hinging entirely upon one's performance immersed in a language vastly different from yours, which even after six months you can only understand when spoken slowly. Some might object that a stereotype of mental dimness is somehow more of a barrier to learning than a linguistic difference—but then would not many of them at the same time support claims like the Oakland School Board's that black children are hindered from learning to read by the small differences between Black and standard English? If black children are barred from learning to read, and thus learning in general, by the fact that they say *I'm a answer dat person firs'* instead of *I'm going to answer that person first,* then surely we can muster some empathy for the Vietnamese child whose rendition of that same sentence at home is *Tôi sẽ trả lòi cho nguòi dó truòc!*

Then some might argue that a stereotype of mental inferiority is more crippling than anything this Vietnamese student undergoes—but upon what grounds? How comfortable would we be telling this student to his face that having been wrenched from one's homeland to make one's way in a country where one is inarticulate and physically small, and where his efforts to assimilate into American peer culture often create sharp frictions with his parents, is somehow less of a sociological burden than being associated with mental mediocrity (and even being occasionally trailed in stores)?

Crucially, these confidence problems are not seen as a sentence for scholarly mediocrity outside of the black community. Every year I have a few Asian immigrant students in my larger classes who dutifully ask me questions in their foreign accents after class, having missed a word or a cultural reference; students like this are legion in California, and they tend to be good ones. They, like women and so many students of other backgrounds, overcome these problems as often as not, even if some get stalled.

In short, certainly racial stereotypes undermine confidence, but confidence cannot be a *significant* reason why even black children of doctors and lawyers make the lowest average grades and test scores in the United States. The minimal effect stereotyping has on so many other students, and the particular tenor of so many black students' attitude toward school, simply do not square with an analysis claiming that confidence is the heart, or even one of the hearts, of the problem we face. To argue that confidence is anything more than a background factor sits well in the Victimologist groove, but only at the expense of implying that black children are congenitally mentally inferior or possess a tragic dearth of emotional strength. None of us could name a whole ethnic group stalled permanently by mere problems with confidence, and if this were what holds black students back, the gap between white and black students would have virtually closed twenty years ago, with the underprivileged minority creating a small lag.

## Underfunded Schools

It is widely believed that the discrepancy between black and white school performance is because suburban white schools are liberally funded while inner-city primarily black schools make do on starvation budgets. Jonathan Kozol's *Savage Inequalities,* widely and closely read by concerned observers and policymakers, has helped to crystallize this perception, such that "Black students are disproportionately represented in underfunded schools" is a virtual mantra one hears in discussions of affirmative action, for instance. However, there are three things which, predictably but hurtfully, are almost never mentioned on this issue.

First, the funding gap is a real one, but its extent over the past thirty years, and the purported lack of effort devoted to closing it, have been greatly exaggerated. Federal funds for schools increased by 122 percent (*with* adjustment for inflation) from 1965 to 1994, with much of the increase shunted to inner-city schools via Head Start and Title I. Contrary to popular belief, this has as often as not meant that inner-city schools got *more* funding than suburban schools. In 1989–90, the National Center for Education Statistics reported that nationwide, heavily minority districts got 15 percent more school funding than predominantly white districts. For example, in 1992, Marion Barry's "underfunded" Washington, D.C., public schools, with 96 percent minority enrollment, were given 55 percent more funding per student than those in nearby ritzy Prince George's County. Moreover, figures like that are not last-minute emergency measures making up for decades of denied funds. "Saturation-level services for ghetto schools, including reduced class sizes, two and sometimes three teachers per class, reading specialists and extended class hours"—sound like a program instituted as an emergency in Newark last year? It is actually a description of New York's More Effective Schools program from 1964!

Of course, often, even liberally funded inner-city schools give substandard educations. Many point out that the pathologies rampant in such schools require even more money, and the unfortunate truth is that inefficient but politically entrenched bureaucracies often misappropriate educational funds so broadly that no amount of increase would effect more than cosmetic improvements. Along these lines, it is often assumed that black students are disproportionately represented in *bad* schools, regardless of funding, and that their school performance is thus due to "underpreparation." Even this claim, however, is filtered through Separatism.

In mediocre schools throughout the country, children from other groups excel or at least do okay alongside black students failing in large numbers, such as in the classically troubled Oakland schools where black failure rates motivated the Ebonics resolution in 1996. More than one study has found that children of poor refugees from Southeast Asia, arriving with limited English and going to school in the very crumbling, blighted inner-city public schools considered a sentence to failure for black kids, did excellently in school and on standardized tests. Try telling an immigrant from Saigon that a mediocre school bars all but the occasional *Wunderkind* from failure—it simply is nowhere near true; black students are dragged down by something extra.

Finally, the underfunding issue is generally discussed as if such a large proportion of black students attend bombed-out, violent schools that those who do not are barely worth referring to in a general discussion. In fact, however, only a fraction of black students attend such schools—as I have noted before, in the year 2000, *most black Americans are not poor.* Unfortunately the proportion is larger than that of whites, and this is a serious problem—but too often that fact is distorted into a shorthand conception of all but a lucky few black students stuck in inner-city schools. This simply is not true, and as we have seen (and will see even more graphically shortly) overall black students in solid schools do little better than the ones failing in poor schools. Once again, I intend that not as a mere critical charge, but as an indication that our search for the true cause of the black-white scholarly lag must proceed elsewhere.

### Tracking

It is also widely assumed that excellent black students are so rare because teachers tend to "track" them into lower ability groups and discourage them from advanced placement tracks. In any discussion of the black education problem, shortly after someone mentions inequities in school funding, one is sure to hear someone talk about how in their high school they remember walking down the hall and seeing all-black low-ability classes and all-white advanced placement tracks. The assumption is that black children begin school as interested in learning as the others, but that teachers, based on racist stereotypes, dump them in unchallenging tracks and snuff out their commitment to school.

The fact is, though, that when we see an all-black low-ability track, there are two logically possible reasons for it. One is that most of the kids were put there inappropriately out of racist bias. That possibility is predictably assumed to be fact by most black commentators on the subject, because Victimology trains black people to assume that racism rages eternally. We have seen why this thought pattern has set in, but while having empathy, we must also acknowledge that there is another logical possibility.

This alternate possibility is that the students are there because this is what their school performance suggested. This very notion is considered unworthy of address by so many, but as it happens, it is this alternative that not just one, but several studies show: Overall, teachers place students not according to any detectable racial bias, but simply on the basis of prior performance. (See the references section for a partial listing.) These studies have appeared mostly in obscure academic journals; none of their authors have been profiled in *The New York Times* or presented a précis of his findings in the *Atlantic Monthly*. Yet they are all detailed, sober studies by trained practitioners, and they point to something quite opposite from the consensus that tracking is founded upon racism.

At Berkeley High, for example, there has indeed been a long-standing tradition of overrepresentation of black students in the low track, but then 70 percent of the black students generally enter reading below grade level (whereas about 90 percent of the whites enter reading at or above grade level). Tracking critics often suggest that black students are assigned to low tracks on the basis of appearance and a quick interview. That is reasonable fodder for controversy, but it is not the usual basis for tracking when the practice is actually observed and studied. Is a teacher a racist when she decides that a student who reads poorly is unlikely to do well in an advanced placement class?

Of course, one may have encountered the occasional teacher who unreflectively tracks students based on a "horse sense" founded upon stereotypes. But study after study shows that in general, race bias is not a *significant* factor in tracking—i.e., that this could not explain the nationwide, cross-class lag in black school performance.

Most important, there is a phenomenon that clearly demonstrates that black children dissociate themselves from "the school thing" *before* being tracked, rather than because of it, their wariness of school well-developed long before they have been tracked or, in many cases, even gone to school for very long. I spent most of my childhood living in one of the first deliberately integrated neighborhoods in the country, West Mount Airy in Philadelphia. As it happens, the very first memory of my life is an afternoon in 1968 when a group of black kids, none older than eight, asked me how to spell *concrete*. I spelled it, only to have the eight-year-old bring his little sister to me and have her smack me repeatedly as the rest of the kids laughed and egged her on. From then on, I was often teased in the neighborhood for being "smart." Importantly, however, none of the white kids ever challenged me like this (on the contrary, most of them knew how to spell *concrete* and were proud of it), nor did they tease any white child this way. What was important here was that these kids had only been in school for a few years at most, and none would be "tracked" for several more. Obviously, children who consider *persona non grata* the black kid who likes spelling are not on their way to embracing school with open arms.

It is not uncommon for people who grew up in progressive, treesy West Mount Airy to consider it the most wonderful neighborhood on earth; I do, and I revisit it often. On one of these visits, I recently ran into one of the ringleaders from that scene in 1968 now grown up, smoking on a street corner at two in the afternoon in jeans and a T-shirt. The tensions of our days in the driveway were ancient history, vastly overshadowed by the basic kick of encountering a "blast from the past." "John-John?!" he called (my old neighborhood nickname, I suppose inspired by John F. Kennedy's son). We shook hands in joyous shock; when I asked him what he was doing these days he said "not much." He is not the only one of that old crowd who has not gone on to much, and yet he grew up in a quiet middle-class neighborhood, and went to a solid public school nearby where many of the teachers were black mothers from the surrounding blocks. What did this guy in was not racism but a culture, which was passed down to him just as it was that afternoon to the eight-year-old's sister, who in that episode was carefully and explicitly taught what she was not supposed to do—spell, or by extension, give too much effort to school. A boy lifting his sister up to smack somebody for spelling *concrete* is a funny little story today (yes, that is *exactly* what happened, and I don't quite remember why I didn't run away), but it was symbolic of something much larger.

My story is not unique; in telling it I join legions of other black people who have reported in myriad articles and books that they were teased for being "smart." Reports of the strong tendency for young

African Americans to discourage one another from doing well in school are numbingly common both on paper and in oral anecdote from blacks. These reports are significant because they show that quite commonly, black children are disengaged from school *several years before they even confront tracking*.

There is a case study that shows very clearly that black students' aversion to school is brought to school from the outside rather than learned on the inside. In the excellent public schools of the affluent Cleveland suburb of Shaker Heights in Ohio, $10,000 a year is spent per student. Students track themselves into advanced courses rather than the teachers doing it for them. There are after-school, weekend, and summer programs to help children whose grades are slipping, and even a program where older black students help younger ones. As early as kindergarten, students needing help with language arts skills are specially tutored. There are coaching sessions on standardized test-taking. A counselor works with students who have low grades but appear to have high potential.

Shaker Heights is obviously so beautifully tailored to helping black students excel that if one didn't know it was real one might suppose it was a fiction. An observer would be hard pressed (and rather insolent) to call the black families sailing through these wide streets in their Saturns "struggling blue collar"; it would be difficult to see what else the teachers could do to boost black children's confidence; there is obviously no problem with funds; and the only tracking is self-chosen.

According to the traditional assumption that black children are hindered from doing well in school, rather than culturally chary of doing so, we would expect the black children in Shaker Heights to have no major problems with schoolwork. That prediction is not borne out. Black students are half of the student population, but in four recent graduating classes constituted just 7 percent of the top fifth of their class—and 90 percent of the bottom fifth. Of the students who fail at least one portion of the ninth grade proficiency test, 84 percent are black.

None of the old explanations work. The only one that might even retain any influence is "societal racism," but here I will reiterate: To think that the mere whispers of racism that black children in this town experience are enough to forever extinguish their intellectual ability is an infantilization of black people. The Shaker Heights case makes it painfully, but incontrovertibly, obvious that the reason black children underperform in school is that they belong to a culture that discourages them from applying themselves to books and learning—regardless of income level or class, and regardless of intervention by even the best-intentioned people. The centrality of this factor is quite empirically evident: for example, a black student in Shaker Heights reported that she began as a good student, but that her black friends called her "acting white" and "an oreo" for doing so, and that in order to get back in their good graces she let her grades plummet; meanwhile, a white student at the school felt nothing less than pressured by her peers to succeed.

Finally, Shaker Heights cannot be dismissed as an isolated case. The story actually came as no surprise to me when I found out about it, because it squares so neatly with what I grew up seeing among black students in the private schools I attended in Philadelphia. White teachers and administrators in Shaker Heights are perplexed by the performance of their black students, but few black Americans would be—to be a culturally black American is to be familiar with how commonplace this disengagement from school is among black young people; all of us have seen it, felt it, and possibly even participated in it—*even if we grew up in plush suburbs rather than the ghetto.*

The temptation to blame "class," racism, lack of confidence, underfunding, or tracking is powerful. Not only are so many trained to frame the black student as a victim, but straying beyond racism-based explanations is uncomfortable because it smacks of feeding into the stereotype of black mental inferiority—"If it's not racism," we think, "then what else could it be?" As I will now show, however, this phenomenon has nothing to do with mental power and everything to do with modern black identity. We must confront the task of realizing that the "usual suspect" analyses of this problem miss the target, and address ourselves to the true "root cause" of black underperformance in school.

## The Cult of Anti-intellectualism: A Cultural Disconnect from Learning

As I noted at the beginning of this chapter, my aim here is neither to simply point out unpleasant things nor to gripe that black students need to just "buck up" and that's the end of the story. That would serve no purpose and would waste trees. My project is to build an argument that a cultural trait is the driving factor in depressing black scholarly performance. We first saw that the inner city is but a sliver of the problem, and that scholastic underperformance bedevils the race as a whole. Next I showed that the causes generally adduced can only be considered triggers of the problem by casting black students as innately feeble and stupid, because (1) students of other groups (including ones of African descent) readily surmount these factors and (2) the problem continues even when these factors are absent.

Based strictly upon the arguments made so far, I propose the thesis of this final section, which is the point of this chapter: that a cult of Anti-intellectualism infects black America.

Namely, the main reason black students lag behind all others starting in kindergarten and continuing through postgraduate school is that a wariness of books and learning for learning's sake as "white" has become ingrained in black American culture. Segregation and disenfranchisement, withholding learning from most blacks, had long created a sense of alienation from learning. Separatism, however, which in defining "black" as "that which is not white" cannot help but exclude learning along with more expendable things like rock music and polenta, has focused this alienation into a rejection. To be culturally black, sadly, almost requires that one see books and school as a realm to visit rather than live in.

This analysis in itself is not new. Signithia Fordham and John Ogbu noted in 1986:

> One major reason black students do poorly in school is that they experience inordinate ambivalence and affective dissonance in regard to academic effort and success. This problem arose partly because white Americans traditionally refused to acknowledge that black Americans are capable of intellectual achievement, and partly because black Americans subsequently began to doubt their own intellectual ability, began to define academic success as white people's prerogative, and began to discourage their peers, perhaps unconsciously, from emulating white people in academic striving, i.e., from "acting white."

Fordham and Ogbu, however, focused on rough urban schools. Especially since their article, it has long been accepted that children in this environment actively reject school. It is less acknowledged, however, that this tendency continues into all classes among black students, and not as mere background noise, but as a pivotal factor, central to the shockingly poor performance of most black students in places like Shaker Heights. Growing up culturally black in America under *any* circumstances typically entails that children learn at an early age that "black" and "school" do not go together, or at least exist in a delicate, charged relationship. Black students categorize themselves accordingly, take on corresponding attitudes, and are almost always rendered to some extent permanently wary of learning. This is usually overt only in the ghetto and somewhat beyond, but its filtering effect colors the orientation toward school of most black students of all circumstances.

Indeed, like Victimology and Separatism, this current manifests itself in degrees. There are certainly black students who shine brightly. Those at the Browns and Cornells are often barely distracted if at all from wholehearted engagement with learning; there are certainly equally committed black students at other schools; and importantly, my claim is not that all black students besides these have flatly rejected school. Overall, however, the only significant difference between how Anti-intellectualism manifests itself in the inner city versus a tony suburb is how explicitly it is espoused. Only the inner-city casualty is likely to consciously reject school completely; the black child in Shaker Heights—or Mount Airy, Philadelphia, or Brooklyn Heights, New York—rarely does. Yet it is the culture-wide operations of this largely subconscious sense of separation from the scholarly, which misses so few and affects to various degrees almost all, which keeps all but half an airplane full of black students from hitting the top in any given year, and specifically leads to the phenomenon increasingly baffling educators in which even middle-class black students lag behind all others despite active interventions.

The subtleness of the operations of this cultural inheritance is such that it hinders the dedication even of black students who are giving their best efforts, not extinguishing, but quite commonly diluting, their fundamental commitment. As such, as often as not even their strongest effort is unintentionally, but decisively, less than the strongest efforts of other students. In a great many cases, what one sees in black students is less a refusal to contribute any effort, than a sad tendency for their efforts to stop before the finish line. This tendency stems not from laziness or inferior mental power, but from a brake exerted upon them by a cultural inheritance that whispers eternally in their ear that schoolwork is more a pit stop than a place to live.

To the extent that it is acknowledged at any length, this factor is generally referred to by terms such as "oppositional identity," a misleading term. It implies that the culprit is alienation from racist behavior on the part of whites, when in fact today it thrives and is passed on even in the absence of significant experiences with racism. This term furthermore carries a subtle implication that the problem is located among the disadvantaged rather than being a general black American cultural inheritance. A preferable term is the one that my friend spontaneously used: A "Cultural Disconnect" from learning endemic in black America.

## Positive Evidence of the Cult of Anti-intellectualism

So far I have arrived at the Cult of Anti-intellectualism via a process of elimination, arguing that class, tracking, etc., are seductive but insufficient explanations. At this point I could be accused of being like the researcher who says "Okay, colds are not due to cold air, crowding, or stress, so it must be. . . . *squirrels!*" In other words, my argument is incomplete without actual *positive indications* that the Cultural Disconnect from learning is the culprit.

I will now show that there is a great deal of such positive evidence.

### Teasing

As I have noted, it is a long-established and well-documented feature of black American culture for children to tease and harass black kids who show an affinity for school. We recall the black student in Shaker Heights. Similarly, a middle-class black student opting for advanced placement classes in an integrated high school in Evanston, Illinois, recounted being told "Oh, you're an oreo" because "getting good grades was always connected to white people." Similar comments were amply reported in the Bay Area in a series on black educational failure in the middle class in the *San Francisco Examiner* in 1998. Meanwhile, across the Bay from San Francisco, Berkeley High School principal Theresa Saunders (who is black) notes "We see it time and time again: [black] kids come in quite talented, and by the end of ninth grade year, they're goofing off. The peer culture is such that it doesn't acknowledge or reward academic achievement." "Oh, Joey thinks he's all bad, 'cause he's gettin' a A!" as one Berkeley High teacher quotes hearing among black students.

Note that we cannot simply dismiss this as an inner-city pathology—it is culture-wide. Shaker Heights is a quiet, crime-free middle-class area, and while some of the students at Evanston Township High School and Berkeley High School are of modest means, both are solid and integrated schools with a great many middle-class black students.

And what happened to me in Mount Airy was not a neighborhood fluke. We later moved to a manicured all-black suburban town in New Jersey, where the first friend I made was as nerdy as I was and then some (he was, in fact, that one other black person I knew at the time who had taken Latin). He was regularly surrounded by groups of black kids and asked how high a building was or how far it was to Florida, and then jeered at and physically taunted when he knew the answer. I must emphasize that this took place, regularly, not on the narrow row house blocks of a "struggling" "urban" neighborhood, but in a quiet, squeaky-clean, airy development of big, beautiful houses, which looked exactly like the set of *Leave It to Beaver*. Furthermore, none of these kids knew the kids back in Mount Airy; they were subconsciously expressing a national subculture. Universally, teasing is one form of cultural maintenance, in this case, unfortunately, of Anti-intellectualism.

### Lower Expectations from Parents

The Cultural Disconnect from learning does not dissolve after childhood, but manifests itself in different ways. Studies suggest that one of them is that black parents tend not to require as much of their children in school as white and Asian parents do. When asked in one study (not an inner-city study) what the lowest grade their parents would tolerate their bringing home, black students' average was lower than whites' and Asians'. Asian students often said that the lowest grade their parents would tolerate was an A- (!), and regardless of our feelings about race and education, few of us could realistically say that this is something a black student would be likely to say. In Shaker Heights, while the district is half black, white parents vastly predominate in parent-teacher organizations and as volunteers at the schools. The black parents are surely deeply committed to their children's well-being, but these discrepancies simply reveal the lower priority that "the books" have in black culture—and recall that our subject is not beleaguered welfare mothers but two-parent families living in a plush suburb. A similar tendency has been reported at Berkeley High School.

Certainly black parents want the best for their children; the issue here is one of culturally ordered priorities. In a Jewish or Asian family, if a child is not a great student, then while the child is certainly loved, this is often considered a flaw, one of that child's downsides. In most black American families—*of any class*—if a child is not a great student, it is not "an issue" to this extent. If a black child *happens* to be good in school, then this is considered a nice bonus, like a Jewish or Asian child who turns out to have a great singing voice. But if the black child is not good in school, it is no more of an "issue" than whether or not he turns out to be a good cook. This cultural difference is indicative of the general ambivalence toward books and learning that black Americans have been saddled with.

### Comfort with Low Bars

There are fewer surer ways to get a whoop out of a black audience than to refer to how strong black people are, how we have survived. *Success Runs in Our Race,* as the book says. Yet somehow, school is reflexively and resolutely considered an exception here—permanent affirmative action is considered a moral absolute even for black children of doctors and lawyers. Asian immigrants' children take on school as a challenge, learning English via immersion, helping one another in study groups, refusing to accept anything but their own best efforts. Black Americans, however, generally consider the particular challenge of school utterly insurmountable without special set-asides (be this in Watts or at Duke); black students are not considered to have even the potential for "Success in Their Veins" when it comes to "the books." One only need imagine the condescension the black community would feel if the National Basketball Association began accepting black players of lesser ability than the best white players out of a sense that this was the "just" thing to do given the racism that young black men suffer and the crumbling courts an inner-city black man learns the game on. It is no accident that all convictions about black strength fall immediately away when school, and only school, comes up. Black people are taught from the cradle that books are not us.

### College Graduation Rates

William Bowen and Derek Bok in *The Shape of the River* report that in three freshman classes from each of twenty-eight universities that they studied over a four-decade period, black students' overall dropout rate was 25 percent, as contrasted to 6 percent among whites—in other words, black students' dropout rate was four times that of white students. Our first suspicion is that this is due to black families having lower aggregate income and wealth than white, and this surely contributes.

Yet if finances were the only significant factor in this discrepancy, then one thing we would expect is that black dropout rates would decrease among those with higher SAT scores, since black SAT scores rise with income level. Yet in fact, the rates decrease only slightly at higher income levels, suggesting that money is only part of the issue.

This correlates with something I have observed quite often, which is that black college students are more likely than white ones to leave school after two or three years simply because they are not enchanted with "the school thing," and I refer to thoroughly middle-class students, not students from the inner cities who may be uncomfortable in an environment dominated by mainstream culture. I have often heard stories like this one about middle-class black people I knew growing up: "He went to Syracuse for a while but after a couple of years came back and started working"; "Oh, she's working at such-and-such; yeah, she went to Penn State for a while." Generally when I ask why such people dropped out, the answer is "I'm not sure." Common wisdom tells us that such cases are a matter of finances, and I cannot deny that this may have played a part in instances I did not witness personally. But as a college student, I observed many such cases at close hand where the issue was definitely a lesser personal weighting of getting a degree than is typical of other students—one who left to train as a police officer, about four who left after a year or two for "time off" and never came back, one who was tired of the tight budget of student life, etc. None of the people I remember but one was stymied by the work itself; all of them were smart— and middle-class—people who college did not exert the hold on that it tends to for other students.

White students can doubtless be unenthusiastic about school. Yet they most often see completing their degree as a milestone on the way to adulthood, even if they are not precisely scholars, while black students often see completing their college degree as a less central part of adult identity. This reflects a lesser weighting of education in the black community in contrast to the white one.

### Classroom Attitudes

I've noted that it is hard to miss an almost alarming pride in disengagement from learning among many black students, arising more from a sense of cultural identity than problems with confidence and "Stereotype Threat." A (black) friend of mine was frustrated after his first year of teaching in a mostly black, but stable, public school by black students' strong tendency to resist schoolwork, many even going as far as declaring that a given assignment was just "too much work" rather than engaging the challenge of tackling it. (Notably, this man also mentioned, without any prompting from me, the smirk I referred to.)

This issue of attitude is borne out by studies; Lawrence Steinberg found, for example, that across nine high schools of various racial compositions and levels of quality, black (and Latino) students spent less time on homework, cut class more often, and reported zoning out in class much more than Asian and white students.

Some people I talked to while I was struggling with my all-black classes suggested I might need different methods for teaching black students. The sentiment that there is a "black" learning style lies underneath a great many black people's opinions about race and education, and it is neither limited to a few Afrocentric "cranks" nor always thought to apply only to inner-city kids. Derrick Bell, for instance, is reported to have given a speech to black Harvard Law students—*Harvard Law School students*—claiming that they should not expect to do well on their upcoming examinations because they had been written by whites to ensure white hegemony—and this from a man who had previously taught in that law school himself.

But bringing this notion down to nuts and bolts, what exactly would a "black" way of teaching my Black Musical Theater History class have been? Wasn't the very subject matter of the class "black"? Should I have delivered my lectures as Baptist sermons? Brought in a drummer from Senegal to accompany classes? (The ironic thing is that I sincerely believe that if I wrote a grant asking for funds to do just this, UC Berkeley would approve it and duly grant me an award for "innovative teaching.") More to the point, supposing that my teaching was at fault once again requires that the students were thirsty for knowledge but somehow unable to attain it because of their "black" mindsets. The actual problem was one of dismissal rather than confusion, and as such, I did end up using a "special" method to avoid flunking most of these students: making exhaustively explicit what needed to be retained, speaking more slowly and repeating often, and teaching less material. This was treating them not as "Africans" but as people incapable of learning as much or as easily as white students. (Students of African immigrant parents, in fact, would rarely have required these "special" methods, in my experience.) That I had to do this was evidence not of a problem with teaching, but with a culturally based resistance to learning.

When the underperformance of black students beyond the inner city is acknowledged at all, the general "Civil Rights" consensus is that the students generally are trying as hard as others, only scuttled by "lack of preparation," "stereotype threat," and the fact that their parents did not subscribe to *Harper's*. However, I know what black students look like who are giving their all but are hindered by true underpreparation and a social context where school was a marginal factor in the lives of most of the people they knew. I have had the occasional student of this kind, and what one sees is first, a bright-eyed commitment to getting something out of the class, and second, a sad frustration at how hard this can be when society has not provided the tools to take advantage of it. This, however, is not the demeanor of a great many of the black students I have known. There is a subtle disconnect from the whole enterprise—an air of "Okay, what's next?" rather than the bright eyes; complacence instead of frustration. Even those who overtly want to do well only rarely seem to develop the minor fixation that leads so many white and Asian students to success. Beyond the inner city and maybe a bit further, the problem is much less societal inequity than the "disconnect" my teacher friend refers to, and it is this which must be addressed if we are to break the cycle of black scholastic underperformance.

## "There's Some of That"?

Finally, we must ask why we would *not* suspect that a strong and obvious Anti-intellectual strain in a culture would not be the *dominant* factor in its educational underperformance. What precisely would lead us to suppose that any other factor was more important, when other groups suffer from these same other factors and keep their heads above water in school, while black students continue to fail in large numbers even in places like Shaker Heights?

I emphasize this because a natural tendency might be to suppose that the problem might be due to all of these things—i.e., why can't it just be that "There's some of that but . . ."? Some problems indeed pan out that way—the destruction of the rain forest is due to a combination of overpopulation due to improved nutrition and health care, imperialism, and the increasing centrality of meat to human diets (which requires land to be cleared for cattle to graze). But all problems do not pan out that way. Some problems that appear to be caused by many things are actually caused properly by only one of them, with the other "causes" actually mere facilitators and by-products. To return to colds, for example, they are caused by a virus. Stress, crowding, other sicknesses, and drafts all make one more susceptible to that virus, but take away the virus and no one would catch cold even in a stressful, crowded, freezing-cold roomful of lepers. Take away the black cultural keystone of alienation from books and learning, and things like racism, teacher bias, and school funding would have no more effect than they do on other ethnic groups.

More than a few people might say that this analysis is "naive" without my having spent years teaching in elementary, middle, or high school. We must first note, however, that if I had concluded that black children were indeed done in by funding inequities and racist tracking, not a soul would claim that I was unqualified to make *that* point without having been a public school teacher—I would be received as one more voice "telling it like it is." In that light, to make the "naiveté" charge without being able to explain (1) the success of other minority groups alongside black students under all conditions or (2) the poor performance of black students in places like Shaker Heights, reveals one to be driven more by an understandable reluctance to give short shrift to black victimhood than by a truly comprehensive assessment of the problem at hand.

The holding pattern forcing so many thinkers to reflexively link all black-white disparities to active, present-day racism can even be found in the reasoning of the best-intentioned and most richly informed thinkers on black education. One sociology professor and educational consultant, for example, can go as far as to acknowledge that there is a culture of Anti-intellectualism among black students at Berkeley High School, saying that "Black and Latino students aren't suffering when they're failing. They're having a party. That's a real problem." However, he is dismissive and irritated at the idea that this might suggest that a cultural trait is the central, driving factor in need of address, claiming that such a position:

> treats those attitudes as if they exist in a vacuum. Part of it does lie in the fact that among many black parents, the emphasis on doing well in school isn't getting the priority that it should—I'll be honest about that. But part of that is that often the parents have had bad experiences with the school and don't feel as comfortable coming in and meeting with the teacher to talk about what's going on with their kid. With a lot of parents, there's not enough trust there to want to engage on that level.

This professor is an admirable and inspiring figure, having spent a career at the front lines of addressing the black-white achievement gap in school with a dynamic combination of scholarship and activism. Yet his perspectives are founded upon a conviction that black children are prevented from doing well in school by external forces rather than internal, and this conviction rules despite the rich evidence to the contrary that he experiences at uniquely close hand. For example, he considers parents' lack of commitment to school to play a significant role in black students' Anti-intellectualism. This at least addresses something other than manifestations of racism—but it still couches the students as victims of outside forces despite dissonance with the nature of the actual phenomenon. Wouldn't parental disengagement lead to simple lack of interest, rather than the particularly pointed teasing and active dismissal we have seen, and which he is surely familiar with? Furthermore, a sociologist is deeply familiar with the role of peer culture, as opposed to parents, in shaping a child's views.

The professor even reveals the operations of this mental filter in his guilty hedge "I'll be honest about that" when acknowledging the Anti-intellectualism cult at all—to even hint that a culture-internal factor has any bearing upon the issue is a potential faux pas requiring an immediate apology, and significantly, must quickly be followed by a link to racism, in the vein of "I think O.J. did it, *but.* . . ." He does not say explicitly that black parents' "bad experiences with the school" were based on racist discrimination, but since white and Asian parents take a much more active role in their children's education at Berkeley High and thus apparently do not suffer unduly from these experiences, we can presume that racism is indeed the purported issue. The professor's position appears to be that the nationwide disparity between black and white school performance, regardless of income level or class, is due in some large part to black parents' having suffered racist treatment from school administrators, and that rampant Anti-intellectualism is a result of this underlying racism, rather than a root cause of the problem.

An interesting thesis: But is perfect harmony between parents and teachers really a *sine qua non* of children's scholastic achievement? What about the subtle discrimination Asian immigrant parents surely suffer in such parent-teacher interactions, with their often limited English and slight acquaintance with the system? They tend strongly to make sure that their children do their best nevertheless, by hook or by crook. Does this not suggest that something—and something dominant and crucial—is at work beyond quality of parent-teacher interaction? Also, Berkeley High was one of the United States' first high schools to voluntarily desegregate, and remains a bastion of commitment to integration. Surely there is most likely the occasional white teacher there who is not crazy about "ethnics"—Life Isn't Perfect—but especially in Berkeley, California, at Berkeley High in the year 2000, are there really *enough* such teachers as to create a *general disinclination* among an *entire city's* black parents to schedule meetings about their children's performance in school? Most important, one cannot help but miss that advocates like this professor, despite rich expertise and commitment to improvement, almost never address uncomfortable questions like these—because of a guiding assumption that racism absolutely must be the pivotal issue, utterly unquestioned in the same way that all work in astronomy is couched upon the earth revolving around the sun.

None of this is to imply that these points are anything approaching the sum total of this professor's work. However, when it comes to this particular issue, the focus on racism is rather as if someone doing a study of colds had devoted her life's work to studying the benefits of relaxation. Even if she knew that the virus was "a factor," at the end of the day you can be sure that de-stressing would play a larger part in her analysis than it would in any unbiased report—and that following her advice, an awful lot of people would be tipped back in their lawn chairs coughing and blowing their noses. It is indicative that Claude Steele's work on confidence was quickly established "on the vine" among black educators, while Shaker Heights is rarely mentioned. Because the Shaker Heights story cannot by any stretch of the imagination be interpreted through the Victimologist filter, it doesn't fit with the program and makes no lasting impression.

There is no reason to pretend that class issues, societal racism, confidence, school quality, and bias-based tracking play no role whatsoever in black underperformance in school. Nor, however, is there any reason to suppose that these things play anything but an extremely subsidiary role—and I want to stress that this is not a mere guess, but a conclusion based upon (1) the performance of other groups under similar conditions and (2) situations like Shaker Heights. If every black child in the United States came from a book-lined suburban home, met only the kindest and most enlightened of whites, was infused from birth with confidence, and attended a school awash in funding with only voluntary tracking, the average black American GPA and SAT scores would mysteriously remain the lowest in the country, rising slightly only because of the disappearance of truly poor schools and active hostility toward learning engendered by inner-city conditions. Overall, black students would continue to "mysteriously" turn in mediocre school dossiers because of the Anti-intellectual strain in the culture. The Haitian immigrant children succeeding in crumbling urban schools on one hand, and the rampant black American school failure in places like Shaker Heights on the other, allow no other interpretation.

In this chapter, my aim has been to argue that a culturally embedded wariness of scholarly endeavor is the primary cause of the alarmingly persistent achievement gap between black students and most others. So far, I have shown that the problem is culture-wide rather than class-related, and that its impact is pivotal, rather than marginal, or a mere epiphenomenon of other causes routinely appealed to in addresses of the issue.

In the following chapter, I will explore this crucial phenomenon further, examining the tragic roots of the problem, the forms in which it manifests itself, and its unfortunately defining place in modern black American culture.

# 4

## THE ROOTS OF THE CULT OF ANTI-INTELLECTUALISM

As Victimology leads naturally to Separatism, Anti-intellectualism follows from Separatism out of a sense that school is a "white" endeavor. One can often hear this sentiment quite explicitly expressed: Here is a black Berkeley High student in 1999:

> When I walk in that gate every morning and I look up and see all those names for poetry and drama and Einstein around here, that doesn't reflect my culture. When I go to chemistry, and they teach me about Erlenmeyer and his flask, I don't know nothing about him. But they won't teach me about people from my culture that have done things that are wonderful. When they teach me about math, they tell me about Pythagoras, but the pyramids were there hella long ago. The Mayans had pyramids, but it's all the Pythagorean theorem? No! That's a lie. And then they teach me all this stuff and then they say, "Oh, I don't know what's wrong with you."

Obviously this particular rhetoric is one this student has inherited from the late 1960s and been Carefully Taught, and her views are far from rare (I have heard similar sentiments from any number of black Berkeley undergraduates); the deep-seated ambivalence toward school that Separatism conditions is clear. Its roots in Victimology—victimhood at all costs—are clear as well, in that Berkeley High in fact has the only secondary school Ethnic Studies program in the United States.

Yet the modern Cult of Separatism merely focuses and reinforces a trait that was indigenous to black culture long before the late sixties. Separatism alone, after all, does not always lead to rejection of the scholarly as "alien"; French Canadians, for example, are not known for lagging scholastically.

Anti-intellectualism has attained such a hold on African Americans first because of how severely the slave system severed Africans from the models in their indigenous cultures of black people living lives of the mind. The Jewish person can look back to countless generations of Jewish scholars; even the most uneducated Chinese person knows that China has been home to millenniums of Chinese scholarship. But African slaves were drawn from dozens of different kingdoms and societies. "Africa" is not a single culture but a continent; Senegal, Ghana, and Angola are as distinct in language, topography, and culture as Belgium, Italy, and Russia. These slaves were then dispersed to thousands of separate plantations, and mixed randomly together. Most American-born slaves grew up on plantations where Africans came from too many different nations for any single culture to predominate and be transmitted, and were usually born to parents from different regions on top of this. Thus certainly black American slaves retained a rich *generalized* African cultural heritage in aspects of language and cultural mores. In a very few cases, there were enough Africans from just one or two regions, and they lived in conditions isolated enough, that specific African traditions have been preserved faithfully enough that inhabitants are overtly aware of their African origin, such as in the Sea Islands where elders can sing songs in the African language Mende (although no longer aware of the meaning of the words) and weave baskets in styles reflective of ones still in existence in Africa. Typical circumstances of slavery, however, so hindered the transmission of specific African cultures that the African heritage survived only as a subtle, generalized, background element in a new, American-bred mix processed as "black" but not "Yoruba," "Wolof," or "Kongo." For example, the black American is not generally conscious of our music and dance styles as rooted in African traditions; it has required scholarship to bring this back into our awareness. Under these conditions, certainly it has been impossible for a concrete memory to survive in black American culture of, for example, the Mandinka griots who memorized and passed down knowledge and cultural lore.

Perhaps more significantly, in America, blacks were then almost all brutally relegated to the margins of society and denied education for centuries. Generations and generations of blacks lived and died in a cultural context in which books and learning were actively withheld or lent only grudgingly.

Because of both of these historical factors, black American culture emerged in contexts that could not emphasize the ways of thinking necessary to scholarly success, and thus naturally has come to classify these ways of thinking as "other." A working-class Jew knows that there are and have always been very "Jewish" people who are scholars; not even the most hardscrabble Chinese peasant family would see a Chinese professor as stepping outside of what it is to be Chinese. Black people, deracinated from scholarly models in Africa and until recently encountering only the occasional ones here, cannot help but see scholars and all associated with them as "something else." History has screened us from the scholarly state of mind, and the Separatist trend has only crystallized something that has existed all along. In the late 1940s in segregated Atlanta, decades before the Black Power movement, my mother was constantly teased by the neighborhood kids for being a "walking encyclopedia"—ironically, exactly what the Mandinka prize as a griot.

These facts make it not only likely, but even guarantee, that black children tend, as stated in a New York State Board of Regents booklet about diversity of learning styles, to prefer "inferential reasoning rather than deductive or inductive reasoning" and show "a tendency to approximate space, number, and time instead of aiming for complete accuracy." Given that "inferential" means deriving conclusions from premises already known or assumed to be true, we can sum up these two descriptions as that black students (1) tend to be open more to confirmation of truisms rather than to new ways of thinking, and (2) tend to be leery of precision. In other words, they are less likely than students of many other ethnicities to dwell spontaneously in the post-Enlightenment ways of thinking that education is founded upon and is dedicated to fostering.

Such essentialist generalizations make many of us uncomfortable, but many black educators have made similar points, and one reason they have is that it would be difficult for any black American to say that he did not recognize the culture to some extent in those two descriptions. On inference over innovation, in the 1998 *San Francisco Examiner* series on underperformance of middle-class black students, black psychologist Edmund W. Gordon suggested that a factor was that black parenting does not allow the kind of "backtalk" that often doubles as exploratory discussion—in other words, he was saying that black parenting styles tend to discourage one from thinking "out of the box"; studies by black psychologist Elsie Moore were also cited in the article as supporting this. As to both the inference issue and precision, in my work on creole languages I myself have been told that I was "arguing like a lawyer"—i.e., being very precise and drawing conclusions from the facts that contrast with the common wisdom—only by black colleagues (plus one working-class, stridently anti-elitist Australian white one). The implication that this particular brand of thinking is "different," and even somehow not "sporting," is not an accident—it follows from an unfortunate kink in our cultural heritage.

*Inference over Innovation*

I have seen exactly these tendencies holding black students back in the classroom. The resistance to new ways of thinking, in favor of seeking confirmation of the already known, is the hardest of the two to change in a mature person.

One student, with an unquestioned assumption that the police were in the wrong, wrote a paper for me that mentioned that certain Caribbean immigrants often had run-ins with the police over their traditional slaughtering of livestock as sacrifices. I thought that this issue would be a useful way to introduce him to the classic conflict between diversity and common national values, as a demonstration that many issues in our world admit various interpretations. This is a central part of my mission in teaching all college students, and I urged him in his next draft to try to come to a personal solution to this problem, trying to see the issue from the side of the police as well—in particular, considering how he might feel to watch a goat's throat slit in cold blood in someone's backyard, which is not, after all, a minor consideration, whatever one's ultimate judgment on the issue.

In the next draft, he had simply added to his original text "I'm not saying I believe in animal sacrifice, but God will have to decide who wins this battle."

I now asked him to imagine himself as a police commissioner assigned to decide whether to do anything about the sacrifices. After deflecting the issue with a few jokes, he finally chuckled that he would tell the police to pursue the practitioners, but meanwhile hope that they could manage to clandestinely continue the sacrifices. The problem here was an internal resistance to thinking "out of the box." His response was based upon two truisms: that preservation of African heritage is a good thing, and that a society has laws. Faced with an incompatibility between the two, his most ready response was to cobble together a fragile solution that preserved both. No amount of gentle prodding could get him to leave the box and consider either that the cultural practice could change, or that one could protect the practitioners by arguing that it is arbitrary to persecute people for slaughtering goats when healthy dogs and cats are "put down" at animal "shelters" all the time—both of which would have been plausible positions. Formulating an *innovative* argument was not his style, and he was not frustrated, but rather amused at even being asked to do so.

Not every white or Asian student is exactly ravenously inclined to ponder issues either. Yet this unfamiliarity with the possibility of, and even quiet resistance to, thinking in new ways, as opposed to mere memorization, reportage, and mechanical execution of set procedures, is a problem overrepresented among black students in my experience. Few students like essay questions, for example, but I find black students often especially at sea in applying facts to actively grappling with an issue rather than simply reciting facts, and never have I had a white or Asian student resort to God in a written argument.

In a class of 230 students that I have just finished teaching as I write this, there were two black students. Early on, one turned in a homework assignment several days late. He wasn't the only student to do this, but he was one of the few who did not have a viable excuse. I took him aside and as genially as possible explained that he was risking failing the class if he did this as a habit, and to feel free to use my office hours or my teaching assistants if he needed extra help. A couple of weeks later, however, he turned in a homework assignment only half done, and it was unfortunately by far the poorest of the sixty others I had seen. I do not know this student's background, but aspects of his speech, dress, and demeanor make it extremely unlikely that he grew up disadvantaged to any significant degree. Also, I feel obliged to restate that one thing I am not in or after class is an intimidating presence—students often designate me "approachable"; furthermore, the subject matter did not involve any of the ugly sociological topics I am discussing in this book, and thus I was unlikely to have made him uncomfortable on that score.

Once again, the problem here was one of simple effort. Linguistics is not rocket science, but its basic principles are rather counterintuitive at first, and take practice, being taught via problem sets with exact answers in the vein of science courses. Many students this semester have told me, as they often do, that this is a way of thinking about language they have never encountered before, something they have to wrap their heads around.

And thus what the ones who excel do is come to office hours, ask me and the TAs questions around the clock via e-mail, catch us around campus, some of them almost obsessively. The black student I have mentioned did not do this, and I think it is another example of a culturally based disinclination among so many black students to delve into new ways of thinking when it comes to schoolwork. I find myself recalling Philip Uri Treisman's study of black students in calculus courses here at Berkeley. He found that it was not that the black students did not work hard, but that while they were diligent about checking their calculations against the answers in the back of the book, they were less inclined to approach the subject via internalizing the guiding concepts behind the calculations themselves, the extra step that determines success in something as initially counterintuitive as calculus.

In this light, it is impossible for me to pretend that the contrast between this student and the many others who came to my office hours every week, asking question after question in an almost Ahab-like quest for the highest possible score on the midterm, and e-mailing me questions deep into the night, was the fault of "underpreparation," or due to the fact that one of his parents may not have gone to college, or due to subtly racist overtones between him and the professor (I am, after all, black myself, and the teacher in the discussion section the student attended was a very soft-spoken, unfailingly pleasant woman from Thailand). Nor can I accept the possible objection that I am drawing general conclusions from what may be one idiosyncratic case, because sadly, this intersection between "black American" and poor schoolwork is *not* idiosyncratic: As I noted earlier, I have encountered this problem to some extent in *most* black students, class after class, year after year. (For example, the other black student in the class was the one I had to ask not to read the newspaper during my lectures.)

The first student was unlikely to be deliberately shirking commitment to the class, and was most likely putting in a certain amount of effort. The reason he was handing in incomplete homework—and as the semester went on simply did not hand in two assignments at all—was a kind of block on approaching the class as a matter of mastering the comprehension of *an overriding logic behind* what the assignments ask, as opposed to the more mechanical tasks of identification (which he had no trouble with). Notably, the two homework assignments he did not hand in were the ones that most required applying facts to solving "brain teaser"–style problems. It is mastering this kind of thinking that the other students pushed their way toward in haunting me and the TAs in our office hours. This student, however, lacked a basic inclination toward pushing that hard, and the reason was neither stupidity nor laziness but a subtle yet damning factor in his cultural heritage.

In the end, this student did not show up for the final. I had to flunk him.

The authoritative "don't backtalk me" style common among black American parents has its benefits (one rarely sees black kids running up and down aisles on airplanes), but in discouraging out-of-the-box thought, it can dilute black students' awareness that higher learning necessitates extending mental boundaries. Add to this the association of this kind of thinking with "whiteness" and students like the one above are less a puzzle than a prediction.

## Leeriness of Precision

Meanwhile, the other tendency among black students, the leeriness of precision, is clearly demonstrated by Eleanor Orr's experience with black students in a fine private school in Washington, D.C., described in *Twice as Less*. Black students were doing surprisingly poorly in math, failing to process the requirements of word problems in particular. Orr's hypothesis that Black English was interfering with these students' processing of basic adverbs and prepositions is untenable, sympathetically intended though it is. These misreadings of Black English do not stem from any differences between black and standard English that might cause "off" translation, but are indeed strikingly reminiscent of how black students, all of them quite comfortable in standard English, often misread questions on my tests.

The issue here is that these students do not readily fall into the necessary habit of painstakingly precise engagement with text or ideas required to figure out which of two trains is going to get to a crossing first. As with the inference-over-innovation issue, because of a culturally determined distance from, and even wariness of this style of reasoning black students are often unaware that this kind of hair-splitting will be needed to master a subject. Orr's students improved with coaching, in corroboration with my experience that the precision issue, unlike the tendency to resist new ways of thinking, is one that students can be taught out of with sufficient attention.

These two factors trace back centuries, but as John Ogbu shows, it is typical of dispossessed groups to first lag behind in scholastic aptitude, but quickly catch up through schooling and upward mobility. What hinders black American students from making this jump is the operations of the Separatist impulse, which paints "nerdy" thinking as incommensurate with membership in the group one considers home. New ways of thinking and close engagement with the written word entail an openness, a sense of integral commitment and belonging, to the realm of school that black students tend to teach one another out of.

Clifton Casteel did a study that illuminated this check on wholehearted dedication to the scholarly. This important study showed that in the eighth and ninth grades, white students were more likely to say that they did schoolwork to please their parents, while black students were more likely to say they worked for their teachers (this was not an inner-city study). This was an ingenious, and extremely important work. If you are trying to please your parents, you are trying to please yourself, essentially, and thus you bring yourself to school. If you are trying to please the teacher you are not pleasing one of your own, i.e., yourself. As such, as diligent as you might be in trying to please the teacher, chances are you are not going to get beyond jumping through hoops. You reserve "yourself" for the weekend or phone calls at night—in school you are basically checking in. The very nature of checking in is that one can do it with all due assiduousness and dedication *without being truly present in a spiritual sense*. This was how most of the black kids in my elementary and high schools seemed—I, like most of the white kids, was very much "alive" at school; it was half or more of what I considered life to consist of. Most of the other black kids were doing a job; you felt that life never really began for them until 3:00 P.M. To the extent that this wasn't true, they did better in school (and were usually ripe for the oreo charge).

## A "Black" Problem or a Black American Problem?

There are those who find it very difficult to accept that black American culture, rather than racism and societal inequities, is the locus of this problem, and there are also those who, mostly within the privacy of Internet chat rooms, suspect that all of this simply means that black people are not as intelligent as others (although *The Bell Curve* brought this view to the light of day after decades of being kept largely under wraps). Yet nothing indicates to me more strongly that both positions are mistaken than the fact that black Caribbeans in America tend strongly not to exhibit this subtle remove from schoolwork. Specifically, in my teaching career thus far, every black undergraduate I have ever taught who has been one of the best students in my class has been of Caribbean extraction. I have certainly had black American students who made good showings, but Caribbeans have been most comfortable thinking "out of the box" rather than just incorporating information, and they were also most comfortable with nit-picking precision. Perhaps if I had been teaching for a longer time, I would have encountered black American students of this kind, but it is significant that thus far I have not. My experience is also collaborated by an observation by a (black American) admissions officer at an Ivy League university that about half of the hundreds of black students admitted to that school over twenty years were children of immigrants rather than black Americans.

Some might suppose that this was because the Caribbean students grew up in mostly black Caribbean contexts and had been shielded from racism. However, of the four Caribbeans constituting the best black students I have ever taught, in fact three grew up here, and one of them grew up in England; none of them spent enough time growing up in the Caribbean to even have Caribbean accents. Indeed, the three who grew up in America were not readily distinguishable as Caribbean outwardly. Nor were they extremely "assimilated" types essentially white culturally—all four were quite committed to black concerns and social life. The difference between these four and black American students was that they had grown up in a home context that worked against, rather than reinforced, the ambivalence toward school that black American culture tends to inculcate.

One of these Caribbean students was particularly interesting and, for our purposes, instructive. Well-ensconced in the campus black community, he had unfortunately developed the poor attendance and perfunctory dedication sadly common among black students. However, his tests were still excellent. Because his heritage had imprinted him from early life with a basic openness to thinking in new ways and a spontaneous alertness to the exact, he could barely help making good grades even when spiritually phoning it in. Holding school at half an arm's length was a second language to him, and thus he had never mastered it fully.

All four of these Caribbeans certainly were black, and yet for all the assertions of some that Africans and their descendants have substandard IQs, their work was quite commensurate with the best white students'. Moreover, all four certainly knew racism, two of them quite readily designating it a scourge in their lives. Yet this racism did not bar them from scholarly competition. It is not "being black in America" alone that creates a friction with school; it is black American culture specifically.

## Misconceptions About Black Anti-intellectualism

The lenses through which so many are led to view black problems distorts most engagements with the Cult of Anti-intellectualism in ways that weaken or misdirect attempts to solve the problem.

### It Is Not Merely an Inner-City Problem

I cannot emphasize enough that I am not contributing one more observation that ghetto kids tend to reject school. I am much more interested in the prevalence of the same attitude, just less explicit, in blacks of all classes—because it means that if we could abolish the inner cities tomorrow, black school performance would continue to be the weakest in the country.

From seventh through tenth grade, I went to a private school in Philadelphia where there had always been about eight black kids in each class of roughly sixty-five from kindergarten through twelfth grade. In this school, ninth grade, the beginning of high school, was the year school got "serious"—real papers, harder math, more and heavier reading. It was this year that homework came to dominate five nights of every week, rather than being something I spent an hour or so on before the sun went down, and the difference from eighth grade was stark enough that even I was scared for the first few weeks. However, almost everybody rose to the challenge.

No fewer than four black students, however, did not come back the following year, and schoolwork was the main problem in all four cases. One of them early in ninth grade had quite explicitly told me, with a memorably full-blown version of that smirk of disbelief I mentioned, that she had no intention of doing the extra work now being required, and was looking for shortcuts. Black students had certainly come and gone at Friends' Select just as white students had, but such a large number leaving at this particular time was significant. There was no tracking at this school, and if any of the teachers' approaches to these students were colored by racism at this Quaker institution, it can only have been of the subtlest kind—I can remember not a single interaction with a teacher there where racism played any discernible role.

More indicatively, in these students, two things went together. First, all but one had a quietly dismissive attitude toward schoolwork, rather than exhibiting the frustration that we would expect if they were "done in" by outside influences. Second, all four were among the "blacker" of the black students in body language, dress style, speech, etc. Yet I suspect all of them, with parents coughing up private school tuition, would have been surprised and insulted to be considered "struggling blue-collar children"; the issue was not indigence but cross-class culture.

In other words, this Cultural Disconnect is almost always evident to at least some extent regardless of class lines, conditioning vastly different life trajectories for black students growing up with the same advantages their white classmates had. A white Berkeley High student recounts:

> There's this guy who works with my mom. He has a daughter who's the same age as me, we grew up together, but she's black and I'm white. Last year, she went to East Campus and dropped out. We have similar home lives, but completely different social groups. Our friends have very different goals; pretty much

all my friends knew they were going to college, but a lot of her friends just wanted to party on the weekends and hang out. So even with the kind of support she had at home, she still slipped through the cracks when she got here.

Examples of this problem outside of the inner city are nothing less than ordinary. I once heard a young black professor who grew up in a stable two-parent home with a solid public school education say that "Academics just aren't a priority for me." (This person has also mentioned having been called "white" by black students for liking school when he was a child.) At another time, a black man told me of when he was recovering from an infection and called the head of a graduate program he was hoping to join. The professor suggested some books that he could read for background while he was recovering, and the man was offended that someone would make such an imposition upon him when he was not in full health. For many academics, being unable to get about is a perfect opportunity to catch up on reading. This man had embraced the scholarly enough to seek a graduate education, but the sense of distance from books endemic to his culture continued to play its hand in how alien the thought of books was when he had anything but all of his strength.

### It Is Not Limited to Black Youth

The Cult of Anti-intellectualism is usually referred to as a matter of "peer culture," but it does not suddenly cease once black people reach adulthood: it is endemic to all age groups. There is no reason, for instance, why the Separatist disparagement of school we saw in the Berkeley High student will mysteriously evaporate when she turns eighteen or twenty-one, and in fact, as we have seen, Separatism intervenes between black people and the scholarly even in the realms of academia.

### It Is Not Fear

Many discussions of this issue propose that black students are "afraid" to do well in school because of fears of rejection. There is compassion in this analysis; it is easier to couch black students as *driven* not to do well than to charge them with subconsciously not *wanting* to do but so well. However, this approach will distort solutions. If we suppose that black students would gladly reach for the top if only it weren't for their friends, then we are led to sloganeering about the joy of reading, seminars where successful blacks are brought in to speak, and other things designed to show black children the benefits of sucking in their guts and "braving" an embrace of school.

These approaches have had no effect on the problem for thirty years, because the Cultural Disconnect is based not on fear but, unfortunately, dismissal. Typical black students refraining from full engagement with their schoolwork are not constrained by "fear" of being called "white." They have a spontaneous disinclination to embrace school too whole-heartedly, because it is inherent to the culture they have been immersed in since birth, long before they were part of a "peer group," to consider school a "white" and therefore alien realm (regardless of class). Indeed, some black children are called into line by being teased as "acting white," but they are the minority; most black children are never teased in this way because, as members of their culture, it would never have occurred to them to step outside of that culture by embracing books. The black student who analysts often couch as "afraid" of being a good student is often one of the very kids participating in calling fellow black students "white" for putting effort into school.

It must also be remembered that the black sense of separation from books and school is an angry, resentful one. As I mentioned in an earlier chapter, the black person who embraces something "white" is not seen as simply doing something "not black," but as implying that she is *better* than "black." The move is considered not horizontal but vertical. African-American students even often harass black Caribbean and African students, whose history has not misled them into adopting a cult of Anti-intellectualism, for excelling in school, and when they do, the typical charge is not only, "You think you're white," but also, "You think you're better than us?" Black students castigate the black student who embraces school not simply as an attempt to "maintain cultural distinctiveness in contrast to the model of the oppressor" but out of a sense of insult.

Beverly Daniel Tatum describes this as "the anger and resentment that adolescents feel in response to their growing awareness of the systemic exclusion of Black people from full participation in U.S. society." However, besides the decidedly anachronistic notion of black people being systemically restricted to only partial membership in society, Tatum misses that this anger kicks in long before black children have even developed a wide-lens view of race relations. Anti-intellectualism is not a response to racism; it is a cultural trait passed along like religion even when one has encountered little or no racism. Neither the little girl smacking me for spelling *concrete* nor her eight-year-old brother knew a thing yet about black people's "participation in society." What they knew was what their people were like, and that is all that is necessary for Anti-intellectualism to take hold.

### It Is Not Overt

Some analysts have concluded that black Anti-intellectualism beyond the inner city is a myth because most black parents and students say that they value education. However, we can be sure that almost no black person in America other than a young person in the inner city and similar areas would explicitly say "I do not value education." The connection between education and earning power and status is too obvious to ignore, such that black adults, having seen and experienced this concretely, are particularly likely to overtly espouse education. For example, while my mother was teased as a child for being smart, decades later her schoolmates as adults regularly exulted when we visited Atlanta about how she had always been "smart as a whip."

In fact, in the overt sense, partly because it is seen as something one accomplishes in an alien realm, academic credentials have a *higher* value in the black community than the white. My black students almost always respectfully address me as "Professor" at the outset, where white ones are more likely to commit the unintentional gaffe of "Mr. McWhorter" (this is not a racist slight; they do it to white professors too). Because being called "Professor McWhorter" makes me feel 100 and I have a fear of aging, I encourage all of my students to call me "John" as the semester progresses and I get to know them, but most black students have a hard time getting comfortable with this and either maintain "Professor McWhorter" or change this to the wonderful "Doctor John," which nicely manages to convey some camaraderie while maintaining the appelation of respect. (I feel compelled to remind readers that, despite the grim nature of the things I am covering in this discussion, this is not a matter of my demeanor; black students tend to address all professors this way. For example, one thing distinguishing social norms in Berkeley's African-American Studies Department from those in others is that undergraduates tend to address professors using their title even after long-term acquaintance.) Thus it is not that most African Americans actively disdain education; the Anti-intellectualism in question is a subtler affair, which is best observed indirectly.

Roslyn Mickelson, for example, found that among black twelfth-graders, who overtly agreed with a list of variations on the basic idea that "Education is the key to success in the future," while we might expect that most would be high achievers, in fact there were just as many low achievers. An overt belief in the power of education does not correlate meaningfully with success in school. However, students who agreed with a different set of statements indicating that racism pervades black Americans' lives tended to be lower achievers. This experiment shows that expressed support for education reveals little about the powerful antipathies lying beneath the surface in a great many black students.

### It Is Not a Defense Response Against Whites

It is also sometimes suggested that the presence of a threatening white majority in schools leads black students to build an Anti-intellectual shield around themselves, in a quest for the sense of protection in a Separatist world. definition This analysis confuses effects with causes. We know this because the Cultural Disconnect reigns even in the absence of whites. The kids teasing my friend in Lawnside, New Jersey, lived in an all-black town, went to an all-black school with an all-black staff, and rarely had sustained interaction with white children or adults—one could spend months in this neighborhood as a child and barely ever see white people except while shopping in the neighboring towns. Furthermore, it is an issue always "on the vine" at Morehouse and Spelman, two of the best all-black colleges in the country, that there is a tendency for many students to nickel-and-dime their way through school, Anti-intellectualism thus remaining a problem even among elite all-black student bodies. Anti-intellectualism is not imposed from the outside; it is today a self-sustaining cultural trait.

## Blaming the Victim?

For many, the idea that the main reason for black underperformance in school could be due to anything but various shades of victimhood is extremely distasteful. I do not want to brand black American culture "guilty" of its own academic failure, but simply as the locus of it, so that we can more effectively solve the problem. It is not the *fault* of black Americans that they have inherited Anti-intellectualism from centuries of disenfranchisement, followed by their abrupt inclusion in American life before they had time to shed the internalization of their oppressor's debased view of them. It is not the *fault* of black people that the consequent focus on victimhood, while perhaps alleviating self-doubt, has encouraged the defensive construction of a sovereign "nonwhite" identity. A wariness of school and learning is a natural part of this sovereign identity, given that learning had been withheld from the culture since its inception.

Nevertheless, the fact remains that today, Anti-intellectualism is not foisted upon black Americans by whites, but passed on as a cultural trait. Black kids in suburban middle-class schools are teasing the black "nerd" as you are reading this not because white people have subjected them to abuse, but because nerdiness is considered external, and even an insult to, the culture. As such, addressing this trait will entail addressing black culture, not white attitudes—even if white attitudes created this cultural trait, they did so long ago, and today the trait has developed a life of its own within our community. We know this because even when white attitudes are dedicated wholeheartedly to black scholastic success, as in Shaker Heights, the rates of failure continue. It is not pleasant that black school performance is today held down by black culture itself. But it is also true.

No one would deny that cultures can have negative traits as well as positive. We have no trouble identifying good cultural traits (Jews value education); we can also sadly identify bad ones (rural Albanians nurture blood feuds). We are reluctant to designate any negative traits in black American culture out of a sense that a people who have suffered so much historically have enough to bear already. But especially in the year 2000, black culture can take some honesty—Success Runs in Our Veins, after all—especially when this honesty is aimed at helping us to be the best that we can be. We must neither behave as children by resisting honesty, nor allow ourselves to be treated as children by having honesty withheld.

## It Isn't the Only Way

We are faced with the problem that maintaining a diagonal relationship to school and learning is a bedrock element of black American identity. An exception is made for using books to chronicle black history and achievement as well as black victimhood. To indulge in the academic solely for its own sake, however, is processed as "something else." I cannot resist saying that in folk conception, it has a similar relationship to blackness that athletics has to Jewishness.

To be sure, this conviction is not as overt as the Victimologist and Separatist ones. Many blacks would openly argue that a focus upon victimhood, and a Separatist reading of all black behavior through its lens, are key and healthy components of black identity, although they might not phrase it in just that way. Yet very few blacks would *explicitly* say that treating books and school as a necessary evil is essential to blackness.

The Cult of Anti-intellectualism operates more subliminally than its progenitors Victimology and Separatism. Black people are "American" enough to feel an *overt* allegiance to school; Anti-intellectualism mani- fests itself much more in action than in word. Yet there are clear signs that deep down, a great many black people indeed feel that the black stu- dent who tolerates nothing less than top grades and aces the SAT is step- ping outside of what it is to be a proper African-American. One must listen closely to hear this underlying sentiment given explicit expression by black people beyond their teens, but it can be heard there, too.

## Black People Are Not to Excel in School

*1.*

Affirmative action in admissions was banned at University of Califor- nia schools in 1995, and the first freshman class chosen without racial preferences entered in the fall of 1998. Predictably, the number of blacks admitted to Berkeley, considered the best of "the UCs," fell sharply. The spring before, talking to a black undergraduate involved in recruiting the black admittees, I asked why no one seemed to be terribly excited about the black students who had made it in, a not inconsider- able number. The student soberly responded that *there was a general fear that black students who performed at such a high level would not be con- cerned with nurturing an African-American presence at Berkeley.*

This showed that the dissociation of "blackness" and school is so deeply ingrained that the black student admitted to Berkeley according to the same standards as other students was regarded with suspicion by black students admitted under preferences. In other words, black stu- dents are not *supposed* to be star students, because then they're not ex- actly "black," are they?

Along these lines, after talking to this student I predicted that the fol- lowing fall when the first black students admitted without racial prefer- ences came to Berkeley, they would encounter some social coolness from black students in classes above them. As it happened, come Sep- tember I heard two of these new black students, quite unprompted, re- port just this. Both were disappointed, having come to campus as outraged at the ban on affirmative action as the older black students and having expected to take their place within the campus black community. Yet that community was, predictably, wary of them: In having embraced school openly enough to present a dossier competitive with whites' and Asians', the new black students had unwittingly signaled a disloyalty to the community they wanted to be a part of. The black Cult of Anti-intellectualism casts top scholarly achievement as treachery—and not just in "struggling neighborhoods," but even at the best public university in California.

2.

When I was a graduate student, I gave a report on the verb *to be* in Swahili. Many languages, like Russian, use *He a mailman* instead of *He is a mailman*. Some use *He a mailman* but then, if the sentence is about location, do have a *to be* verb and say *He is in the house*. In some languages, the *be* in *He is a mailman* and *He is in the house* are different words. In some, there are even other *be* verbs for *God exists* or for specific sentence types like *His name is John*. In others, where we would say *He was a mailman,* they would say *He became a mailman* or *He stood a mailman*. In lots of others, *be* is not even a verb, but a pronoun, prefix, suffix, or some other part of speech. The variations and combinations are endless worldwide—actually, as languages go, English's *to be* verb is pretty boring, and in the meantime, Swahili's is just all over the place, including doing most of the things I just described, and is changing all the time.

After the talk, a black graduate student in the department told me, good-naturedly but pointedly, that he and some other black students who had been listening had begun to wonder, because I seemed so enthusiastic about the subject, whether I was a "brother" or not. The student did not mean this as a hostile criticism; it was said with a smile. Yet it was an important comment. A great many black linguists have studied the verb *to be* in Black English and creole languages of the Caribbean, but the main motivation behind this has been the exploration of the black American and Afro-American linguistic heritage, with the focus on *be* connected to demonstrating (correctly) that the absence of *to be* in some Black English sentences is not a "mistake" but an innocent feature constrained by grammar rules just like the one telling us when to say *the house* as opposed to *a house*. This in itself is a rich, useful, and fascinating endeavor that I have done some work in myself. However, that day my take on what I was discussing was based simply on the fact that I found it interesting in a universal sense (Swahili was rarely if ever spoken by slaves brought to the New World). The implication that being entranced by a subject simply for its own sake suggests a lack of black identification was another rare direct glimpse of the quiet sense in African-American culture that pure bookishness is "not black." By no means was the student "calling me out" the way the black "nerd" is so often challenged in junior high; the inquiry was made with a jolly combination of sincerity, challenge, and play, and the students had no problems with me in general. Yet saying it at all was in essence simply a civil, adult version of the schoolyard scenario—something made particularly clear by how implausible it is to imagine a Chinese-American student even joshingly wondering whether another one was "Chinese or not" for delving into a subject not related to Chinese identity. Recall also that this episode occurred in a graduate program at an elite university, not a high school hallway in Detroit.

3.

During a meeting of a mostly minority educational advisory panel, the topic arose that a work by a black scholar had finally been published, the scholar having taken many years longer to finish it than had originally been promised. No problem there in itself—any number of white scholars miss their deadlines in academia; I would even venture to say that in this business, missing deadlines is pretty much the norm! However, what was more interesting was something one of the panelists, a black American educational sociologist, said: "See? This shows we can do just as well as whites. It only takes us twice as long to get it done."

This was meant as a bit of a joke, sure. But importantly, it also reveals an underlying sense of a certain distance from the scholarly endeavor. "Just as well as whites"—as if for black scholars, writing a book is a kind of party trick, a mimicking act, rather than a deeply felt expression of one's life's purpose. And the "twice as long" part is on one level an affectionate in-group reference to the "C.P.T." ("colored people time") syndrome, a supposed tendency for black people to be rather loose about doing things on time (Mexicans have a similar in-group joke about the "mañana" syndrome). But here, the subject was producing academic books, which for a Ph.D. is one of the signposts of a career—not just "clocking in" nine-to-five, but a career, a métier, a mission. White professors constantly joke about how far past the last deadline imposed on them is, but always within a general assumption that this is not ideal, a slip, a messy closet, an unpaid bill. This man's expansion of this from the personal to a group trait, and significantly, with less of a sense of jolly humility than of proud ethnic identification, was revealing. There's a lot in a joke. We are often told that even the silliest little race joke signals bigotry deep down in the mind of its teller. To the extent that one believes this, one must also consider that this man's comment, even if meant as casual social libation, was an echo of a sense that for black people, the scholarly is a costume rather than skin. We can do it "just as well as whites" if we feel like it, as a kind of performance, but as fundamentally Separate from whites, we must not be expected to do it as often, or with as deep a spiritual commitment, just as we expect Dana Carvey to talk like George Bush on the occasional talk show guest shot, but certainly not day in and day out, because Carvey is, after all, not George Bush, and only George Bush *really* talks like that.

4.

Certainly white high school students often brand studying and good grades as "uncool," but this tends to be a mere fashion statement compared to the more trenchant implications of selling out to an enemy that nerdiness so often has among black students. Furthermore, among whites it is largely a matter of the teen scene, while in modern black American culture, the sentiment often continues to play its hand out among adults.

For example, Berkeley's black professors and administrators dutifully agree that they want black students to excel, but with the same sense of polite adjustment with which we all classify the black corporate lawyer as an "American." Their concrete efforts after Proposition 209 were mostly dedicated to formulating ways to get around the ban on racial preferences and continue admitting most minority students with lower qualifications. Pointedly, it was Chinese former Berkeley Chancellor Chang Lin Tien whose response to Proposition 209 was to institute the Berkeley Pledge, dedicated to helping black students in secondary school become competitive for application to good schools. This policy meanwhile rarely entered black Berkeley faculty's discussions of or statements on Proposition 209 and the course to take in its wake. These people's actions, betraying their words, reveal a distinctly subsidiary investment in black scholarly excellence.

The black recruiter undergraduate, graduate student, and sociologist, as well as Berkeley's black faculty illustrate, unintentionally, a paradoxical sense many black Americans have that Anti-intellectualism is, in its way, healthy. Even the most well-intentioned people may find themselves sensing an almost willful intransigence in statements like the recruiter undergraduate's, for example. However, in the end that statement is not only natural, but in the America we live in, nothing less than reasonable.

We want to say, "Come on—why can't a black person like school?!" but this student is responding to concrete experience, having every reason to see the death of black culture looming behind a sincere love of learning for its own sake. For the sad fact is that, because the Anti-intellectual current in black American culture is so strong, it is true that as often as not, *the black person who chooses to truly embrace school has indeed had to all but leave the culture.*

More often than not, such a person has little black inflection in her speech, cannot dance any better than most whites (sorry!), socializes primarily with whites, and eventually marries one. I will never forget, for example, the handful of black undergraduate women at Stanford who joined white sororities, had few if any black friends, had hairstyles carefully nurtured to look as much like white girls' as possible, and whose romantic ideal was Brad Pitt rather than Denzel Washington. Our recruiter's ironic commitment to black scholarly mediocrity is based on having interacted with people like this.

I once saw a black astrophysicist commenting on a television talk show about the importance of a comet's impending pass by the earth. I found it so shocking that I put down what I was doing and turned up the volume. Astrophysics is inherently objective and centered upon precise measurements and answers, and there is no allowance for substandard astrophysics in the name of "diversity." There is no such thing as "Afro-centric astrophysics"—the field cannot be adapted to illuminate specifically black concerns, and there is no conceivable way in which it could be improved by opening itself up to a "black point of view." Therefore, there is no such thing as a black astrophysicist whose interest in the field is less in helping to illuminate the interactions of celestial bodies than in chronicling the oppression of blacks via the apparatus of an advanced degree; the black astrophysicist does not have the option of segregating himself into "Black Astrophysics" conferences where at the end of the day, cultural fellowship and uplifting ideology are weighted more heavily than intellectual rigor. When we see a black person on TV billed in white letters on the bottom of the screen as "Astrophysicist," we are seeing that rare bird, a black person of advanced scholarly credentials who has at every step of the way had to be in there pitching with the very best of them.

In the America we live in, it follows naturally that black scholars who devote themselves to a realm of inquiry so utterly disconnected from ethnic identification, and in which there is no room whatsoever for bending intellectual standards, is extremely unlikely not to have had to leave some "blackness" behind. To embrace such a career and also remain immersed in the black community requires an exquisitely delicate balancing act of which very few people are capable. The sad thing is that by definition, the culturally black person in the year 2000 only rarely engages with a realm of inquiry requiring innovative deductions rather than confirming truisms, and founded upon something as relentlessly precise as advanced mathematics.

This black astrophysicist was clearly brilliant, with every bit the command of his field that his white colleagues had—but predictably had not a trace of black inflection in his speech, nor did he reflect black culture in coiffure, dress, or body language in the way that the biographer of Elijah Muhammad I mentioned in the Separatism chapter did. I have since met this man, when we appeared on a television talk show exploring the tension in America between nationalist and community sentiments. In his enthusiastic promotion of astrophysics as exploring the place of humankind as a whole in the universe as opposed to reinforcing intergroup boundaries, he was expressing a sentiment extremely difficult to reconcile with the black American mindset today designated the "coolest."

On a train, I once heard a group of white undergraduates behind me talking animatedly and at length about their classes. After a while I got up to go to the dining car (as if one "dines" on rubber hot dogs and Pepsi), and on my way back to my seat noticed that one of the women, who had actually been talking the most, was black. The women were wearing Harvard sweatshirts, and it occurred to me that a black student as avidly and unquestioningly committed to her classroom experience as this woman was likely to be one of the tiny number of black students each year whose scholarly credentials qualify them for admission to an Ivy League school. The fact that she, like the astrophysicist, had no black inflection whatsoever in her voice was also telling. Speech is a strong indicator of one's social affiliation, and I could not help suspecting that this student was probably not the kind of person our Berkeley recruiter undergraduate would have considered "authentic." As it happened, I was on my way to Boston, and a few days later happened to espy this very student on the streets of Cambridge, happily ensconced in a crowd of white students, and looking comfortable in a way that strongly suggested that she was in her "crowd." It is highly likely that she, like so many black students I have known—as well as, yes, me—has found that being truly in love with school, and being unable to frame it as just "getting that piece of paper," as often as not requires stepping considerably outside of the black world.

Thus our undergraduate recruiter's sense that Anti-intellectualism is a necessary component of cultural blackness responds to a real opposition of the scholarly and the black in the world we live in. Not only the recruiter, the black graduate student, the black sociologist, and Berkeley's black faculty, but also the astrophysicist, the "oreo" sorority girls, and the student on the train, are all innocents, their choices virtually forced by the constraints of modern black American culture.

But—it doesn't have to be this way. It is natural that so many black Americans quietly think that to be scholarly to the core of one's being, to be uncompromisingly precise, has at best a delicate and fraught relationship with the core of being "black." But this sense of incommensurability between being "culturally black" and doing "white" things is the product of blinkers forced upon us by our moment. Millions of years ago, there were camels with little trunks. Such a creature is biologically possible; we just don't happen to have them anymore, just like Ford no longer makes Falcons. In the same way, the only reason the bookish "brother" or "sister"—other than one who studies black victimhood and victories—raises the antennas of many blacks is that current conditions tend to discourage such persons from emerging.

In Philadelphia, for example, students in both black and white public schools are traditionally well-immersed in classical music. In my teens, in the summers I went to a music camp where about half of the students in the orchestra I played in were black. Very few of these black kids were from the tony private schools; most were working-class kids from row home neighborhoods, with names like Dwayne and Tomika.

Shelby Steele in *A Dream Deferred* notes that contrary to Separatist dogma, blacks have become jazz virtuosos on classical instruments. Excellent point, but even here we can't help noticing that the music they play on these instruments is "black"—dazzlingly deft and profound, but also heavily dependent on intuition and created by men many of whom were musical illiterates. Because the creation of jazz entailed adapting classical instruments to an art form springing from black traditions, Steele's point in its way bolsters a sense that the culturally black person can pick up the *gist* of European traditions, but only to then fill them out with hot, spontaneous impulses rather than engaging in the reproduction of the stolid European tradition itself.

But Philly's youth orchestras did not bear out this idea. Year after year there were decidedly "black" kids playing thoroughly respectable renditions of the works of the dead white European masters, and then putting down their instruments and capping on each other in Black English, the boys in their muscle shirts with hair cut close, the girls sashaying down the hall in their halter tops and coiffed with shiny cornrows. And make no mistake—these were not exceptional prodigies of the sort we could put aside as marginal "static." They were just decent players who had chosen this as their after-school activity rather than the track team; almost none of them went on to become professional musicians. Nor were they concentrated in the brash, "Dionysian" brass and percussion sections blowing on trumpets and beating drums—in other words, being jazz musicians once removed. On the contrary, the black kids were concentrated in the string sections—happily playing the most demanding instruments in the orchestra. This skew was so pronounced and so consistent year after year that the inevitable social separation between black and white was also the one between the strings and the other instruments. As a cello player, for example, my social circle there was exclusively black (except for one white violinist)—the brass and percussion sections, not to mention the winds, I generally knew only by name and face, if that. And finally, the black kids were not just the back-benchers sawing away dutifully behind white and Asian section heads. The head first violin, viola, and cello were all black. Nor was this an accidental constellation. Before I came to the camp, there had been a head cellist who lived in legend as a great player. He visited one day, and he was a husky, down-with-it black guy from West Philly who most of us would mistake for a varsity wrestler.

Many people white and black have trouble shaking a sense that to expect serious dedication to on-paper endeavors, and the precise abstraction required, from black students is an imposition upon people of a different "culture." But there was black culture aplenty at this camp and we played Schubert and Wagner. Statements like the student recruiter's at Berkeley—which we should recall was meant as representative of the feelings of the black recruiting staff in general—reveal that many blacks have a nagging sense that to expect more than the occasional black student to embrace the European this wholeheartedly will compromise black identity. But this legendary cellist was pure homeboy, and yet could also make a sterling showing not on the sax and not on the drums, but on the violoncello.

Settlement Music Camp not only illustrated that "black" is not incompatible with the kind of precision, concentration, and discipline we have no trouble expecting from whites or Asians. It also supported my point that it is culture that is central to why black students lag behind in endeavors of this kind. Philadelphia happens to have a tradition of putting classical instruments in young black kids' hands, and thus hundreds of black kids in the city at any given time are playing the violin just as around the country others are playing basketball or jumping double-dutch. My father was a violinist in a student orchestra when he was a child in the 1930s. Because this tradition runs so long and deep in Philadelphia, these kids are not steeped in a sense that to play Mozart is "white." Black culture does, however, steep its children in the idea that school is "white," at best a tool, not a lifestyle. Without this aspect of the culture, we can be sure that black kids would do math, write compositions, and take tests as well as kids of other races—and the happy string players I knew show that they could do such things without shedding cultural blackness. We only suspect otherwise because current conditions do not allow us to see the range of possibilities ethnicity can manifest itself in.

But the Cult of Anti-intellectualism does worse than simply blind us to our own possibilities. In courting "authenticity" at the expense of scholarly achievement, black America sabotages itself in a much more concrete way.

Namely, a race preferring to reaffirm common wisdom rather than innovate, and distrusting precision as "white," is in a poor position to formulate strategies for its own advancement. Why, for example, have almost all of the most influential programs aimed at ameliorating the misery of the inner cities been created and developed by whites? Because black American culture trains its best and brightest to devote more time to crying victim—i.e., once again, affirming a truism—than to grappling with the details of a complex problem (i.e., embracing precision) and formulating innovative solutions (i.e., transcending inference from the already known). Ralph Ellison put this better than I could:

> During the '60s students had been given a facile name for their unhappiness, and one which provided many of them an excuse for rejecting academic discipline. Those who worked on their studies while they protested I could respect, but what on earth could I do about the many who appeared to be throwing away a much better opportunity for an education than that for which my mother and I had had to make such great sacrifice. No ideological catch words could blind me to the fact that they were wasting a valuable opportunity for learning how to convert their anger into forms of conscious thought and creative action. The need to control and transcend mere anger has been our lot throughout our history, and for many years failing

to do so, as the saying goes, got you dead. Nor are things essentially different today, for no matter the headiness of our slogans, an unthinking indulgence in anger can lead to a socially meaningless self-immolation and to intellectual suicide.

## Walking Against the Wind

As students today, young black people are walking against the wind. Even when trying to stride ahead with all of their efforts, the message their culture inculcates that "books are not us" is a wind blowing at them from the opposite direction. This wind keeps them from getting as far as the whites, Asians, Indians, and even Caribbeans and Africans who stroll along opposed by no such wind. The aggregate effect of this wind is the direct cause of the scarcity of black students in the sciences, the rarity of black students at the top of any class, and the strikingly low test scores one sees on college applications submitted even by earnest middle-class black students year after year.

The saddest thing is that the Anti-intellectual cultural inheritance hobbles even the great many black students who are trying their best. As often as not, they are less participants in teasing black nerds than observers, and regardless, by high school or college, the schoolyard and the driveway are distant memories. Yet their culture, their inalienable comfort zone, now handicaps them in subtler but equally powerful ways, as often as not in what is not done or said as in what is. Rarely will they meet a black student as besotted with a class or subject as many white ones are. Rarely will they see a black student using every possible strategy to do well in a tough class. Immediately they will be bombarded when they get to college with conceptions of blackness emphasizing victimhood and Separatism, which cannot help but reinforce a sense that school is more a matter of "getting that piece of paper" from an alien institutional construct than a personal rite of passage. Quickly they will notice, except at the very top schools, that their friends tend to be rather cavalier about attending classes. The fact that they encounter a deeply committed black student or two will have negligible effect amidst the overwhelming uniformity of the message they receive from the black student body as a whole. Such things combine to put a kind of subconscious scrim between black students and school, quietly blocking them from the committed, open-hearted engagement vital to top-rate performance *even when they give their best efforts.* This operates like any num-

ber of subconscious mental blocks, such as a deep-rooted fear of inti-
macy ensuring that a person unwittingly holds other people at arm's
length even when actively seeking friendships.

Most black students are barred from shining brightly in school by a
similar subconscious sense of separation from the realm of books and
learning. If a black student sees a fellow black student who aces school
as a sell-out, then how likely is he to be able to truly give his all to schoolwork, *even if he tries his hardest*? It would be remarkable if that student
*could* turn in top-rate work. This is the root of the Shaker Heights
dilemma. Why, after all, would it not be? The teasing of bookish black
students, aiming at pleasing the teacher rather than one's parents, "Now
you're arguing like a lawyer," the suspicion that black students who don't
need affirmative action will not be "down with us"—none of these things
are just inner-city phenomena; on the contrary, all of them permeate
black American culture as a whole, and all of them lead to the question:
Why would a people burdened with this tragic cultural legacy *not* post
the lowest scholastic achievement record in the country?

It is absolutely vital that we address the Cultural Disconnect from
learning for its own sake in black American culture honestly, directly,
and relentlessly. Just as this legacy itself is a drag on the race, to deny its
pivotal significance is cultural self-sabotage. To insist that black students cannot be expected to operate on a lucid mental level in anything
but near-perfect societal conditions is, in broad view, to imply that black
Americans are the planet's most dimwitted and constitutionally impo-
tent ethnic group. It must give us pause, for example, to see teachers
and administrators at Berkeley High claiming that black students are
done in at the outset by the vast and impersonal bureaucracy one must
negotiate to settle into courses, when for white, Asian, or other students,
grappling with this system is seen simply as part of growing up. The ease
and comfort of analyzing black students as barred from scholastic
achievement rather than leery of it, even with constructive intent, is in-
validated by the condescension and infantilization such positions entail.
Moreover, to avoid the unpleasant glare of the Cult of Anti-intellectualism is cultural suicide, since by doing so, we allow the central factor in
black scholarly failure to rage unchecked.

In sum:

- When a race is disparaged and disenfranchised for centuries and
  then abruptly given freedom, a ravaged racial self-image makes Victimology and Separatism natural developments.

- Victimology makes mediocre scholarly achievement seem *inevitable*.
- Separatism, casting scholarly achievement as "what white people do," *sanctions* mediocre scholarly achievement.
- It is a short step from *inevitable* and *sanctioned* to "authentic," and authentic is just another word for "cool."

History created the quandary as inevitably as flour and water make dough. The question now is how to undo it.

# 5

## African-American Self-Sabotage in Action: The Affirmative-Action Debate

> We told them that it's a very hostile environment and that we're not welcome here, and they don't want us here because they are not letting us in. We weren't pushing them to come to Cal.
> —Director of UC Berkeley Black Recruitment and Retention Center, spring 1998

\* \* \*

WE WILL NOT GO QUIETLY!

OUR COMMUNITIES ARE BEING DENIED
ACCESS TO EDUCATION WHILE BEING
RELEGATED TO PRISONS AND GHETTOS.

STAND UP!

MARCH & RALLY WED.

APRIL 15TH ON SPROUL

So read one of the flyers decorating the UC Berkeley campus in the spring of 1998, after it was announced that the number of black students admitted for the following fall had fallen 43 percent from the previous year's total, as a result of Proposition 209, which banned the use of racial preferences in California university admissions. The tone of this flyer typified the general sense of outrage among black students and faculty over the drop in minority admissions, aired in various rallies furiously decrying the imminent "resegregation" of the undergraduate population. Campus buildings were plastered with flyers like this one, while the student body was abuzz with rumors of a racist takeover of administrative policy.

Whether minority students ought to be admitted to universities with lower grades and test scores than others is one of the most complex and difficult issues to decide in America today. In a country with such a racist past, surely we can do better than the blinkered and unfeeling line that all people ought to "pull themselves up by their own bootstraps."

Moreover, to reject the institution of affirmative action in the 1960s as "discrimination against whites" is an almost willfully unreflective position that I can never quite believe the person making the charge means sincerely. This argument suffers from ignoring the realities of recent history, particularly in anyone old enough to have lived through it: affirmative action was instituted as a response to the fact that as late as the mid-1960s, open racism in elementary and secondary schools as well as colleges and universities themselves kept the black population of many institutions of higher learning to a small fraction. After all, in 1966, *Brown v. Board of Education* was as recent as the inauguration of George Bush or the premiere of *Roseanne* will be by the time the reader reads this.

UC Berkeley Chancellor Robert Berdahl recounted to me a WASP professor at a Northeastern university in the 1960s casually saying over a faculty club lunch that he was in favor of any number of the changes in university culture then blowing in the wind "as long as we don't have to let in any more niggers than we already do"—and this was before black students began violent campus demonstrations. In a world like this, the issue of greater good surely trumped "discrimination" against whites almost always able to attend some other school of their choice.

There are those who argue that black Americans were advancing socially and financially even before the institution of affirmative action, and obviously, many oppressed groups rose in America without it. Yet it is reasonable to question whether these groups' having to face brutal bigotry in a society that turned a blind eye to the injustice inherent in it was an ideal, as opposed to a more primitive stage in the country's ethical trajectory. Applied reasonably, affirmative action is a badge of moral generosity and sophistication—"leveling the playing field," as Bill Clinton is fond of putting it—of which our country ought to be proud.

However, history marches on, and the country we live in is vastly different from the one in which affirmative action was established. By the time you read this, 1967 will be about as far from the present as the election of Franklin D. Roosevelt and the premiere of the film *42nd Street* were from 1967. Sadly, however, over the decades, a common wisdom on affirmative action has established itself in most of the black community that is as ahistorical as that of many of the policy's opponents, in a way that has come to proffer more harm to the race than good.

In fact, the response among most black students, faculty, administrators, and pundits to the reassessment of affirmative action in the light of a new America is a clear demonstration that the three currents of thought I have discussed in this book are not simply fringe extremes typical of politicians and various "characters." The supposed national "debate" over affirmative action is in reality a stalemate—partly because of the limited vision of many "conservatives," but in equally large measure because those currents in thought hinder so many African Americans from even perceiving that any debate could possibly be necessary.

## Affirmative Action and Victimology

### The Poverty of the Black Middle Class

The Cult of Victimology enforces a cognitive dissonance between the rapid and manifest recession of racism by the year, and a mythological conception under which the only difference between black American life in 1950 and today is that we can sit anywhere we want on the bus. Because the black contribution to the affirmative-action debate is filtered almost exclusively through Victimology, the foreign observer listening to most black speeches, rhetoric, and punditry on affirmative action would come away with the impression that all but a tiny minority of modern black Americans still grow up idling on ghetto front stoops. "Few African-American students receive adequate education," I heard a black professor at an elite institution casually intone, as if it were 1940. The liberal media reinforce this conception, such as a *New York Times* piece on the aftermath of the ban on affirmative action at University of California schools, musing that:

> Minority students look around and realize that they have had to fight their way through thickets unheard of in North Hollywood. Saul Mercado, a senior, said "I come from a family of 11 kids. My father got as far as third grade; my mother stopped at second grade. There was no talk of school. I was swimming against the tide at home, and societal expectations as well." As far as Mercado was concerned, triumph over adversity easily trumped test-score meritocracy.

At Berkeley, one is almost sure at any rally against the affirmative-action ban to hear indignant references to the policy's barring admission to black children growing up in shabby neighborhoods in next-door Oakland, and official and unofficial discussions of affirmative action at Berkeley are always centered on concepts such as "outreach," "the Community" and other terms implying that black Berkeley students have been primarily children from, if not precisely the 'hood, then only a few blocks over.

Yet almost none of the black students attending rallies like these, and precious few of the black students at Berkeley in general, have grown up in circumstances anything approaching the unfortunate ones in bad sections of Oakland, nor even "struggling blue collar." Most of the black students at Berkeley have long been children of middle managers, municipal administrators, management consultants, educational administrators, and even doctors, lawyers, and college professors—not food service workers, airline attendants, or bus drivers. The figures bear out what is readily observable after half a semester on the campus. For example, of the 257 African-American freshmen who entered Berkeley in the last class before the ban on racial preferences took effect, only 83 had parents whose total yearly income was $30,000 a year or less, a commonly used metric for "lower income." No less than 174 of the 257—65.2 percent of the class—came from homes where the parents' income was *at least* $40,000 and usually much more. For those who resist considering even this a middle-class income, the parents of 107 of the 257 made *at least* $60,000 a year.

Importantly, these 1997 figures were nothing less than ordinary, looking much like those throughout the 1990s. Year after year, only about a third of the black entering class could be considered lower income even by the most liberal metric, while the parents of about half and often more of the class made *at least* $40,000 a year, with quite a few in brackets much higher than that. The only significant change over the years is a general gradual increase in the proportion of students whose parents made $40,000 a year or more. In other words, only a small fraction of black students have had to "fight through a thicket" to get to Berkeley— at least not a thicket any denser than those faced by any number of other Berkeley students. The Mexican student quoted in the *Times* piece is clearly something of a hero, but he is an exception at top schools, by no means anything approaching a rule.

There is no reason why Berkeley would be unique on this score among elite universities. Of the black students admitted in 1989 to the twenty-eight selective universities surveyed by William Bowen and Derek Bok in *The Shape of the River,* just 14 percent came from homes earning $22,000 a year or less. Just as many and a bit more came from homes earning $70,000 a year or more, with the rest—71 percent— coming from homes earning incomes in between. To be sure, the proportion of white students coming from families earning $22,000 a year or less was lower, and the proportion from families earning more than $70,000 was higher—as we all know, black Americans have yet to achieve financial parity with whites. This, however, does not in any way signify that the black student populations at Columbia, Oberlin, and Swarthmore were, or today are, islands of ghetto culture plunked amidst scions of the white elite.

In response to the typical objection that income does not correlate exactly with class, we must return here to an important point. Many affirmative-action advocates are only comfortable claiming that for black people, anything short of growing up in a mansion is on some level "struggling" until a white person says it, which reveals this notion as the Victimologist distortion of reality that it is. When my best friend, a black man, went to college, his white roommate asked him whether he intended to go back to the neighborhood "to help out" after he graduated, casually assuming that any black person grows up in the 'hood. Given that George and I grew up on the wide, tree-lined, integrated streets of Mount Airy in Philadelphia where there is precious little "help" needed, we found this hilarious—as well as ridiculously insulting. Similarly absurd was the time the two of us were at a wine shop choosing a bottle to take to a dinner party when an old white woman asked us whether there were any more of a certain brand in the back, under the impression that any young black men in the store could only be the help (we were neither wearing smocks, affixing price tags, nor lifting anything at the time).

Among black people, these are "Mmmmm-hm!" anecdotes—two more stories showing the lens through which we are so often viewed by whites. Yet affirmative-action advocates can be sure to get whoops of support from an audience with claims implying the same equation of black with lower class that they find so insulting when whites listen to them and take it to heart. For instance, one Berkeley professor at a teach-in on the affirmative-action ban angrily noted that "the people most likely to be taught by emergency teachers are disadvantaged minorities." That is true, but the question this man considers irrelevant is how many of the minority students *at Berkeley and like schools* have ever been "disadvantaged," and why, if we are to designate anyone who does not grow up in outright plush surroundings "disadvantaged," certain minority students such as Asians manage to excel in school in representative numbers regardless of life circumstances.

In general, then, statistical approaches like "blacks make x percent of what whites make" or "x percent of black youth are unemployed" require a logical sleight of hand revealing how Victimology trumps truth, because they have little to do with the students being addressed. If 40 percent of New York City's streets have potholes, we do not deem it illegal to drive over twenty miles per hour anywhere in the city. If anyone claimed that such a policy was justified because there just might be a new pothole somewhere, we would not consider that possibility worth traffic jams and preventing people from getting to work on time. Victimology forced this man into a fundamental conception of "minority" as "poor," regardless of the middle-class black and Latino students dominating his audience, most of whom had grown up no more, but no less, comfortable than Moesha, Urkel, Mickey, and Judy or Bart and Lisa.

### "I Don't Feel Welcome"

Even black students themselves are Carefully Taught by Victimology to conceive of themselves as somehow cosmically "disadvantaged" regardless of their life circumstances. One way this is revealed is in the often heard observation that the ban on affirmative action makes black applicants of all walks of life feel "unwelcome." This complaint was aired often when UC Berkeley's Boalt Law School admitted its first class without preferences, and all of the black admittees declined to attend because of a sense that the new policy suggested that black people were not welcome on campus (one black student enrolled who had been admitted the year before but had deferred).

The "unwelcome" charge contains the underlying implication that the administrators in question are bigots who do not want black people around. However, the expression is in fact a euphemism for the expectation that in order to "welcome" black people, an admissions committee must allow black students to enroll with lower grades and test scores than other students.

The purported justification for this is that black people face obstacles to education that would make it unfair to evaluate their records as stringently as other students'. However, this position fails because (1) it implies that all but a few black students go to poor schools, when this is not true, (2) in the meantime even black students from good schools tend to make lower grades and test scores than other groups, and (3) it begs the question as to why students of other groups manage to succeed in the same schools.

We cannot expect black students concerned with the extent to which they are "welcome" to necessarily have point 2 in their heads, which is something one is most likely to pick up only as a "buff" on the subject, paging through doorstop books and interminable newspaper articles. Point 3 is the kind of thing that Separatism discourages many from considering, out of a sense that "black" is under all circumstances a thing apart. Point 1, however, is glaringly clear to any African-American person on a college campus today. As often as not, the black student today who declares that she only feels "welcome" if admitted under the bar is comfortable in standard English, has barely known overt discrimination in her life, went to school alongside whites, interacts with them with ease and has often dated some, and while most probably did not grow up in anything we would call luxury, has known the same vacations, new cars, and spending money for CDs and clothes that her white and Asian schoolmates have. Indeed, the correlation between these externals and class is not precise, but neither is it nonexistent (as we have no trouble acknowledging in reference to whites). Clearly it is valid to question why a black student who displays none of the cultural traits that suggest a life on the margins of society is entitled to dispensation in scholarly evaluation over, for one, black people suffering in terrible schools, or more pointedly, to white and Asian students who have led very similar lives.

That this is not processed as incongruous by any but a tiny minority of blacks is due to Victimology, which requires us to assume that the "default" black person grew up on the other side of the tracks, and channels our vision so strongly as to keep it from ever occurring to us that there is a lack of fit between this conception and the actual black people around us at a school like Berkeley, two generations past the Civil Rights Movement. It follows from this that it becomes impossible to even conceive how a good person could see any question at all about exempting *all* black students from serious competition.

Too often, the white person bringing up that not too many of the black students around him appear to have grown up suffering is simply dismissed as "not getting it." To the extent that "it" is a belief that regardless of outward circumstances, all black people suffer under a cloud of racism too oppressive to expect top performance in school, or that a student can only reach the top if his parents talk about Arab-Israeli peace negotiations at the dinner table, I reiterate that the claim has serious problems. However, most whites have simply learned not to ask too many questions on this score for fear of being called racists. Of course, when they eventually begin to wonder whether black people just aren't very bright, they are told that their sentiment betrays that the racism at the heart of slavery lives on. But today, sadly, African Americans are too often driven to reinforce this impression themselves right here in the present tense, in few cases more vibrantly than a poised, well-dressed African American telling a media interviewer that she only feels "welcome" on a campus where her scholarly records are evaluated according to lowered standards.

### Professional Indignation Trumps Truth

At UC Berkeley after the racial composition of the first freshman class admitted under Proposition 209 was announced, minority students were particularly indignant that a large number of minority students with 4.0 GPAs and high SAT scores had not been admitted. The fact was that even larger numbers of white and Asian students with similar records had not been admitted, as has long been par for the course in admissions to top universities. The race-blind admissions process had exposed minority students for the first time to the same luck of the draw that other students have always had to cope with. Although the admissions committee could not have prevented minority students from suffering this fate under a race-blind procedure, many minority students instead suspected a racist plot.

At a meeting of minority faculty called by the chancellor, one professor informed us of this feeling among the students, and passionately urged us to let the students know that the administration welcomes minorities. This, however, would obviously have been a pointless objection to a student who saw the figures as evidence that the administration did not. Why did this professor, who had even been on the admissions committee himself, apparently consider it so beyond the point to simply explain to the students that even more white students had suffered the same fate?

Because this would not have served to fan the flames of Victimology. I couldn't help suspecting that this professor would *rather* simply tell the students "we welcome minorities," thereby reinforcing a scenario of good-hearted souls helpless in the face of a racist cabal pulling the strings up in the administrative offices and beyond in this, our eternally racist country. Indeed, a few months later he stood before a cheering audience comparing the ban on affirmative action to the Ku Klux Klan, the Chinese Exclusion Act of 1882 that barred Chinese from immigrating to America, and the similar Gentleman's Agreement that excluded the Japanese. "They're not wearing hoods anymore, but . . . [applause]", he preached, reinforcing his impressionable students in the kind of Victimologist paranoia that thwarts initiative and keeps the cycle going, all in the name of higher education. Moreover, this man is not a self-conscious strategist "utilizing" Victimology for "access to power"; he holds these sentiments quite sincerely—he began crying during an interview for Berkeley's faculty and alumni magazine about the ban (and he is not a drama professor).

### Professional Victimhood Trumps Action

Nowhere are the Victimologist roots of today's pro–affirmative action stance more vibrantly demonstrated than in the Berkeley student group By Any Means Necessary (BAMN), formed in response to Proposition 209. In the organization's flyers, all of the usual-suspect arguments are hauled out: "black median income is lower than whites'," SAT tests are "biased," Proposition 209 is part of a backlash against minorities designed to take us back to Reconstruction—"DID YOU KNOW . . ." intones one flyer, "that the attack on affirmative action, if it were to succeed, would roll back all of the gains of the Civil Rights Movement and throw American society back to the days of forced, legal segregation?"

Indeed, it is difficult to avoid sensing at BAMN meetings, as well as in their literature and in conversations with their members, a yen for indignation rather than constructive engagement with the actual facts and positions surrounding university admissions and race. Nothing indicated this more strongly than the organization's treatment of a group committed to class-based, rather than race-based, admissions who tried to make a statement at one meeting. The head repeatedly refused to allow the representative to speak, and when he finally managed to say his piece, predictably with a certain degree of exasperation at having been silenced for so long, she dismissed his position as "an attitude." This group's ideas were considered beyond the pale not on any logical basis, but because class, an inchoate concept in America, is less easily harnessed into personal, identity-based grievance, and is thus only fitfully commensurate with Victimology.

Something else that strikes one about BAMN is that few blacks are present at meetings or at the tables where they distribute literature on Sproul Plaza, and this was also true at the first campus-wide faculty meeting addressing possible ways to reverse Proposition 209 when it passed some years ago, where out of about 150 faculty members I was one of the only black ones present. Certainly there have been any number of individual meetings among black faculty and administrators in the wake of the ban. However, the pan-faculty organization officially convened to work against the ban was headed by whites, the largest meetings among black faculty were convened by Chancellor Berdahl, and there has arisen no black-led student organization against the ban as visible, active, and persistent as the mostly nonblack BAMN. It appears strange that black people have played so little role in the organizations devoted to concrete action against Proposition 209—until we remember that Victimology is devoted not to action but to grievance for its own sake.

While there is plenty of room for debate about the wisdom of affirmative action in admissions, the commonly accepted argument that the policy is morality incarnate because black equals poor is based on a conception of black America that is now decades out of date. There can be no intelligent or constructive debate about affirmative action that operates upon the notion that most black students at selective schools are shell-shocked people drawn from "the Community," virtual heroes for even making it to campus—for the simple reason that most black students at top schools are middle class by any definition. True, *nationwide* a larger proportion of black students than white are saddled with lousy educations. However, it is no longer true that this proportion is so large, and the discrepancy between their educations and many white students' in middling schools is so vast, that any body of black students larger than a dozen must logically be a group of undereducated "struggling blue collar" statistics, rubbing their eyes in the glare of a hitherto unencountered white world and dumbfounded by stringent academic expectations.

## Affirmative Action and Separatism

Victimology spawns Separatism, a particularly damaging manifestation of which is the sense that, both as an acknowledgment of their eternal victimhood and as a check on cultural cooptation, blacks must be subject to different and weaker standards of evaluation and judgment than all other people. As we have seen, one of the most pervasive manifestations of this evaluation filter is in the realm of scholastic achievement; Chapters 3 and 4 covered the effects of this upon young black people in the classroom. The sense of separation from the academic plays an equally vital role in shaping the most commonly encountered black positions on affirmative action. The value of competition and excellence in school is certainly not an alien concept to people with these positions, but crucially, they give it much less emphasis than issues such as head-counts, role modeling, and earning power. This is not an accident: it is an expression of a cultural *meme,* in the term of Richard Dawkins, conditioning a sense that to take The Books too much to heart is something other people do.

Certainly these people do not actively want black students to fail— this will not be an argument that black teachers and administrators secretly allow black students to do poorly because it keeps extra salaries and resources flowing from on high. Black support for affirmative action is not a cynical, deliberate ploy, but a natural expression of burdensome Separatist standards of evaluation.

Most of these people would claim that their furious support for racial preferences is due not to Separatism or its descendant Anti-intellectualism, but to the purported fact that all but a marginal few black students are prevented from excelling in school because of poor schooling. But this position is an outdated distortion: the main cause of the black-white scholastic gap is the Cult of Anti-intellectualism.

However, for our purposes now, let's pretend that 90 percent of African-American children are indeed going to bombed-out schools where teachers pop in videos and go out for coffee while their students vegetate. Even if this were true, there are various potential solutions that one might pose to such a problem. In our America, though, one particular response has predominated: racial preferences, the response most compatible with Separatist thinking.

We can see how Separatism channels approaches to the affirmative-action problem in various ways.

### Campus "Discussions"

In the wake of Proposition 209, there were various meetings of concerned faculty, minority and non, on what possible responses might be. The theme of these meetings was generally how the ban might be reversed, circumvented, tweaked, or relaxed, the consensus being that the affirmative-action policy of previous decades had been nothing less than a moral absolute. The guiding assumption at these meetings was that the policy had been necessary because as a rule, black students are not given the opportunity to excel. This was so much a part of the bedrock that the conviction was never spelled out, but the endless talk about "outreach"—as if most affirmative action had gone to people difficult to "reach"—and rapt attention paid to suggestions such as that black students are done in by racist guidance counselors, made the context clear. As a firebrand Latino professor bridled at an affirmative-action teach-in, "We cannot have philosophical discussions about merit in a society still so riddled with inequality."

What was more important, however, is what one did *not* hear at these meetings. For example, one possible response to a backlash against affirmative action would be to spread the word that SAT scores correlate only weakly with college performance, or that black students do as well as others once they get to Berkeley. Indeed, neither of those things is true—but *most affirmative-action fans think both are,* and thus it is not inconceivable that they might bring these conceptions to bear on the issue. Yet it was almost bizarre how meaningless these two simple points were to the movers and shakers at these meetings; they also at best tended to hover at the margins of most campus statements against the ban (BAMN's claim that the tests are "biased," though untrue, was a rare exception).

This gap in argumentation is not a chance lapse. It reveals that whether or not minority students are as good as white ones is considered much less important than whether or not they are simply present in healthy numbers. Whether or not black students rate with white ones, and how well, cannot help but seem a rather secondary issue when viewed through a lens teaching one to be wary of "The Books" as anything but tools for earning power. The focus, then, on mere head-counts—"diversity"—is predictable: The underlying position is "Beyond a certain point below which even blacks are not admitted, just being *there* is more important than how good we are."

Another possible response, if one believes that the secondary schools are to blame, might be to attack the issue from that end, and commit oneself to the improvement of these schools so that black children will be more likely to present competitive records when applying to college. Of course, legions of people have been fighting for reform of America's schools, especially those serving minorities, for decades. However, there has been much less attention focused on turning these schools specifically to preparing students for admission to good schools. Only recently in California have there been developed such programs as the Berkeley Pledge to help prepare minority high-school students to present competitive applications to Berkeley and other top schools. Crucially, however, efforts like this one only took flight *after* it became clear that Proposition 209 was here to stay; the general shift of mood against quota-based affirmative action has spurred similar movements in other states starting in the late 1990s. Before this sea change forced attention in this direction, however, racial preferences of indefinite duration was widely considered to be a suitable solution by almost all minority faculty and administrators, and this had shown no signs of being about to change.

Preferences, excusing black students of all life circumstances from true competition, was a wise policy when instituted in the 1960s, but has always been, at heart, a Separatist affair, steeping an entire culture in a sense of local, sovereign standards of evaluation. Addressing how the schools might make black students more like the others is, obviously, not a Separatist idea. Separatism, then, neatly determined which of these ideas became so entrenched over thirty years that most African Americans now perceive it not as a strategic choice but as pristine moral judgment. The strategy aiming to make black students, in this area, like everyone else only came to the fore as an emergency measure, and the saddest thing is that many faculty appear to process this, rather than preferences, as the necessary evil.

In these meetings and conversations, a consensus becomes clear that the sheer presence of minority faces at Berkeley outweighs all other considerations by a wide margin, and that as long as there is some cut-off point in scores and GPA below which even minorities are not admitted, all talk of merit or excellence or rising to a challenge or fairness is, at worst, racist and backward, or at best—and it is this which I find most alarming—utterly unimportant. The reason for this is the operations of Separatism and, ironically enough among elite tenured professors, Anti-intellectualism.

It is clearly unfair to expect shining grades and test scores by black students who have struggled through life in ways unthinkable to most white students on campus, even if their problems were not as concretely oppressive as violent schoolrooms or chronic hunger. Why, however, do black affirmative-action advocates see no problem whatsoever in the black child of a municipal lawyer and a high-school principal in San Diego being admitted to Berkeley with lower grades and scores than the white child of an insurance executive and a travel agency manager? Why is it considered so absolutely unthinkable to even consider that a policy of brute, across-the-board set-asides may have come to require revision when applied to such students?

The sad truth is that Separatism conditions a quiet but fundamental sense among many African Americans of influence that top-rate grades and scores are somehow part of another world, external to the essence of being a black American. This is a depressing charge to make, but the lack of interest these people consistently show in presenting arguments to the effect that black students are as adept as white ones, their serene comfort with preferences contrasted with thirty years of only fitful interest in approaching the issue from the bottom up via the schools, and the central place that the concept of "diversity"—which, whatever its merits, has nothing to do with brain power—occupies in their arguments admits no other explanation. What we are seeing is the adult manifestation of black children's distrust of the nerd, which we already saw in the undergraduate black recruiter worried that the first black students admitted without preferences would be orcos.

The frantic support for affirmative action among so many African-American educators is conditioned not only by the misconception that most black people grow up "struggling," but also by an unstated sentiment that middle-class black America, at the pain of losing its essential blackness, should only be expected to produce so many nerds. In other words, we have reached the tragic apogee of the Separatist vogue: an unstated feeling among this cohort that the black student who aces the SAT and tolerates nothing less than top grades is stepping outside of what it is to be a proper African American.

### Graduation Rates

Affirmative-action advocates at Berkeley often defend preferences on the basis of the fact that black students, even if admitted with lesser qualifications, go on to graduate. Actually, William Bowen and Derek Bok show that black students in the class of 1989 at twenty-eight top universities were about three times more likely to drop out than white students. However, the very reliance on the broad issue of graduation is another indication of a sense of incompatibility between blackness and high academic performance.

Most criticism of affirmative action is centered less upon whether minority students reach the finish line—which in top schools most students of any color can nickel-and-dime their way to even if they are not star students—than whether or not it is fair to reject qualified white students in favor of less qualified minority ones, and whether or not affirmative action solves the problem it was intended to address. Graduation rates attract some attention, such as in Stephan and Abigail Thernstrom's *America in Black and White*, but the general thrust of the rising sentiment against affirmative action addresses the more fine-grained issues that loom as the black middle class gets bigger by the year.

One may or may not agree with conservatives' criticisms in this area; however, for one of the most often heard responses to these criticisms beyond "diversity" to be "Well, the minority students graduate, don't they?" is analogous to asking someone how a symphony performance of Beethoven's Fifth was last night and receiving the enthusiastic answer that the orchestra managed to get to the end of the piece. One could not help suspecting that this listener was not terribly concerned about the quality of the playing. The fact that so many minority advocates of affirmative action consider that kind of answer to be a compelling defense of the policy reveals, again, the lowered importance of the quality of black scholastic performance.

### Stigma

In American society as a whole, being good in school is considered a badge of accomplishment, a good trait, a gift. As such one would think that a race requiring dispensations for admission to good schools would consider this, even if necessary, to be a problem. Even for those convinced that the low performance of black students was due to racist inequality (rather than a cultural wariness of the scholarly in general), one would imagine that they would be indignant that societal conditions saddled their race's students with a handicap like needing preferences to make a showing, denying them one of the most positively valued facets of any human being in a technologically and intellectually advanced society.

Yet one detects very little sense among black students, faculty, or administrators that affirmative action is an inconvenience, an albatross, a necessary evil. It is instead thought of simply as part of the scenery, as unremarkable as covering our feet with shoes or eating with a fork. Even black college students who have suffered little or no discrimination in their lives often have a deep-seated sense that to have been evaluated according to the standards of white children would have been an injustice. They feel that as members of an oppressed group, they are in an inchoate but powerful sense are "oppressed" themselves by virtue of being part of that group.

Yet the fact is that a group with a legacy of oppression does not inevitably come to consider exemption from serious academic competition a birthright; in fact, not even most postcolonial African-descended people develop this mindset. Black American culture is infused with this comfort with lowered bars as a local development, not as a natural outgrowth of oppression.

We see this in the Cape Verdean student's statement in Chapter 3 that if she had been admitted according to lower standards of evaluation, it would have lowered her opinion of herself as a scholar. Cape Verdeans, descendants of African slaves who in Cape Verde still suffer discrimination from their former colonizers the Portuguese, share a legacy of slavery and disenfranchisement with black Americans, and in America take their place alongside other darker-skinned peoples as "other." However, they have not undergone the unique historical experiment black Americans have, under which abrupt enfranchisement from on high seeded professional victimhood as a balm for the insecurity that can only be erased by personal achievement, this followed by the natural developments of Separatism and Anti-intellectualism.

As a result, Cape Verdeans certainly have a sense of what it is to be "Cape Verdean," encompassing various cultural factors. However, when it comes to school, they largely share the conventional American attitude that excelling there is a positive trait, like athletic or musical ability, with the natural correlate feeling that to be given a permanent "handicap" in academic competition would be condescending and embarrassing. We also see this native sense of personal responsibility in school in Caribbean and African immigrants, whose children often find themselves in conflict with their African-American classmates who revile them for working hard in school.

It is for this reason, for example, that *New York Times* reporter James Traub found that affirmative-action beneficiaries at University of California schools tend to feel no stigma about having been admitted under the bar. If excellence in school were valued as deeply in African-American culture as in white or Asian culture, then affirmative action would be seen as a necessary nuisance to be endlessly evaluated, renegotiated, and gradated, with its demise breathlessly awaited—not as something to rejoice in.

## Affirmative Action and Anti-intellectualism

The Anti-intellectual strain stymies the affirmative-action debate not only in conditioning an unspoken sense of separation between black people and serious academic competition, but also in a guiding sense that careful reasoning is somehow beside the point when this issue is discussed. This is evident even among university professors who in other realms of inquiry have built careers upon sophisticated, cosmopolitan analysis.

An affirmative-action advocate in support of reversing Proposition 209 in one speech dutifully advised minority students to learn how to listen to opinions other than their own about the ban on preferences without facilely calling the other person a racist. Minutes later, however, he showed his hand by shouting that "Ward Connerly is a pimple on a cancer!" the cancer being a supposed backlash against minorities. Connerly is the black UC regent who spearheaded Proposition 209. The man is not precisely the king of tact, but his justifications for his actions raise important points worthy of discussion. Yet despite the professor's dutiful genuflection to the value of civility in constructive exchange—as one would expect of a university professor—on this racial subject he felt quite free to suspend civility and careful reasoning in favor of audience-baiting schoolyard name-calling, thereby inciting students by example to do the same. In general, despite his careful instruction that we not call each other racists, his speech was primarily concerned with warning us that Proposition 209 was part of a surge of racism in national culture.

At a meeting of By Any Means Necessary, one of the few black speakers, a graduate student, laced her speech with references to Ward Connerly as Wardell, noting that this is his given name. "Wardell" has a "blacker" sound than Ward, and her using it was a sly implication that Connerly goes by "Ward" to skirt his racial membership in the same vein that Michael Jackson lightened his skin tone. Translation: Connerly's opposition to affirmative action is invalid because he probably just doesn't like black people.

But this is not an argument. I have no idea how Connerly feels about black people, but even if he thoroughly despised every one of us, this in itself would not invalidate the points he has made about affirmative action, all of which center upon equity and incentive. The notion that the soundness of a person's viewpoints on racial preferences stands on whether or not he "likes us" is an Anti-intellectual one, avoiding grappling with the meat of the issue in favor of the easy score of subjective grievance. The speaker also regularly intoned "Wardell" with a particular black American intonation pattern almost impossible to transcribe on paper, but which conveys simultaneously a "calling out" and a diminishment, the implication being that Connerly is not a man with a reasoned opinion to be addressed, but simply a bad boy "acting up," his ideas so inherently dismissible that they could be vanquished by some good old-fashioned black mother wit.

Shortly before this meeting, Connerly had suggested that Ethnic Studies and African-American Studies departments be eliminated at UC campuses. Connerly definitely went to the limit on that one, but our speaker closed with the insight that she thought old Wardell was pulling this just because he was "scared" of the potential power of the minority students and faculty united in such departments. In other words, Man, he just scared he gonna get his ass whupped. There are plenty of reasoned justifications for "identity" departments (I espouse them in theory). But once again this woman simply chose the backyard instead of actual argumentation (her one attempt at this was to say that she felt "comfortable" in classes in such departments). There is nothing wrong with a little vaudeville in a speech or presentation, of course—I use it all the time. You can not compel a live audience by simply reciting a list of arguments. But the problem here was that vaudeville was all there was. This woman—a graduate student at UC Berkeley, no less—did not present one reasoned argument in the whole fifteen minutes of her speech. Needless to say, she got a big round of applause.

Casual unreflectiveness of this sort smacks of the lack of concern with reasoned, inclusive argument we see in "Afrocentric historians," even more in the tongue-clicking dismissal anyone who questions the paradigm receives. After a while one gets the feeling that the notion of looking into the issue any further than "diversity at all costs" comes from another world, as if trying to break down this rich and mighty issue with a neutral approach were somehow a faux pas, not done, not the way we do it in these parts—even among people who constitute some of the world's most eminent and credentialed thinkers. Instead, discussion is carefully limited to a small set of endlessly reiterated declarations— "Athletes and alumni's kids have been slipping in the back door for years," "Berkeley is a public institution and therefore should reflect the ethnic composition of California," "We are seeing a return to the past," etc., all richly seasoned with the mantra "diversity."

The blissful *comfort* with such patently incomplete, line-in-the-sand argumentation can only stem from a sense of unaccountability to the rules of enlightened exchange—that is, a basic sense that when "black" is involved, close reasoning is at best optional, and always disposable in favor of signifying and name-calling.

I began teaching at Berkeley the fall that Proposition 209 was passed to sharp indignation and great dismay among minority students, faculty, and administrators. This was long before I thought I would ever write a book like this one, or had had much reason to learn or think much about race in education. I considered it urgent business to come to an informed opinion about the issue based on taking in all of the facts.

Statements on campus against the ban were—and still are—couched so consistently as calls for "diversity" that an outside observer would suppose that Berkeley's administrators had decided to bar minorities from admission altogether. Since this was not the case, I assumed that the "diversity" chant was a totem that had come over the decades to symbolize a series of viewpoints addressing the actual issue at hand—that is, whether minority students should be admitted to the university under a lowered bar of evaluation—and if so, upon what basis. In other words, I thought "diversity" stood in the same relationship to the actual substance of the viewpoint as the opening vamp of "New York, New York" (*plink plink plink ee-dink, plink plink plink ee-dink . . .*) stands to the whole song. I could not imagine that headcounts alone was the paramount justification for affirmative action in the minds of tenured professors serving as standard-bearers for one of the United States' most eminent temples of scholarly training and achievement. I assumed that such people's adamant support for the policy was based on other factors, which had been discussed and validated in the decades before I became a professor.

Around this time, an African-American professor called a meeting of concerned minority faculty. Besides him, two professors showed up, myself and another. I was perplexed at the low turnout, but thought that at a meeting like this I could become better informed about the roots of the ardent support for affirmative action assumed of all Good People on campus.

After a while, I mentioned that over the years, the debate had changed such that "diversity" alone was losing its potency as a justification, and that for better or for worse, the charge that affirmative action had been "discrimination" against whites meant that our task now was to present a direct and sustained justification for admitting minority students with lower grades and test scores than other students. Since this was long before I had studied the issue, I imagined that statistics were available showing that SAT performance had no significant correlation with performance in college, or that students admitted under affirmative action performed as well as other students, or that all but a small number of black students in California went to terrible schools.

After I said this, the two professors were silent for a few pregnant seconds, looking at each other and at me as if I had just brought up wallpapering technique or the latest dinosaur finds in Mongolia. Finally one of them genially said that when he came to Berkeley decades before, he had rejected affirmative action as tokenism. He then stopped and turned slowly back to the other professor, upon which they continued their initial conversation exploring possible methods of getting around Proposition 209. This subject occupied the rest of the meeting.

That little episode was my first encounter with the reality of most support for affirmative action. I spent the next couple of years waiting for other affirmative-action advocates to fill in the gap that this man had not, explaining the justification for indefinitely suspending minority students from serious competition. I gradually realized that these people had no historical precedent to refer to, no concern over the damage to incentive and confidence in a group exempted from the need to strive for the top, and only the slightest sense of sociohistorical trajectory. Their only justification for their position was statistics showing that a greater proportion of minority students attend poor schools.

The charge from opponents that the solution is to see to it that children are educated better, or to allow them to go to solid second-tier schools, grew ever louder as time went by. Yet affirmative-action advocates had little interest in engaging these arguments, instead passionately devoted to racial set-asides of indefinite duration. After a while I even began to suspect that these people would not even *want* minority students to truly excel more than occasionally, and shortly after this occurred to me, the undergraduate black recruiter came to my office one afternoon and concretely demonstrated just this, suspecting that the new black freshmen admitted without preferences would be sell-outs. This was presented as a sentiment representative of the black recruitment office in general, and the following week the director of the very office this student was working in proudly recounted to *The New York Times* that the office was discouraging black prospective students from choosing a "racist" school like Berkeley—despite the strident daily protests against the ban led as often as not by whites. (One of the director's statements on this score was quoted at the outset of this chapter.)

As it happened, a few days later on my way to teach a class, from a distance I saw the professor from the meeting some years ago making a speech at one of the many anti–Proposition 209 rallies on campus that spring, underscoring a point by thrusting his fist into the air and arousing a big roar from the student crowd. I was not close enough to hear what he was saying, but I didn't have time to go find out and, in truth, I no longer needed to. I was quite sure that it was about either diversity, poverty, or impending segregation, and most certainly not about fixing California's schools, urging minority students and parents to put forth their best efforts, or fostering constructive discussion. I now knew what had brought this man from a suspicion of tokenism in the 1960s to impassioned and unquestioning support for permanent set-asides in the 1990s. Victimology, Separatism, and Anti-intellectualism had guided this man, as they have so very many others, into being *comfortable* with minority students being the weakest performers on America's university campuses.

# 6

## African-American Self-Sabotage in Action: The Ebonics Controversy

> It underconceptualizes what occurred to simply label the discourse of the mainstream media about the Oakland resolution as racist . . . White Americans . . . are repulsed by the people, by Black people, their language, their aesthetics, their rhythms, their history, that is represented, symbolized, interpreted in the African-American literary and scholarly traditions and commodified in popular culture.
>
> —Theresa Perry, *The Real Ebonics Debate,* 1998

Near the end of 1996, the Oakland school board issued a resolution declaring that African-American children speak not English but a separate African language called Ebonics, and that the district would henceforth attempt to raise black students' poor scholastic performance by treating Ebonics as their native tongue, in the vein of bilingual education programs. The resolution took its cue from a quiet tradition of thirty years' standing among an assortment of education specialists and linguists, who see the differences between black and standard speech as a prime culprit in black children's poor classroom performance.

For the general public, the media hoopla that ensued, over what was generally perceived as a cynical exploitation of identity politics to nab some bilingual education funds, was a passing episode, good for a few laughs and some jokes passed around on the Internet, now dimly remembered by most.

For me, however, it was a much larger experience. The morning the story hit the national news, I was awakened by a call from *ABC World News Tonight* asking my opinion on the school board's resolution, and by the time this interview was over, three more messages had accumulated in my Message Center from other major media outlets asking for similar interviews. Over the next several days while the story was "hot," I could barely get through a meal without the likes of NPR, *Dateline NBC,* local talk radio shows all over the country, or *The New York Times* calling, and over the next few weeks was quoted even in Europe.

Many linguists were asked their opinions on the Ebonics issue during these weeks, but almost none of them were all but besieged as I was. Why was I, an unknown linguistics professor, consulted so relentlessly that by just two weeks after the early-morning call from ABC, I had appeared on *The Today Show,* guested on NPR's *Talk of the Nation,* and been quoted in *Newsweek?*

For the sole and simple reason that every single other African-American linguist or education specialist supported Oakland's resolution.

The media, predictably, tended to cast the issue in terms of "pro" and "con." Finding the "pro" was always easy—all they had to do was call an African-American education specialist or an African-American linguist who was not me. As far as "con" went, however, a media organ who had a white professor question Oakland's policy would of course risk the racist charge. What was thus needed was a black linguist to express an opposing viewpoint, and there turned out to be only one.

I was initially surprised to be the only voice of black dissent among linguists. I learned the reasons why over the next few months, and what I encountered was another demonstration that Victimology, Separatism, and Anti-intellectualism are not mere fringe phenomena local to disaffected inner-city residents and certain colorful powermongers. As with the affirmative-action controversy, these thought patterns strongly channel the perspectives of legions of concerned and well-meaning African Americans, distracting attention from potentially effective solutions while rendering seductive other solutions that in fact only perpetuate the problem they address.

Like affirmative action, the Ebonics issue is richer and trickier than it looks on the surface. Just as one cannot fully understand the Ebonics controversy outside of the context of the ideological holding patterns currently infecting black America, it gravely distorts our view of the debate to operate under the general misconception that Black English is simply "slang" or a bad habit. Thus despite my preference for a straight-through line (I hate footnotes for that reason), here I cannot proceed before a quick detour for a brush-up on the subject of all the controversy: specifically, what *is* "Ebonics"?

## "Why Don't They Just Use Proper English?": Background Information

One might think from the general thrust of this book so far that my position on the "Ebonics" issue would be that Black English is mere lazy speech, and that the people supporting it as legitimate were just being apologists for black mediocrity as usual.

Not quite, this time: The basic contention that Black English is not "bad English" is in fact correct.

## Black English Is Not Bad English

There is a common misconception—among blacks as well as whites— that black speech differs from mainstream speech only in terms of "slang," colorful expressions that change by the decade like *word up* for "that's right" and *freak* for "pretty woman." This, however, is not what the resolution meant by "Ebonics," usually called African-American Vernacular English or Black English by linguists (I use the latter term).

For one, the dialect has several *sentence patterns* of its own. When black people say, *Ain't nobody even be seein' her on weekends* instead of "Nobody even sees her on the weekends," they are not peppering their speech with "slang," but using a different grammar. Like French uses two negatives at a time, as in *Je ne parle pas* "I don't speak," where both *ne* and *pas* mean "not," so does Black English. The *be* in the sentence looks "unconjugated," but note that the standard English version of the sentence doesn't even have a verb "to be" in it to be "unconjugated." Black English uses this *be* in a very specific way to express events that happen on a regular basis (in this case, the woman's disappearances on the weekend). A great many languages in the world have a special word or ending or prefix to do this, too; standard English just happens to be one that doesn't. Slang comes and goes, but black Americans have been saying things like *Ain't nobody even be seein' her on weekends* since way back into the mists of time.

Black English also differs from standard English in terms of *accent*, which is why we perceive there to often be a black "sound" in someone's voice even if she is using standard English sentence patterns and no slang. Some of these differences are very subtle aspects of vowel pronunciation; others are more obvious, such as a tendency to replace *st* with *s* at the end of words (*bes* instead of *best*).

Yet the understandable but mistaken inclination to see all of this as "lazy speech" or "bad English," the inclination is not what "becomes clear" only becomes clear from a historical perspective.

As animals and plants are always evolving, so the words and even basic grammar of all speech varieties are always changing. No one today could have a conversation with the people speaking their language more than about a thousand years ago—this is much of why we study Chaucer primarily in translation into modern English. Also like evolution, language change can take place in any number of directions and combinations. Language evolves in particular ways in each region where it is spoken and among each of the groups who speak it. As a result, any language viewed close up is a bundle of variations upon its basic theme, that is, dialects.

One of those dialects is chosen as the standard one not because it is somehow "better" or "more correct" in the eyes of God, but because it happens to be the one spoken where the center of power coalesces. All of today's British English dialects, for example, developed alongside one another from Old English via the same innocent processes of gradual change. Today's standard English is simply the variation that happened to evolve in the region of England where London was located. Black English, like Cockney English and Appalachian English, is one of the variations on the theme that did not happen to be chosen to be featured in the shop window, so to speak.

The things that look "sloppy" in Black English only look that way because we cannot help seeing them as developments *from* standard English, when in fact they developed alongside and separately from standard English, making Black English one of hundreds of the world's variations upon not standard English, but the *now extinct ancestor of all Englishes*.

Yet we still have a hard time shaking a sense that Black English is somehow "lesser" than the English we learn in school. This is largely because inevitably, the dialect chosen as standard becomes perceived as "the Language" while the others appear to be sloppy violations of it. However, they are simply alternates to the standard, having evolved in the same way as the standard did but in different places and among different people. The cat family is a useful analogy. All of today's cats great and small evolved from some ancestral, now extinct Ur-cat. We have no trouble understanding that a tiger is not a "degraded version" of a leopard but simply another variation on "cat"; we do not see house cats' lack of a mane as meaning that they are "broken" versions of lions. In the same way, Black English is not "bad standard English" but just another kind of English, according to the same basic processes of change that elsewhere produced not only Standard English but Russian, Chinese, and Tagalog.

Thus it is true that black people's speech is not "lazy English." Because linguists, like most modern academics, are committed more to sharing ideas within the halls of ivy than to communicating them to the public, even many black intellectuals, like Shelby Steele and Stanley Crouch, are not aware that Black English is not a failing, but it is true. One might naturally suspect that I am taking this tack because I grew up hearing relatives and friends talk this way, and perhaps because of the "Up-with-people" politics of modern academia. Personal experiences and politics can certainly thwart even the sincerest attempts at impartiality, but in this case, we are dealing with a view that any trained linguist on earth would unhesitatingly espouse, regardless of race or even political tendencies. The status of Black English, like all English varieties of all social statuses, as alternate rather than degenerate is not an opinion but a truth, founded upon basic tenets of linguistic science. There is no more question about this than there is as to whether a Burmese is a "degenerate" cat while a Siamese is a "real" cat.

The drafters of the Oakland resolution were correct in treating black speech not as a mistake but as a legitimate entity of its own. People all over the world speak home dialects quite different from the standard language of their nation, using the home dialect in casual situations and the standard in formal and public contexts, and this is not seen in any way as a "problem." For example, the Italian dialect of Milan, like a number of others, is so different from standard Italian that it might as well be a different language: For example, the Milanese person who says *M'è piasú* (may pyah-SOO) for "I liked it" at home will write *M'è piaciuto* (may pyah-CHOO-toh) in a business letter.

## The Ebonics Case

It is the implications that Ebonics advocates draw from these facts which is where the issue gets dicey. The resolution itself did not specify exactly how Black English was to be used in the classroom, but the "Ebonics" idea has long been used here and there, and the tradition has been in part to teach black children to read from primers written in Black English, the belief being that reading skills will develop more easily without the added burden of "translation" from the mother tongue Ebonics into the separate language standard English. Contrary to the widespread impression that the aim was to always teach black students in "jive," however, the intention has been to use this as a *transition* to standard English, as in bilingual education programs. Second, with the same aim of transition, there are workbooks directing black children to give standard English "translations" of Black English sentences, such as *She is my sister* for *She my sister*.

In fact, however, the conviction of these educators and linguists that the differences between Black English and standard English are the cause, or even a significant factor, in the black-white classroom lag is based on a highly distorted view of the facts.

For instance, the Oakland resolution described Black English as a "Niger-Congo African Language System," a characterization reflecting an idea that Black English uses English words within a grammar that is African. As it happens, there are languages like this, the European-African hybrids called creoles, especially common in the former plantation colonies of the Caribbean. The problem is that Black English is nothing like these languages in sound or structure. For example, in the creole of Surinam called Sranan, the way to say "That hunter bought a house for his friend" is *A hondiman dati ben bai wan oso gi en mati.* That sentence might as well be Korean to anyone who does not know the language, but in fact every word of it is from English: That hunt-man that been buy one house give his mate. Much of why the words look so unlike their English source is because this creole, like many African languages (and Japanese and many others), has sequences of consonant-vowel-consonant-vowel instead of cramming consonants together in words like *sprite*—therefore *da-ti* instead of *that,* etc. The sentence structure is also African-based. Languages have different ways of ordering words, and just as Spanish has *te amo* "you I-love" instead of "I love you," the native languages of the slaves who created Sranan say "buy house give him" instead of "buy house for him," and "hunter-that" instead of "that hunter."

Black English, however, is obviously not this kind of European-African hybrid; the Sranan sentence above in Black English would be roughly *Dat hunta done bought a house for his frien'.* There are some light African influences here and there in Black English, but overall, it is obviously what it looks and sounds like: a kind of English.

In the meantime, in claiming that the differences between Black and standard English are a barrier to learning for black students, advocates of Ebonics are neglecting the fact that all over the world, children bring home dialects to the classroom just as different from the standard dialect in their country and very often even more different (such as the Italian example). Yet they learn the standard dialect through simple daily immersion without special readers or workbooks. This is true in Germany, Italy, Finland, Japan, Francophone Canada, and a great many other places. What this suggests is that what holds black children back is not language but something else—and we have seen ample evidence in this book for what that might be.

Finally, Ebonics advocates often claim that there are studies showing that black students perform better when taught with Black English materials. However, most of the studies in question concern related, but distinct issues: One shows that black children do better when not relentlessly corrected about their speech, but does not include dialect readers and translation exercises; another one shows that translation works in an area of Sweden where the local dialect really is so different from the standard that it might as well be a separate language, barely comprehensible to a standard speaker even on the page, etc.

Only three studies address the actual issue of teaching African-American students with Black English materials. In one, the students did better, but standard English materials were used as well as Black English ones, muddying the result. Two used only Black English materials: in one, one group did better but the other did not; only in the other did students' reading scores rise overall. What is never mentioned, however, is that no fewer than nine other studies have found that using only Black English materials had no effect, and in the meantime, in Los Angeles where the Ebonics approach has been used since the early 1980s, students' performance has not only not improved, but declined over the years.

It is extremely difficult to conclude from these things taken together—how similar Black English is to the standard dialect, what students in other countries effortlessly do, the results of the studies—that Black English is a significant factor in why black children tend not to perform well in school. As we all know, there are gifted teachers who would inspire their students to learn under any circumstances. Between this and the fact well known in the social sciences that sometimes, sheer novelty can spark curiosity for brief periods only for old patterns to settle in after the novelty wears off, it is not hard to see how every now and then, the Ebonics approach might have some effect. However, out of twelve studies, for it only to have worked unequivocally once, and to have half-worked twice, is clearly not the most compelling record one might seek.

All over the world, the way children who speak a nonstandard home dialect learn the standard one is by being immersed in it in school. My opinion is that teaching standard English via dwelling at length upon Black English as a "separate language" in the classroom is ill-advised not because there is a thing "wrong" with Black English, but because it detracts from the immersion in standard English that is the best way to learn it. The ideal is for black children to be bidialectal in Black and standard English just as Milanese kids in Italy are bidialectal in Milanese and standard Italian. The reason black American children tend to do poorly in school is not that they cannot jump dialect gaps the way students in Milan do, but because there is a psychological barrier between them and school in general.

Some more nuanced Ebonics advocates claim that this psychological barrier is just the reason translation is necessary. They note that while Bavarian teachers do not treat their children as speaking "bad," but just different, German, Black English is thought of as a bad habit children ought be taught out of.

There is an important point here. Like many Americans, I often pronounce *your* as "yer"—I am less likely to say " 'yore' book" than " 'yer' book." None of us see this as "bad English"—on the contrary, few of us have even noticed it, and if we do, we just see it as a harmless variation on the "yore" pronunciation. Once a director of a play I was in told me to stop pronouncing *your* in my apparently "flat Northeastern" accent and say "yore." This was not a race issue: I am one of those black people whose speech is "white" sounding (when I started dating, a girlfriend told me that I had made her mother nervous when I first called because I sounded like a fifty-year-old white insurance salesman on the phone). Yet this was hard—*your* is a common word that popped up in quite a few of my lines, and even though I could correct it if I thought about it, the more comfortable I got with the part the harder it was to correct it, because "yer" is, after all, my more spontaneous, "native" pronunciation of that word. Being corrected on this was a minor annoyance, because it made me a little insecure about saying my lines.

Now imagine if your (yer) most spontaneous speech included something like "yer" roughly every three words, and that it wasn't only sounds like the last one in "mouf" as opposed to *mouth,* but whole sentence patterns like "ain't got" instead of *doesn't have,* and finally that the difference was not perceived simply as "flat," but as "wrong" and ignorant. This is the plight of Black English–dominant children in classrooms being "corrected" by white teachers under the impression that the black students' most comfortable mode of expression is bad English rather than different English.

This is a real problem, but some Ebonics advocates suppose that explicitly teaching students how to bridge the dialect gap is a way of addressing it. However, it is an equally ready solution that teachers ought be taught not to condemn students for their "bad" Black English, thinking of standard English as something to add alongside Black English rather than replace it. This goal, a laudable one, does not in itself presuppose dialect readers and translation exercises, which, after all, children all over the world learn standard dialects without. The idea that approaching standard English as a foreign tongue is a necessary component in addressing the problem with black students is based less on the actual issue at hand than on the fact that the translation approach has so dominated discussion that it has gradually become tacitly thought of as a *sine qua non* in any address of the issue. In the meantime, it is hard to see how teaching black children that they speak a tongue separate from English would do anything other than strengthen, rather than lessen, the psychological barrier in question.

## E Pluribus Unum: The United Front

My arguments on the Ebonics issue were certainly not delivered from the Mount by Moses; an issue this rich leaves plenty of room for discussion. However, I think I can claim that my points are worth being brought to the table at least, following basic lines of logic and based on a familiarity with the topics at hand. In that light, what is significant within the theme of this book is that my position was processed not as simply a differing opinion, but as a heresy. I remain in bad odor among several Ebonics advocates to this day. One of the contingent's gurus, a medical school teacher named Ernie Smith, circulated a paper among black education specialists close to the issue around the country surmising that I suffer from a subdural hematoma (a swelling of brain tissue following a blood vessel rupture) polluting my thought processes (yes, really!), and followed this up with a series of letters to me laced with epithets, insults, and obscenities, often concerning his purported sexual exploits among female members of my family, each time furthermore having a friend come to my department and distribute copies of these letters to each member of the faculty. In other words, not only were my views not considered worth being brought to the table—there was not even perceived to be a table at all.

Support for the Ebonics approach is by no means monolithic. A small number of vocal advocates insist that Black English is a separate language and heartily endorse dialect readers and translation exercises. Radiating outward in waves are larger numbers of teachers, administrators, and speech pathologists committed to a more general "acknowledgment" of Black English. They are less interested in dialect readers and translation than in various approaches bringing Black English stories and poems into the classroom alongside standard English ones. This, in my opinion, can be a harmless way of lessening the sense of alienation from school that black children tend to have while allowing standard English to prevail so that they can assimilate it thoroughly. However, while agreeing in private that the "bilingual" approach is not necessary, such people share with the more extreme advocates a basic conviction that the black-white scholastic lag is due in some way to the absence of Black English from the typical school curriculum. Thus the sense of a communal mission against racist inequity leads them to publicly remain in staunch support of "addressing the educational needs of African-American children," even though the way this is most vibrantly and frequently presented is in the form of an extreme method they would never use themselves. As such, my having expressed anything except support for Oakland's school board was processed as highly unsavory, even to people who essentially agreed with my public statements.

As with the Berkeley professor's *froideur* when learning that I was not a fan of Johnnie Cochran, the outside observer might wonder why passions would run so high about what is really, in the long view, a mere difference of opinion over an educational policy. The reason is that Ebonics advocates' conviction is based not on a dispassionate assessment of the evidence, but is instead, like all race-related issues in this country, filtered through the lenses of Victimology, Separatism, and Anti-intellectualism. With Ebonics as with affirmative action, this triumvirate of thought patterns have refracted a complex issue into something perceived as an inviolable truism, the saddest thing being that the truism is one that, as we will see, forces us to shoot ourselves once again in the foot.

## Ebonics and Victimology

I was told that at one conference on language and society, it was said of me after the Oakland controversy "That John McWhorter—he just doesn't . . .," followed by a facial expression suggesting that the end of the thought was roughly " . . . *get* it!" That pretty neatly sums up many sociology-oriented linguists' take on my statements at that time, even those not involved in the Ebonics movement. What is it that I am considered not to get? We approach an answer in something a black linguist said to me during the controversy in a genial yet pointed manner: "McWhorter, why are you saying all those mean things in the media?"

Interestingly, a couple of years later he told me that he had always agreed with me. During the controversy, however, he stood in line with all of the others espousing the "needs of African-American children in the classroom." "Mean" things—what he meant was that regardless of the truth of what I was saying, there was an overriding imperative, my neglect of which constituted an incivility.

What ths man meant, and what I have been considered not to "get," is that the main issue in the Oakland controversy was not evaluating an educational policy but defending black America from racist abuse. Nowadays I am occasionally asked by someone at a party or in a play I am doing whether I was involved in "that 'Eu-bonics' thing" a few years ago. They generally say this with a bit of a giggle. I am always struck by the contrast between this and what a grim business it was for most black linguists and educators. To this day, when the subject comes up, such people tend to look off into the distance and shake their heads, in line with a general conviction that the media explosion was a racist onslaught, revealing the eternal bigotry underlying the superficiality of the differences between today and 1950. This view has been enshrined in a number of conference talks and academic articles since.

In fact, the public and media response to the Oakland controversy was based mainly on pan-racial misimpressions about language in general, and the misleading wording of the resolution. The interpretation considered the "correct" one in academia, that the controversy allowed the public to vent the breathless racism always lying just beneath the surface, is only possible through a Victimologist filter.

## What Did They Expect?

It is true that much of the media coverage reflected an exasperation with what appeared to be a callow expression of identity politics. However, the Oakland resolution was often seen this way because of a misconception among the general public, always rued by linguists, that the standard dialect is "the Language" while nonstandard dialects are bastardizations of "the Language" rather than alternate varieties in their own right. I have tried to disabuse the reader of this natural misconception on pages 186–88, but the subject may be best learned and understood in a linguistics class or two.

The general public was unable to see any legitimacy in the claim that Black English was anything but bad grammar, not necessarily because of racism (although this surely played a small part here and there), but because of this general—and importantly, pan-racial—misconception that a language is a set entity rather than a bundle of dialects. This misconception is so easy to fall into and so prevalent in America that there are even people in the Ebonics contingent who subscribe to it unwittingly. Some of them quite casually dismiss the nonstandard white dialects, such as those that slaves heard in the South, as "degraded English." For these people, the appeal of the idea that Black English is "African" is the link with something unequivocally whole and legitimate—African languages. They have no awareness of the general fact that *no* nonstandard dialect is "bad grammar," and without the Africa myth, they would have as hard a time as the general public seeing anything but a joke in Black English. Even a great number of black people, many of them quite black-identified and fluent speakers of the dialect themselves, see Black English as "bad grammar."

Anyone in linguistics, including educators with even a year's training in it, are acutely aware of this inconvenient gap between the assumptions of the general public and what linguists know. The fact is that if it had been rural Southern whites who had declared their "redneck" dialect a separate language, there would have erupted much the same flood of jokes and dismissals in the media. The interpretation of the media hoopla as bigotry required a filter—Victimology, which transforms all criticism, even well-meaning or race-neutral, into racism.

As always, the Victimologist analysis is maintained regardless of concrete evidence to the contrary. A couple of years after the media controversy, an anthology of articles on Black English and the Ebonics approach appeared. In its introduction, the editor frames the controversy as a demonstration of the eternity of racism, at one point ruefully wondering "Where were the essays, op-ed pieces, magazine stories, or panel discussions that systematically laid open the power, beauty, complexities, and pedagogical possibilities embedded in Black Language?" In fact, there were a great many such things: Newspaper editorials by leaders of the Ebonics movement often shared space with critical ones; there quickly appeared a whole issue (Spring 1997) of the accessible and widely circulated journal *The Black Scholar* full of paeans to the dialect; there were short articles praising black people's home language in any number of black magazines; and there were symposia at colleges and universities all over the country (Ebonics was also an extremely popular topic for papers by high school and college students that spring). In general, since the late 1960s there has been a veritable flood of conferences, symposia, and written materials on all levels about the legitimacy of

Black English. The only thing that could have led this editor to miss these things, or to write the comment in the introduction of the same book where the author of one of the articles gives a list of a number of positive media treatments of the Ebonics issue, is a sense of eternal victimization closed to empirical evidence.

## Ebonics: A Natural Outcome

Much of the furious insistence that Black English bars black students from learning to read stems from how Victimology constrains black thinkers' creativity in formulating solutions to problems facing black America, out of a presumption that the only possible logical solutions will respond to white racism.

For example, if one asks why black students overall post the lowest scholarly average in the country, perhaps the first and most natural guess is that the problem is poor schools. But why do black students also lag severely in decent and even excellent schools? Victimology tells us: racism—it must be teacher bias. But Victimology comes up short in the face of further questions: What about black kids in schools where teachers are doing their best to help? What about the fact that black kids do just as badly under black teachers?

Obviously all of this suggests that the problem is located in a historical legacy left to the students' culture itself, and that it is this which we must address. But the sense that victimhood is key to any black problem makes it seem pointless, and even somewhat offensive, to dwell on this at any length. Victimology ensures a common assumption that any informed analysis of the issue simply *must* take as a given that black children have been "denied their rights" to translation training.

One understandable reason for this is that once one strays from this assumption, a suggestion may loom that black people are less intelligent than others. This, however, is not the only way that the problem could be cultural. The other way is that black kids resist school because it is "white." Indeed, this is increasingly discussed, albeit very carefully, in the media and in educational circles. However, Ebonics advocates, to the extent that they acknowledge this at all, perceive it as a background factor at best, because this conception squares only awkwardly with the basic assumption that some form of racism is at fault.

It is therefore quite unsurprising that the next analysis would be that black students have been denied their rights as "bilinguals," because it combines the advantages of explaining why the problem is so extreme among African Americans specifically (since Black English is native to them), and meanwhile entails an indictment of white America. It is not an accident that the Ebonics approach was first developed in the mid-1960s as Victimology and its descendants took hold of black American culture, while the culture argument was not aired until the 1980s, and remains unacknowledged as the pivotal and decisive issue that it is.

The Victimologist filter by no means constrains only black supporters' positions on the Ebonics debate. When I decided to write a book expressing my opinions about the issue, the first publisher I contracted with was a leftist academic press run by (white) scholars, who solicited and accepted it heartily on the basis of a proposal I wrote outlining my two basic opinions: first, that Black English is not bad grammar, and second, that nevertheless, the dialect has been misidentified as a culprit in underperformance in school. In our face-to-face meeting before I wrote the manuscript, the head editor kept anticipating it as "an analysis of the debate." I thought to myself in passing that this was perhaps a rather diagonal designation for the essentially concrete editorial treatment I intended to write, but the proposal made my goals so clear that this slight dissonance was only a passing impression.

When I submitted the manuscript, however, suddenly all the smiles and encouragement had been replaced by precisely the expressions I would have seen on the faces of a ritzy apartment building's tenant committee if they had been about to accept me but had just found out that I was a convicted pedophile—politeness just barely holding disgusted indignation in check. The editor was appalled that I linked much of the support for the Ebonics approach to Separatist ideology. About 98 percent of the manuscript was dedicated to laying out facts about the issue on how languages and dialects work, the history of Black English and related dialects, and experiments with the Ebonics approach over the years; I actually only spent a few pages on the sociopolitical aspect of the issue as I saw it. Yet those pages were enough that the editor was no longer interested in publishing the book.

Typical of how fiercely the black-as-victim perspective is held, the editor did not even pay lip service to the idea that my opinion might be one valid interpretation out of many. Instead, he quite confidently hectored me over the phone about how my opinions about Separatism could not possibly hold water given that they did not square with what his black friends thought, and moreover that my ideas implied that I did not believe that oppressed people were deserving of help. Yet the manuscript included a discussion of inner cities and their poor schools, with my observation that raising educational performance in these areas would begin with addressing these societal problems. I furthermore included a point-by-point discussion of what teachers ought to know and do in relation to the dialect gap even if translation is not necessary, as well as an extended espousal of Afrocentric education outside of the realm of language arts specifically. For this man, however, my breaking ranks at all with the "victim" analysis overshadowed whether or not I concurred with it in some part, just as arguing that *some* women ought be denied the right to vote would have (justifiably) rendered me just as offensive as suggesting the complete revocation of women's suffrage.

What was particularly interesting was that this man was not even American but French. Nevertheless he felt no compunction about telling me that my views about an issue involving a race I belong to, a dialect I grew up around and heard used daily until adulthood, in a country I had lived in for my entire thirty-two-year life without a break, had no value and were even evil, despite the fact that he was white, had no particular experience with Black English, and grew up on the other side of the planet in a country where the race debate is at a much less advanced stage than the American one. What made all of this irrelevant to this man was that though he was neither black, a linguist, nor even American, the credential he could claim was that of a modern liberal humanities academic. Under that tradition it is considered not an opinion but a verity that black people are eternal victims in all aspects of life, and this naturally rendered my criticism of the Ebonics contingent a hideously naive and menacing anathema, which he could confidently reject as *hors de question* even from far outside of any acquaintance with the issue.

What struck me most was that the editor was so surprised by what I had written when I had spelled out my views so explicitly in my proposal. I finally realized what he had actually meant in his anticipation that I would "analyze the debate." He expected that as a black academic, what I was going to do was first argue against the "conservative" take on Black English as "gutter talk"—which I did, even though plenty of liberals labor under the same misimpression—and then second, argue that any factual discrepancies in the position of Oakland's school board and its supporters must be understood in the context of the deathless racist oppression that all black Americans live under. Even a proposal that clearly indicated a different perspective could not distract him from quite casually awaiting this kind of manuscript, because the currently dominant consensus that "black" means "victim" has a way of making it inconceivable—literally, impossible to conceive—that any informed person could harbor any but the very politest of reservations on this score.

Listening to this man smugly hissing at me over the phone that afternoon was quite an experience, and I was angry about it for a while. I was angry not because he did not publish my manuscript; I quickly found another publisher. What bothered me was having had my moral character so witheringly questioned by someone so far outside of the societal issues I had treated. Yet today I think I understand him, and can see that a diatribe like his can come from even people of the kindest dispositions, deepest erudition, and sharpest intelligence and insight. I had barely thought to consider that his talk about "analyzing the debate" conflicted with my intentions, since I took the proposal sitting in front of us as our indelibly concrete point of reference. In the same way, because he took the identity of all blacks as victims as an indelible point of reference, it would never have occurred to him that I would write anything but an affirmation that life is hell for anyone in America with black skin, and that thus all black Americans are exempt from criticism.

## Victims of Victimology: Missing Real Solutions

The saddest thing about how Victimology infects support for the Ebonics approach is that while black schoolteachers, professors, speech pathologists, and community activists dutifully convene in conference after conference discussing the Ebonics approach, a reading program is being used in over a thousand schools across the country as I write called Success for All, which has been shown to work wonders in teaching disadvantaged minority children in poor schools how to read. It is expensive, but the very Title I funds that the Oakland resolution was courting also pay for Success for All. The program uses the phonics approach, widely shown to be a more effective method of teaching poor children to read, as opposed to the whole-word method, which often works better for middle-class children who tend to get more reinforcement in learning to read from home. Success for All also focuses on cooperative learning among small groups, also shown repeatedly to improve disadvantaged minority students' learning abilities. It is often charged that teachers do not challenge inner-city students: Success for All is busy and intensive. We are all aware of the unfortunate concentration of lesser teachers in lesser schools: Success for All is so highly structured that it has been called "teacherproof." And best of all, it works, allowing formerly stagnant schools to raise most of their students to average reading level or above. Critics are put off by the rather mechanical atmosphere, but given the well-known discipline problems typical of inner-city children, it is hard to say that this might not be a necessary approach. But above all, Success for All has been shown to *work*—not just in a study or two out of twelve none longer than a semester in duration, but over entire schoolyears in a great many schools.

Success for All suggests that what will help disadvantaged minority children is not bridging the inch-wide difference between Black and standard English, but compensating for the remove that black American culture puts between child and school with a highly structured, intense program focused upon results. An upper-middle-class white girl may benefit from the free-and-easy arrangement of a Montessori school where children choose their activities, and formal instruction is only one part of the schoolday. For many disadvantaged minority children in our moment, however, a more direct and disciplined approach appears to be effective.

One would think that heavily minority school districts would be clamoring for Success for All, given the urgent crisis in black scholastic performance that motivates Ebonics advocates. Yet year after year, in many districts under the "Ebonics" spell, "exploring" the issue of black language and education is treated as a precious gospel to spread. Given the success rate of Success for All compared to that of the Ebonics approach, why would the latter be deemed more worthy of attention?

Because to support Success for All, created by a white man and entailing no particular recognition of black-white speech or cultural differences, would not embody a statement that a racist oversight—i.e., neglecting to teach black children in their own "tongue" or "acknowledge" it—was being undone. Success for All, in being incompatible with the conception of black children as exotic victims, naturally appears less attractive, which results in depriving many black children of a potential ticket out of the ghetto. This is due neither to cruelty nor stupidity, but to a powerful thought pattern that discourages many black people in positions of power from thinking beyond the Victimologist box.

## Ebonics and Separatism

As we have seen, Victimology conditions a Separatist belief that oppressive victimhood permits different standards of evaluation in black culture than those of the mainstream. Episodes like the Tawana Brawley hoax and the processing of the O.J. Simpson trial demonstrated this in terms of morality. In the Ebonics movement we see this manifested, as with Afrocentric history, in terms of standards of argumentation. The movement is founded upon an unstated assumption that the looming presence of racism renders fact suspendable, or, as Senator Joseph Lieberman so memorably put it in reference to his views on Bill Clinton's sense of morality, fungible.

The problem with this is that while the Ebonics idea responds in part to the tendency for white people to take Black English as a sign of cognitive deficiency—as was actually openly argued by some back in the day—the lack of concern with fact and truth that Separatism conditions in these people's public statements often gives an unintentional impression of questionable reasoning power. This is an urgent paradox, because the group perceived as dim is not equal.

### Ebony and Phonics?

The problem begins with the very term *Ebonics*. It was coined in the early 1970s by a black psychology professor combining *ebony* and *phonics*. The second word usually refers to a method for teaching reading, but it is also rather marginally used to refer to the sounds of a language. This professor was a concerned person with only the best of intentions, but he did not happen to be a linguist, and thus had no way of having gained a sense of how languages and dialects are named. As it happens, languages and dialects are not designated with the suffix *-ics*, nor do language names usually refer to the hue of their speakers' skins. There is a temptation to ask why we are beholden to follow the white man's tradition. Ideally we would not have to. But for better or for worse, we share this society with white people, and as we all know, labels are important. The sad fact is that while "Ebonics" is a great name for a reading program, as the name of a dialect it sounds, frankly, clumsy.

Indeed, it did not catch on at first outside of the educational world. By the late 1990s, it was rarely used by the linguists who had inaugurated a body of academic literature on the dialect, designating it as Black English Vernacular, Black English, or African-American Vernacular English. However, it had been retained by the more ardent advocates of using the dialect in classrooms, and because it was this kind of work that the Oakland school board consulted in drafting its resolution, *Ebonics* was the term that the media picked up.

It was at this point that, in an ideal world, black linguists and educators would have taken their cue and graciously noted when possible that *Ebon-*

*ics* was an outdated term long since replaced by others developed according to scholarly tradition. Instead, however, they revivified it, out of a sense that combatting "racist" perceptions of the dialect was more important than quibbling over its name, and perhaps that, however infelicitous, it was a term coined within our bunker and therefore to be retained.

Yet black Americans are no more deaf to the power of names than any other group; witness how readily the community has adopted the succession of names for the race over the decades—*colored, Negro, black, African American*—or the extremely coded, deflective nature of the term *affirmative action*. It is unfortunate that ideology suppressed that natural sensitivity to labels during the Oakland controversy. I don't know how many nonblack students and professors have asked me perplexedly and with a bit of a smirk why the dialect is called "Ebonics," and every time I think to myself that we could have done better. In a quest to legitimize a stigmatized dialect, how constructive is it to let pass a name which, though well-intentioned, sounds vaguely unlettered?

## "Distracting Noises"

A similar downplaying of the power of words drove Ebonics supporters to subvert their own cause during the Oakland controversy. Much of the furor in the public and the media was due to an assumption that the school board intended to use Black English as the actual medium of instruction, rather than as a bridge to acquiring standard English. Ebonics advocates and their supporters rolled their eyes at this supposed "distortion," but in fact the resolution, at the time widely reprinted and quoted in the media, said quite clearly:

> Whereas, the standardized tests and grade scores of African-American students in reading and langage arts skills measuring their application of English skills are substantially below state and national norms and that such deficiencies will be remedied by application of a program featuring African Language Systems principles in instructing African-American children *both in their primary language and in English* . . . [italics mine]

and later even reiterated:

> Be it further resolved that the Superintendent in conjunction with her staff shall immediately devise and implement the best possible academic program for imparting instruction to African-American students *in their primary language* [italics mine]

Granted, the school board wrote this resolution primarily for the eyes of people familiar with the Ebonics idea, and had no idea that it was going to be broadcast across the globe. Once it had been, however, the words were on the page for all to see, and the easiest solution, which would have done no harm to the school board's cause, would have been to simply say that there were some unintentionally ambiguous passages, and to explain them.

Instead, the school board, led by people of Black Nationalist sentiment, dug in its heels against what it saw as racist abuse and obstinately refused for weeks to reword the resolution. Supporters saw this as an indication of strength, and given how heated the media condemnation was for a few weeks, it most certainly was. However, it also furthered the impression that black Americans are not subtle enough of mind to manipulate or see the value of clear wording. One of the editors of the Ebonics anthology that was released two years later dismissed these sentences as "what some might consider distracting noises," one implication being that "some" are the alien contingent who would be so unsporting as to take a written document by black people at its word.

## Selling Out with Facts

The sense that presenting a united front outweighs acknowledging fact often leads those under Separatist sway to sincerely assume that a black person who airs facts incommensurate with the party line could only be doing so as either a mistake or as active treachery. During the Oakland controversy, for example, I received two letters from black people I had never met suspecting that I was taking my position in order to make money. Crucially, neither of these people took issue with the facts I had presented.

I will never forget an Oakland school official telling me, quite politely, that I should remember that given that I was a professor, the things I was saying to the media did not make the Oakland school board look good. This man literally could not imagine that a black person with authority and an audience could in sound mind "break ranks" and criticize a black-led body, regardless of whether what I was saying was true! He happened to be African, and ironically, he told me this after we had spoken as "pro" and "con" to a group and he had admitted to a questioner that Black English does not sound at all "African" to him, whereas Caribbean creole languages (which truly are "African") do.

Not long ago I attended a Black English conference (with some trepidation), and before long was predictably attacked by one gentleman for the "shocking statements" I had written in an article summarizing my opinion—but not once did he offer a rebuttal of a single point. His pique was due simply to my having said anything but "We must address the needs of African-American children." At the same conference there were a few black professors who would only speak to me on the most utilitarian and polite terms, one of them barely able to bring himself to even look toward me when I tried to strike up a conversation in the elevator. I soon heard that a group of black professors had commented behind my back, as had been said during the controversy, too, that I am simply ashamed of the way black people talk. However, none of these people ever address a single point I have actually made, one of which has always been that I am an avid supporter of Black English.

The critical disinclination to allow facts their weight is thought to be an unselfishly motivated, pragmatic response. But the problem is that racism, while present, no longer determines black American lives strongly enough to justify this response, which, unchecked, does more harm than good.

## Making Our Garden Grow

Separatism also constrains Ebonics supporters from taking a more global perspective on dialects, in favor of concentrating on the "black" topics of Black English and the African connection. Although at first glance giving the appearance of making our garden grow by tending to our heritage, it instead does unintended harm.

What Ebonics advocates rarely consider is that to argue that black children are barred from reading by their home dialect while children around the world sail effortlessly over similar or larger dialect gaps implies that black children are not very bright. Just how much of a burden is it, really, to internalize that on paper you say *She is my boss* instead of *She my boss,* or that the word you usually pronounce as *bes* is *best* on paper? This question is especially pressing compared to rural white Southern children, whose home dialect is so similar to Black English that the two can be difficult to tell apart on the page or on the phone (both Ray Charles and Jim Nabors might say "Ain't nobody tellin me nothin!").

As I mentioned earlier, there are Ebonics supporters who note that there is a unique stigma against Black English that makes the translation approach valuable as a way of validating the students in their culture. That is at least an argument, whether one agrees with it or not. The problem is that this is almost never aired publicly, which leaves white observers walking away mumbling to each other that they say *He don't know* too in their off-hours but that they didn't need any help figuring out that you just don't write that kind of sentence down. The claim that the Ebonics advocates present to the public, simply that black students are done in by small differences between their home speech and standard English, once again hinders integration or, if one prefers, even graceful cohabitation, because it makes us look like mental lightweights. That all Lucy ever had to do to keep Ricky from recognizing her was to put on a wig, fake a dialect, and black out a tooth looks laughable to us. What, then, are we to make of the image of the little black boy sitting at his desk unable to recognize his language because of the occasional little verb "to be" and some extra final consonants?

## Blood Ties

Nowhere are the Separatist, and specifically, Anti-intellectual underpinnings of the Ebonics movement more visible than in the courtesy and exposure accorded to one of its gurus, Dr. Ernie Smith. Smith is notoriously insistent that Black English is not a form of English and must be called Ebonics, and he finds the very terms *Black English* and *African-American Vernacular English* viscerally offensive to the point of regularly spewing invective upon anyone who insists on using them. Even tenured elder statesmen in linguistics and education have stories of being gouged by Smith in this way at symposia and on radio shows. He is also a Black Muslim, and unfortunately inherits from this tradition a passionate antipathy toward white people, one of his writings on the history of Black English calling them "evil incarnate," "genetically recessive," "pathologically deceitful liars," etc.

Smith studied linguistics briefly in the early 1970s, but his doctorate was in something called Comparative Culture, and he teaches at a small medical college. He has not been a practicing scholar of Black English and has not followed the research on it, perhaps in part because of his disagreement with linguists' very treatment of the dialect as a kind of English. Nevertheless, he has developed a "theory" of the history of Black English, according to which African slaves superimposed English words into African sound and sentence patterns, thus creating not a form of English but a new African language. Uninformed by historical research and often laced with racist statements, this work unsurprisingly finds no outlet among academic publishers, and thus Smith has published his main works himself.

Smith has a charismatic podium style, his presentations alternating between seductive black preacherly cadences and furious indignation in a fashion reminiscent of the Reverend Al Sharpton. As a result, he has come to play a central role in dispersing the idea that black students fail in school because their home dialect is not English. He regularly speaks to groups of African-American schoolteachers and has inspired passionate disciples. Smith was consulted by the Oakland school board as they drafted their resolution. Indeed, "Doctor Ernie" has an almost God-like status among many black schoolteachers and administrators, and even linguists and education specialists friendly to the "Ebonics" notion find that in order to be listened to they must address Black English as the "African language Ebonics" when consulting with groups in thrall to Smith.

The problem is that Smith's claims about Black English are not just "controversial," but hopelessly uninformed. He claims that black children are done in by lacks of fit between speech and text like *Did you eat yet?* versus the supposed "Ebonics" version "Jeet yet?" However, not only black kids, but Jeff Foxworthy, Dennis the Menace, and Bart Simpson say "Jeet yet?"—which is not Black English but simply colloquial standard American English. Smith angrily dismisses the widely accepted assumption that the regional British English varieties that white early Americans spoke were important ancestors to Black English, when in fact Black English features like *ain't*, the use of *done* in *I done seen*, the "unconjugated" *be*, and dozens of others trace to these humble white dialects. Smith designates Black English an African language and in one paper gives an imposing list of citations in support, but the list is composed of studies of creoles (like Sranan), crackpot Afrocentric tracts, obscure master's theses by people in fields other than linguistic research, and one article from *Jet* magazine!

Things like this are, unfortunately, only the tip of the iceberg, but since Smith is not a scholar, it would serve no purpose but small-mindedness to belabor the flaws in his work any further. The fact remains that the "research" that "Doctor Ernie" tutors black teachers in is built on sand.

In itself, this power that Smith has over schoolteachers and school administrators is unfortunate but understandable. What comes across is a commitment to helping the race, underscored by Smith's charismatic presence, and it takes a trained linguist to fully comprehend the hollowness of his supposed research. The seductiveness of Smith's Victimology and Separatism is unfortunate, but no more surprising, in light of what we have seen in this book, than the basic respect in the black community for Louis Farrakhan.

What gives pause, however, is that even among black trained linguists and language-oriented education specialists, Smith is not treated as the charlatan that he is. To be sure, in private one will hear from black academics close to the Ebonics controversy that Smith "likes to call names," or that he "doesn't keep up." Yet during the Oakland controversy, when Ebonics advocates with Ph.D.s drafted a resolution at the annual meeting of the Linguistics Society of America in support of the Oakland school board's resolution, they dutifully included Smith's principal manifesto as one of the academic studies in support of teaching black students using Black English as an intermediary. Most if not all of the people in the room were well aware that this piece of work is not valid scholarship. But once again, within the context of a race-based issue, the correspondence of his work with the truth was given less weight than acknowledging "one of our own" (and this was not a matter of social politeness; Smith was not present). The priority of communal solidarity over empirical validity worked against this body's goal of convincing wider circles of the worth of the Ebonics approach, however. How compelling will this philosophy look to anyone interested in the Ebonics movement who is able to sniff out street-corner pseudoscholarship when he sees it, who takes this list at its word and goes to Smith's work as representative of the ideology?

Moreover, when the Ebonics anthology I have mentioned appeared two years later, it included an edgy article by Smith full of arrant falsehoods that do not stand up to even the most cursory scholarly scrutiny, many of which even someone without linguistics training could see through immediately ("Jeet yet?"). The article also comes just before an interview with John Rickford, one of the few Ebonics advocates who informs his statements and work on the subject with linguistic expertise and addresses questions the philosophy naturally brings up to the outside observer. The anthology is titled *The Real Ebonics Debate,* but the notion of a "real" that could accommodate both Smith and a solid, eminent scholar like Rickford at the same time is one that could only follow from Victimologist and Separatist epistemology. Smith's indignation over black suffering is considered, in the end, more important—"realer"—than the veracity of his claims.

Black journalist Carl Rowan once said of Marion Barry: "The mayor may be a cocaine junkie, a crack addict, a sexual scoundrel, but he is our junkie, our addict, our scoundrel." It was sad to see a person of influence urging his own community to settle for less. The spontaneous impulse that keeps even the tenured professionals among Ebonics supporters from seeing anything amiss in Ernie Smith representing their case to academia and the public springs from the same well as Rowan's exhortation. We can do better than this.

## Hypothesis Becomes Verity

But Ebonics supporters continue walking against the wind. At one of the conferences on Black English that the anthology's editor rues the dearth of, a presentation was given by William Labov, grandfather of the academic study of Black English. Labov has been passionately devoted to counteracting the view of Black English as bad grammar, and is also committed to social justice. His position on the Ebonics approach is a careful one. In the early 1970s, he evaluated the possibility that the black-white scholastic lag was due to the dialect gap and discreetly concluded that culture rather than dialect was the culprit. This point, however, was essentially a footnote amidst his very foundation at this time of the linguistic investigation of Black English in all of its aspects. He has since maintained active ties with the Ebonics movement leaders, and lent crucial support to a court case in Ann Arbor, Michigan, in 1980 urging the school district to adopt Black English readers for African-American children.

Along those centrist lines, at the conference in question Labov gave a talk discussing his recent work reinvestigating the causes of black children's low reading scores. The project was couched within a genuine concern about the problem, and was not explicitly framed as a refutation of the translation approach. Yet what he showed was that when examined in detail, the mistakes that the black students in his study made in reading were *not* usually caused by the aspects of sound and grammar that distinguish Black from standard English. In other words, their mistakes were based less on being confused by words like *desk* as opposed to Black English's *des,* but upon more comprehensive problems with sounding out whole words and with processing aspects of grammar that are the same in Black and standard English. In other words, the children were having problems with reading overall, rather than being thrown by the aspects of the words and sentences that did not correspond precisely with their dialect.

I did not hear one person at the conference express an awareness of the implications of what Labov was showing. There were a few questions about school funding and teacher training, applause, and then it was time for a coffee break. I found myself imagining a biology conference where someone showed that some creature was passing on acquired characteristics to its offspring, like its fur having been lightened by the sun or its leg having been broken in a fall, rather than passing on just its genetic endowment according to the tenets of natural selection. If someone presented a study offering counterevidence to a fundamental conviction shared by most if not all of the biologists present, we do not imagine that after a few tangential comments about wildlife preserves and grant application procedures everyone would just smile, clap, and go out into the lobby for snacks.

The fact that this very sort of thing did happen at a Black English conference is a sterling demonstration of how Separatism can block serious engagement with important facts, out of a sense that the depredations of racism are the dominant issue and require our most active attention. Labov's couching of his talk as "on our side," in being concerned with black scholarly failure, immediately dulled the audience's mind to evaluating the actual content of what he was saying.

Yet Labov was suggesting nothing less than a possible path of salvation for the race, in showing that focusing on the dialect gap may be a garden path and that it is other methods that may produce the result we seek. Separatism, however, places the race at risk of missing opportunities for salvation, by blunting focus upon any but the paths that fit with Victimologist ideology. Many would say these paths are the right ones—but the counterevidence to the Ebonics case is only one strong indication that the America of the second millennium is too complex for that to be true any longer.

During the Oakland controversy I appeared on an episode of the now-departed afternoon talk show *Rolonda* devoted to the Ebonics issue. I was, of course, the "con," and the "pro" this time was Geneva Smitherman. Smitherman, author of three books for the general public on Black English, is a doyenne of the Ebonics movement, having trained a number of its supporters and attained renown in linguistics, education, and beyond in spearheading academic support for the Ann Arbor case in 1980. Stridently "black identified," she is also notorious for her indignant dismissal of anyone questioning the African roots of the dialect or its treatment as a barrier to acquiring standard English in classrooms. She shares with Ernie Smith a certain charismatic and even intimidating presence, magnified by loyal colleagues and students, which helped to cow white linguists into silence regarding any skepticism during the Oakland controversy.

I had no illusions that Smitherman would receive me with open arms.

However, it turned out that I didn't know the half of it. Before the taping of the show, she did not return my greeting. During breaks in the taping, since we were seated next to each other I tried to make small talk, which she replied to just briefly enough to fulfill minimal demands of civility. After the taping, she did not return my good-night.

Most shocking, however, was what happened later. The episode was by no means a slugfest, but predictably, the general tone was against Oakland's resolution, with most of the audience viewing Black English either as just slang, or as a scourge that had no business in the classroom. The day the episode was slated to appear a few weeks later, another episode was aired in its place. It turned out that because Smitherman did not like the way the discussion had gone, she had refused to sign the consent form permitting the episode to be aired.

I could not help wondering what Smitherman had expected on a rowdy afternoon talk show: surely she, having presented the Ebonics case to the general public for decades, was well aware of the common misconception that all English other than that of Walter Cronkite is "bad grammar." More to the point, however, was that she had pulled the plug on a show I had flown all the way across the country to appear on without so much as letting me know; if she did not want to talk to me, then basic civility among colleagues would dictate at least a brief electronic mail. That she did not even inform me was, in the final analysis, an eloquent upturned finger.

Most important, though, we had not appeared on the show alone, but with eight other people, including schoolteachers, some nonblack teenagers who spoke some "Ebonics," a Black English–fluent black teenager, and, for some reason, Wynton and Branford Marsalis's father, Ellis. All of us sat on the stage together throughout the show—and thus Smitherman's refusal to allow herself to be shown made it impossible to air the episode at all. By this point, appearing on television was no longer a novelty for me. But for most of these people, some of whom had traveled long distances to get there, appearing on a national television show was one of the most glamorous and important things that had ever happened to them; yet Smitherman felt no compunction about depriving them of their moment in the spotlight—even when some of them were in favor of Oakland's resolution.

The affection Smitherman has inspired in so many people makes it unlikely that behavior this boorish is typical of her. What would make a person behave this way? One story is that Smitherman disapproved of the fact that I was paid for my appearance while she was not (I had to travel farther and was more in demand for appearances at the time). However, I, in all sincerity, simply cannot believe that she, or anyone, would scuttle eight other people because of something so petty, especially since we were all put up at a good Manhattan hotel with all food and transportation paid for. The other story is one she has told more widely, and is much more likely and, in itself, humane: Smitherman thought the episode was a sideshow that did not do justice to the issue.

But let's face it, any episode of any show like this is a cartoon. One does not present a comprehensive exposition of any issue on *Jenny Jones;* we can be sure untold thousands of people have left the sets of shows like these feeling unsatisfied. The *Rolonda* producer (a black woman, for the record) told me that not once had any other guest on the show refused to sign the release form, nor could she remember anything like it happening on the talk show she had worked on previously.

Smitherman's sense that this episode had not sufficiently shielded black America from the depredations of racism is not one I agree with, but it is hardly indefensible in itself. But how casually she channeled her convictions into depriving eight innocent people of their day in the sun on what was, after all, just one episode of a low-rated talk show, was one more demonstration that Victimology and Separatism wield their influence far beyond Al Sharpton and the ghetto. Her behavior was an expression of the potent grip of the ideology I have described in this book, which in this case framed even this ephemeral little television episode as a racist abomination. Such a belief also renders the black person in disagreement as a repugnant, disloyal, self-hating freak.

Shortly after the Oakland controversy, the journal *The Black Scholar* asked me to contribute to a special issue of articles on the topic, most of which supported the Oakland school board. The issue emblazoned the names of all of the authors in capital letters on the cover—except guess who's name was missing? Of course, I was told that the omission of my name was an "accident." Needless to say, Geneva Smitherman's name did make the cover.

For whatever it was worth, however, the *Rolonda* episode was eventually aired, edited with a special technique that neatly sliced Smitherman out of the frame. As it happens, the editors at *Rolonda* may have been prescient in a symbolic way. In the final chapter, I would like to discuss how we might redirect the black American race from the tragic ideological detour that sociohistorical happenstance has driven us into.

# 7

## How Can We Save the African-American Race?

Black America is currently mired in a detour, intended by neither blacks nor whites, from the path to the mountaintop that Martin Luther King envisioned. Having been taught to cherish victimhood over action and essentialism over universalism, a great many people of the second black generation after the Civil Rights Movement are being hindered in continuing the struggle our ancestors initiated on our behalf.

Indeed, it is Victimology, Separatism, and Anti-intellectualism that make it a stretch for whites to think of that suburban black corporate manager as a representative "American" even three decades after the Civil Rights Act of 1964, even though there are millions of black managers, and even though in general most black people are not poor. Surely, remnants of racism contribute to this state of affairs. However, today, the ideology that so many black Americans have been steeped in contributes much more to this sense of "black" as "different" and, most importantly, "less." Victimology, the tendency to exaggerate the degree of black oppression regardless of progress, has understandable roots in the Civil Rights Movement freeing a group with a battered self-image. But white people are no more prone than black people (or any others) to dutifully frame all present-tense experience through a fine historical lens. As such, to the younger white person who never knew segregated America, watching middle-class black people depicting themselves as partners with Kosovar Albanians in victimhood because they are occasionally bypassed by a taxi in Manhattan or trailed by a salesclerk looks like paranoia. Separatism starts as a healthy reclamation of identity and is then distorted by Victimology into what is felt to be a necessary battle posture, but to modern white eyes, Separatism is parochial. Anti-intellectualism has been such an inevitable development of Separatism in black America that its failure to shackle the race would be nothing less than surprising, but just as inevitably, to any outsider it can only look like mental inferiority.

Paranoid, parochial, and dumb: This is how much of white America perceives us on some level. It is not our fault, and it is absolutely unacceptable. In fact, it was indignation at this perception that led me to write this book. However, the reason they believe this is no longer, in any meaningful sense, good old-fashioned racism—the terrain has changed profoundly since the 1960s. I sincerely and regretfully believe that at this complex juncture in American history, black America has unintentionally become as much the cause of this as the racism that led whites to drag us to these shores and treat us as animals for 350 years. Sure, "They started it." Not only did they bring us here as slaves, but they also kept it going—most ironically—by finally seeing the light and letting us free!

As direct consequences of the abrupt unshackling of a crippled race, Victimology, Separatism, and Anti-intellectualism are a person with his eyes sealed shut still pawing frantically at the air long after his attacker has laid off, driven to frenzy by massive assault. But thank God the attacker did let up. And the unjust fact is that once he has, he walks on unharmed, while it is up to us to stand up, rub our eyes, brush ourselves off, and walk on to do the best work and lead the best lives we can. We do ourselves no favor by collapsing again to the ground, shutting our eyes, and pawing at the air some more for the absolution of letting everyone know what the attacker did, and certainly not by deciding that we are to live our lives in that position as a remembrance of history. Sure, every now and then the attacker is going to traipse back and pop us on the back of the head. But we can take it, can't we? Take one look at the classic picture of a slave ship in cross-section and that question is answered.

In the meantime, to continue swiping madly at the air and indignantly insisting that this is one's right in view of an attack that recedes increasingly into the past makes one look not fearsome, but pathetic, a lesser person. In that light, certainly the last thing the African-American race ought do after having come so far is to nurture the very racism that kept us in chains for 350 years. Yet this is what I fear has become the case.

Common wisdom frames black children of all classes as living under the risk of the depredations of racism, enjoying a brief window of childhood innocence before becoming aware of their status as second-class citizens. I find myself seeing black children as living under a concurrent risk, that of being stunted in their ability to make the best of themselves as they are shepherded into a conviction that regardless of outward appearances, they inhabit a fundamentally hostile, alien nation.

There are two black boys who play in the yard behind my apartment. To describe anyone living in this building as "struggling blue collar" would be a stretch by any standard. But I wonder how long it will be before they learn the gospel—that most black people are poor, that white people are generally not to be trusted out of earshot, that school is an inherently "white" endeavor that they ought dwell in only for utilitarian reasons. The torch is being passed on independently of external conditions. We cannot let this happen.

## We're Past "Talking"

I find it sadly unlikely that dialogue, along the lines of Bill Clinton's "National Dialogue on Race," will be of any significant use. The hold of the three currents in thought is so strong that it conditions an assumption among most blacks in power that such a dialogue can only be an occasion for reminding whites that they are racists, and among most whites that their only acceptable participation is to agree.

Indeed, one is forced to conclude that a great many of today's black leaders are unamenable to any meaningful dialogue on race. A disproportionately influential contingent will maintain to their dying day that most black Americans are poor, that there is a racist at the heart of all whites, and that because of these things, regardless of class or opportunity, no black American is to be held to mainstream standards of morality or academic achievement. There are now roughly two generations of African Americans caught in these thought patterns—those who came of age as the Civil Rights Movement dawned, and now a whole subsequent generation who have spent their lifetimes in a climate which encourages victimhood as an identity rather than as a problem.

This frame of mind is so deeply rooted in these people's very souls that to let it go would entail a massive sociopsychological dislocation few human beings are capable of or willing to endure. There are many African-American leaders and thinkers who are fighting the good fight, watching our backs and chronicling remnants of racism while acknowledging progress and refusing to settle for allowing the race to be represented by fruitless melodramatics. Examples include economist Glenn Loury, *New York Times* columnist Bob Herbert, *Atlanta Constitution* columnist Cynthia Tucker, law professor Randall Kennedy, and essayist Stanley Crouch. These people are often dismissed as sell-outs by many who mistake as Doing the Right Thing figures such as Derrick Bell, June Jordan, Manning Marable, Ralph Wiley, Lani Guinier, Maxine Waters, Al Sharpton, and Carl Rowan. Yet while the emergence of this kind of person served a purpose in getting blacks in the door and to the table, ironically, this type is now the main agent in keeping blacks from ever getting up from the table and moving on. Maybe it had to be this way. However, what this means is that we cannot look to them to get us out of these holding patterns. The key is what kind of America we set up for the generation of black people to come, and it would be truly unfortunate if that were an America where people of this frame of mind continued to dominate the political and intellectual leadership of the race.

I have two suggestions that I think will get us back on the only track worthy of this, or any other race, which is progress. Both entail that America enter upon what can be regarded as the second phase of the Civil Rights Movement. The first phase was to level the proverbial playing field. This job is nearly accomplished. The second phase is for us to get out there and play, and in order for that to be worthwhile, or even possible, then *we must be treated as equals, and we must allow ourselves to be treated as equals.*

It seems to be assumed that this was a *fait accompli* once the playing field was leveled. But black American history was run through with too epic an injustice for this alone to accomplish our goal. There remains work no less intimidating, but no less imperative, than that which we have already done.

## The Road to True Equality: Combat Victimology Chic

When the process of bringing blacks to equality with whites began in the 1960s, the conception of blacks as a race of victims was logical and appropriate, for the simple reason that it corresponded with reality. Most black people were poor. Those who were not still faced concrete barriers of discrimination in employment, education, and use of public services in all parts of the country. Open bigotry was common and accepted among whites ("Aw, look at the little pickaninny!" a white woman said out loud to her friend about me in 1967—in Philadelphia, not Savannah). Integration was a new idea considered progressive and somewhat quixotic, with most people casually viewing blacks as an eternal servant class.

Today, about a quarter of black Americans are poor. Discrimination is increasingly rare and subtle, shading ever more from racism into classism, which while indefensible itself, is rampant in all human societies and wounds people of all colors. In the general American consciousness, bigotry certainly has not disappeared completely, but is considered a social stain, its expression regularly costing people and organizations millions of dollars a year in lawsuits. No, things are not perfect—but let's face it: There are millions and millions of people on earth who would kill for the lives of all but a few black Americans today, and there have been untold billions of people who have triumphed amidst conditions unspeakably worse. We sell ourselves short to pretend otherwise.

In short, black Americans are no longer a race of victims *as a whole* in the meaningful sense—i.e., to an extent which extinguishes the potential of a human being. Instead, this is a race a fraction of whom are victims, and victims more as the result of historical than present-day racism—the people who remained behind for various reasons while most of the race moved upward. Surely that fraction is not as small as it must be in order for blacks to be equal with whites. However, a fraction it is, and a small enough fraction that it is no longer logical to conceive of these lives as representative of "the condition of the African-American race." Not only does such a conception not correspond to reality, but it is a grievous insult to the millions and millions of black people who have achieved comfortable and meaningful lives over the past four decades.

There are three new habits of thinking that I suggest will help us get beyond this self-imposed ideological obstacle to success.

## Mantra Number One: Our Successes Are No Longer "Anecdotes": They Are the Norm

If there is one misconception that most perniciously distorts our interracial dialogue, it is that most black people are poor, or, as was found among almost half of the blacks surveyed by the Gallup poll mentioned in Chapter 1, that three out of four black people live in the inner city. Black Americans are rightly indignant when whites evidence this misconception, but then are equally given to equating black with "just getting by" when issues like affirmative action and welfare come up. In *The New York Times,* black activist and scholar Manning Marable's parsing of the state of black America in the late 1990s was that "a segment of the minority population moves into the corporate and political establishment at the same time that *most* are pushed even further down the economic ladder" (emphasis mine). It is time to stop applauding this kind of defeatist rhetoric; it's poison.

As I write, the two statistics commonly used to define the black condition are that blacks make 61 percent of what whites make and that one in three black men in their twenties are involved with the criminal justice system. We should look to the second statistic to remind us of the work that remains to be done, but the first one is a myth and needs replacing. I suggest that we replace it with a positive statistic to keep our progress as front and center in our minds as our problems: only one in five black people live in the inner city, and only one in four black families live below the poverty line. That's not perfect, but progress is being made. Fast.

Because it is unhealthy to turn a blind eye to one's progress, we must resist enshrining stories of misery and discrimination as "the way it is" while dismissing stories of success or normality as unrepresentative "anecdotes." Too often, the black person with a beautiful house, nice cars, and children in private school is processed as "an exception" and almost an inconvenience, the idea seeming to be that to pay too much attention to this "B. Smith" kind of person will detract from the grinding horror of life for 99 percent of the race. This, like the "united front" ideology, was once appropriate (when nine out of ten blacks really were poor), but is now obsolete. Quite simply, there are now far too many millions and millions of black people living comfortable lives to be processed as "lucky." Today such people are nothing less than *normal;* this is exactly the progress that the civil-rights revolution was for, and— most importantly—as I have argued, to acknowledge and even revel in this success does not require leaving poor blacks behind.

Along these lines, for example, my personal recollections are certainly anecdotal; as personal experiences, they could be nothing else. However, today, the recollections of people like Nathan McCall are "anecdotal" as well—Derrick Bell even couches his observations as "stories," forgoing any pretense of actual reportage. If we are willing to accept these people's anecdotes as useful and valid, then we must also accept mine: It simply does not follow in the year 2000 that a black person's Victimologist anecdote is automatically truth while one taking issue with that perspective is simply a fluke.

The truth is that today, all of our anecdotes are valid and representative of the lives of millions of black Americans. I am not "lucky" or "odd" or "different" to have never been barred from a store as a black man in the year 2000—I am ordinary! What all of the anecdotes good and bad spell is the reality—racism is not dead (Nathan McCall, Beverly Daniel Tatum, Patricia Williams), but the situation is strikingly better than it was a few decades ago and is getting better all the time (Orlando Patterson, Glenn Loury, Randall Kennedy). The former view sells more books, fits in with the Victimologist hustle clouding so many eyes, and is a more natural topic for public airing than anecdotes about improvement. But it is only part of the story—and by no means the dominant part.

## Mantra Number Two: Occasional
## Inconvenience Is Not Oppression

The last thing I want to convey is that life is perfect for black people in America. I hope to have shown through my own recollections as well as other observances that I am well aware that this is not the case. However, I do believe that a time comes when drawing some lines, facing the ever challenging but vital issue of degree, becomes not just cordial, not just intelligent, but imperative. This is because to conceive of ourselves today as eternal victims *impedes our progress toward equality*—because there comes a point when refraining from drawing a line between oppression and "occasional inconvenience," as a black cousin of mine perfectly phrases it, is infantilization. The person who one considers incapable of coping with any hardship whatsoever, who one considers capable of achievement only under ideal conditions, is someone one pities, cares for, and perhaps even likes, but is not someone one respects, and thus is someone one does not truly consider an equal.

### An Inappropriate Analogy

In 1987, Guatemalan Mayan activist Rigoberta Menchú wrote an autobiography, *I, Rigoberta Menchú,* in which she described an early life of virtual slavery under the rule of European-descended colonials, including seeing family members murdered. The book won a Pulitzer Prize, and became a signature documentation of the horrors of imperialism, widely read in leftist circles and a popular assignment in college courses.

Twelve years later, David Stoll announced in his book *Rigoberta Menchú and the Story of All Poor Guatemalans* that Menchú had taken a rather creative approach to truth. Menchú's childhood was in fact a relatively privileged one, sparing her the grinding misery that most of her people knew. She did lose members of her family, but fictionalized or sensationalized some deaths for shock value. Her father's conflict was with his in-laws, not white overlords. Menchú describes the police burning the Spanish embassy when guerillas hid out inside it, but in fact the guerillas themselves, who had come to be seen as a scourge by most of the peasantry, started the fire.

Menchú is clearly something of an opportunist, but let's face it, most leaders are, and we cannot help thinking that her personal weaknesses are less important than the larger picture. After all, the Guatemalan peasantry have indeed been tragically oppressed by their overlords; Menchú did suffer to some extent; if the guerillas overstepped their bounds at times this was inevitable given what the Mayans had suffered;

and a book that carefully presented the situation in all of its ambiguities would have been read by a few hundred intellectuals and Central America hounds but would not have mobilized public support for the Mayans. In the name of creating awareness of the injustices of imperialism in Guatemala and Third World nations in general, perhaps Menchú's tactics were not ideal, but we can suppose that her distortions and self-dramatization did serve a higher cause.

I sense that this is the lens through which many Americans black and white today think that the apocalyptic visions of people like Derrick Bell and Lani Guinier ought be viewed. The idea seems to be that being black in America is still such a crushing burden that it is fitting, "understandable," for black leaders and intellectuals to downplay the stupendous progress the race has made, square the corners, round the edges, in service to the greater good of fighting the implacable racism that still thwarts a black person at every turn.

This kind of unstated analogy between a situation like the Menchú controversy and black America may have made sense in about 1970. But today it is hopelessly frayed and inappropriate. This is clear from the inherent impossibility that stupendous progress could have been made if being black were still a crushing burden and racism were still implacable. To the white person who dares point out this incompatibility, our current discourse encourages the black person to say "You just don't know," and the white person is assigned to nod dutifully and then shake his head in pity. But increasingly, if required to explain precisely what the white person "doesn't know," the black person has nothing to offer that belies the central point that life for blacks in America today would look like an alternate universe to black people just fifty years ago, is getting better rapidly, and shows no signs whatsoever of getting worse.

Acknowledging intermediate points, transitions, and historical layers is nothing more and nothing less than one way of making sense, and while this is considered a *sine qua non* of intelligence in any white person, there is a tragic pretense that black people can somehow be exempt from making sense and yet still be considered equals. This isn't good enough because we all know it is a lie, and there are few grimmer fates for a race to await than to be eternally considered (1) mental lightweights or (2) hothouse flowers that fade and die in the face of anything but ideal life conditions.

"How do I know what these people are going through?" one might ask. It would be helpful if we realized that one thing black America is going through is an ideological plague forced upon us as a by-product of the conditions of the Civil Rights Movement, which granted freedom so abruptly that it left behind a tragic combination of unprecedented opportunity and a historical inferiority complex. This was not black people's fault, and the Civil Rights Movement was certainly far better than nothing. But in indulging the resultant chronic self-righteous doubletalk, ironically we are now blocking the integration the Civil Rights Movement sought.

## Concern for the Victim Versus Becoming a Victim

Menchú's defenders propose that her distortions stem from an Amerindian tradition in which the group's experiences are, in a holistic sense, each individual's. A similar sentiment, albeit unspoken, underlies the affluent young black who has never known hardship or discrimination considering herself "oppressed" and rejecting whitey out of a sense that the one out of five black people in the ghettos are in a holistic sense "her," such that she shares their fates on an abstract level. Now, the last thing we want is for blacks who have made it to reject those who have not as "other." The sense that the ghetto is "cool" is entrenched to an unhealthy degree in black culture, but in contrast to the casually dismissive classism one sees in many subcultures on the rise in both the past and present worldwide, one cannot help but see middle-class black America's refusal to dissociate itself from those less fortunate as, in itself, sophisticated and humane.

However, the fact is that one can maintain concern for the victimized members of one's culture without conceiving of oneself as a victim as well. This is the difference between addressing victimhood as a problem and adopting it as an identity regardless of one's actual circumstances— Victimology. When a black person you know has grown up in a war zone of a neighborhood, lost siblings to gunfights, often gone hungry, suffered through drug addiction, and gone to a school so bad that it left him with reading and writing skills too low to get a decent job, he is a victim—but just because you are the same color as he, it does not make you a victim when you are occasionally trailed in stores. While maintaining compassion for the true victim, for you to frame yourself as equally a victim is neither morally required nor even healthy, because in distorting your experiences as "victimhood" you hinder your own capacities of strength and initiative. This is especially true given that today only a fraction of our population are victims in any meaningful sense.

In contrast, Rigoberta Menchú speaks for a people the vast mass of whom are still living semiliterate under an oppression more concrete and resolute than anything many of the black people of influence crying "victim" could withstand for longer than about two days. Menchú really is one of the lucky ones who slipped over the wall. But the time has come for us to reconceive the black college professor who sits in the trendy new restaurant emoting about how oppressed he is between forkfuls of gourmet pasta, his free hand alternating languidly between his six-dollar glass of cabernet and his white significant other's knee under the table, and about to catch a twenty-dollar shuttle bus to the airport the next morning to fly to a conference where he will meet dozens of African Americans just like him, most of whom got special attention on their job searches because of their color, and most of whose research has been funded by universities that bend over backwards to shower grants upon as much minority-oriented research as possible. Okay, four years ago this professor was driving through a white neighborhood in his Honda Accord and a policeman pulled him over on a drug check. But why, if "Success Runs in Our Veins," if we survived centuries of slavery, if we are so wonderful, does that episode negate the victory and richness of the rest of this professor's life? What kind of "oppression" is this? One in four black Americans is poor today; you can bet that a heck of a lot more than one Mayan in four is poor in Guatemala, and I shudder to imagine our black college professor offering his manicured hand to Rigoberta Menchú as a partner in "oppression."

### An Example

Okay, that one was staged. But here is a real-life example. In her widely read book *The Alchemy of Race and Rights,* law professor Patricia Williams recounts a Benetton clerk claiming that the store was closed in midafternoon when she tried to enter, interpreting this as evidence that racism continues to pervade American society decades after 1964, her indignation tacitly colored by the irony of Benetton's vibrantly multiracial advertisements. Let us assume that this clerk really did bar Williams from the store because of the color of her skin. Our question, in our times, is whether this is a typical experience for black people today. In 1960, episodes like this were so common that they barely occasioned comment. However, I can state that never in my life have I been barred entry to a store at two o'clock in the afternoon or indeed at any time of day, and we can be sure that a great many black people could say the same thing. One recent exception was Denny's outlets, discovered to be refusing entry to black groups at night too often across the country to be an accident (although I myself have eaten many a nighttime meal at

Denny's outlets, on both coasts, and as often as not with black people). Yet significantly, because we live in an era where such actions are legally prosecutable, this practice was aired, condemned, and eliminated. This was progress, not reversal or stasis.

Thus Williams's experience certainly shows us that racism is not completely dead yet—but then why would we expect that it would be in an era of *transition,* anymore than we would expect that two hours after we put an ice-cube tray in the freezer, that a couple of the cubes would not still be a little liquid? What Williams's experience in no way indicates is that racism is not receding, or that it will never go away. As such we must question Williams's interpretation of this sad event as evidence that her life's journey is paved with the thorns of a racism appallingly eternal. She, like so many of us, one day in one place stubbed her toe on a remnant of a situation once rife. However, this does not logically require a strong human being to ask "I am a law professor at a prestigious university, but where is the value in that if I was barred entry to a Benetton's?" More properly, an approach to victimhood as a problem rather than as an identity would condition the interpretation "I was barred entry to a Benetton's and this is a disgraceful echo of the past, but in the grand view, I am ultimately a law professor at a prestigious university whereas this would have been impossible just a few decades ago."

Williams's preference for the former approach suggests a sense that to dwell too much upon her success would be to dismiss the suffering of the fraction of the race still mired in true misery, the "authentic" black person being morally required to incorporate the entire race in her self-conception. This ideology, however, has outlived its usefulness. Surely Williams ought neither to lose her concern for the underclass nor discontinue her efforts to help them. Yet it is not only morally acceptable for Williams to distinguish between the degree that racism affects her life versus the degree to which it affects those of the underclass, it is morally *imperative*— lest she infect her readers, almost all of whom have benefited from the Civil Rights revolution and are poised to continue doing so, with a defeatism dampening their ability to see or take advantage of opportunity.

## Mantra Number Three: When a Race Has Urgent Work to Do, People Crying "Wolf" Are Wasting Our Time

Obviously, there are a great many black people who rise above defeatism and are doing their part in moving the race forward by making their way in a tricky, but ever improving interracial landscape. Reading this book, a person might understandably think "Isn't he exaggerating a little? Are all black people in the United States running around shaking their fists at nonexistent enemies and turning their back on mainstream America?"

Certainly not. Not just some, but *most* black Americans can see that there is much of the huckster in Al Sharpton. The problem, however—and the reason I write about Black America rather than "some" black Americans—is this crucial point: manifestations of Victimology are so widely *accepted* at all levels of the black community rather than rejected, even among the many people who would not propound such views themselves. To continue to accept expressions of this ideology as "on the table," as fundamentally legitimate reflections of the race even if one is open to others as well, is to operate significantly under their influence.

For example, reviewing the evidence in the Tawana Brawley case of 1987, one simply cannot avoid the sad truth that this young woman fabricated a story of rape. The vast discrepancies between her narrative and the evidence (see page 77) are too obvious to admit any other explanation. Yet what Patricia Williams considers important about the case is that "Tawana's terrible story has every black woman's worst fears and experiences wrapped into it. Few will believe a black woman who has been raped by a white man." (Note also the use of her first name alone, connoting a taking of her into our fold, a warm, exculpatory embrace.)

In fact, there is quite a bit wrapped into Williams's position. For one, we must ask whether rape by white, as opposed to black, men has been an urgent problem for black women since several decades ago. To focus upon problems of the past rather than those of the present can solve no current suffering, and is thus celebrating victimhood rather than addressing it. Furthermore, all women have traditionally suffered the indignity of an undue burden of proof in rape cases; only recently have lawyer-scholars like Catharine McKinnon made significant inroads into this injustice—and Williams's mention of McKinnon makes it clear that she is aware of her work. Has this been a black problem or a women's problem in general, and has class played as significant a role as race? For Williams to co-opt the battle to amend rape laws as a race issue is a bold move that would seem to at least demand an explanation or defense. Yet all that she offers in this vein is that it is traditionally thought by whites that "black women whore as a way of being." No one would deny that there has been a stereotype of black women as sexually lascivious. Yet our question is how much this has affected white-on-black rape convictions within recent memory as compared to white-on-white rape cases—and in that light, the literature on women in rape cases is suffused with a general problem that women of all colors are too often assumed to have "asked for it" (dramaticized usefully in the film *The Accused* with Jodie Foster, which eloquently demonstrated this as a gender issue, not a racial one). Williams's lack of interest in addressing the issue beyond the level of folk conception, as a professor of law, suggests a fundamental desire to cloak the race in the mantle of victimhood at all costs.

Finally, Williams criticizes Sharpton for not allowing Brawley to speak for herself during the media controversy, but not for duping his supporters for years with the case itself. As such, whether or not she considers Al Sharpton a bit of a "character," in absolving him of a callow, mendacious hoodwinking of the public, she is condoning Victimology. Without explicitly saying so, she reveals that she considers Sharpton's tactics excusable, and that she thus considers this professional Victimologist a worthy leader of the race.

To the extent that people like Sharpton and Louis Farrakhan are considered "cool," to the extent that the black man at the party grousing about the "war on blacks" is considered a righteous brother even by moderately-inclined people present, to the extent that Spike Lee complaining that Hollywood does not want to produce movies about the full experience of black people is considered "telling it like it is" by black people who in one year's time have seen *How Stella Got Her Groove Back, Beloved, Down in the Delta, Foolish,* and *The Wood*—the black American race is in trouble.

There is a deeply felt sentiment in the black community that we are not to disagree in public, and this is a large part of why on the subject of race and race alone, so many millions of moderately minded black Americans are so naturally inclined to suspend logical engagement and accept barely credible depictions of the modern black condition as "valid opinions." The "united front" strategy was a valuable survival tactic in the old days, but we only maintain it today on pain of holding ourselves back. Cognitive dissonance and unfocused resentment are handicaps to emotional health and being all that one can be, and a race conditioned to process posture over action as a reflection of itself is—regardless of the historical reasons—doomed to remain America's poster-child race apart.

## The Road to True Equality: Give Black Students the Gift of Competition

There is in my view no issue as urgent to addressing black Americans' pathway toward true equality with whites as affirmative action. This is because this policy interacts urgently with something central to the soul of all human beings: reward for effort to forge one's place in the world, and the vital role this plays in self-conception.

Some readers may have justifiably wondered just what my position on affirmative action is. As I noted, I believe that the policy was nothing less than urgent when it was instituted in the 1960s. Where I depart from most black thinkers is that I do not think that the policy ought be continued until there is no racism whatsoever in the country and black Americans have achieved complete parity with whites.

## Affirmative Action: A First Step

I consider affirmative action to have been a necessary emergency measure, which was not the sole step, but one of two necessary steps toward the task the policy was instituted to accomplish: affording a race the ability to compete in the mainstream. In completing that task, all would agree that there comes a time when one must allow the group to compete without any more outside help than is the societal norm. Significantly, however, one cannot, by the dictates of sheer logic, direct a group to compete in a context where there still exists no incentive to reach for the very best. In that vein, the second step in achieving the result affirmative action was intended to bring about is to abandon the policy—*before full parity in performance has been achieved.*

### Affirmative Action Where It Is Needed

Of course, instituting the second step is only appropriate when the playing field has been leveled sufficiently to enable the race to successfully compete. For that reason, I support the preservation of affirmative action for the time being in the business realm. Hiring and advancement is based as much on personal contacts and social chemistry as merit. After a mere few decades of desegregation, most African Americans, even when successfully employed by predominantly white organizations, are ultimately more socially comfortable with members of their own race than with whites, and lack the decades-deep networks of contacts that so decisively affect the lives and careers of many whites. It follows from these two facts that left to their own devices, whites will naturally tend to promote other whites more readily than blacks. It is questionable that this is always due to "racism" as much as to a purely human birds-of-a-feather phenomenon. One need not be a bigot to be more inclined to promote someone with whom one feels a certain "click" or who has ties to people dear to one—any black person choosing whether to promote a black person or an equally qualified white one could feel the same way even in the absence of any particular commitment to "doing the right thing" for a fellow black. And sometimes in some places these days, good old-fashioned racism raises its head through the muck—the struggle isn't over yet.

However, things are different when it comes to university admissions, in which case one is dealing not with interpersonal dynamics but with application in writing. Here, affirmative action is not justifiable on the basis of the inexorable realities of social chemistry. Indeed, many argue that the playing field is not level in the realm of education nevertheless; namely, that societal conditions make it impossible for most minority students to achieve the grade-point averages and test scores that whites and Asians routinely do. As I have argued in this book, however, this is no longer true. Racism may play a marginal, background role in black students' academic experiences, but not nearly enough to cause the massive disparities across classes between black and white performance. To argue that less-than-perfect schools or residual teacher bias so decisively cripple a black student's performance is to beg the question "Why not poor Asian immigrants, or even black Caribbeans, going to the same schools?" Many will answer here "Well, they have a different culture"— and that's just my answer: the evidence suggests that most of the black-white disparity is today due to a sense of separation from scholarly endeavor internal to African-American culture.

### A Thumb on the Scale?

The degree of this disparity tends to get lost in the affirmative-action debate, in favor of a misconception that the policy is used as a mere "thumb on the scale," choosing the minority student over the white one only in the case of parallel qualifications, or at best, using race only as a small boost.

I once played piano and wrote lyrics for a student production at Stanford introducing freshmen to campus life. It was funded by the administration on the condition that a "diverse" cast be chosen. As a result, some people were cast who most likely would not have been without this directive, casting often being affected by a preset sense of a given character as white, with favoritism tending also to drift to those in the local theater "scene." Yet the casting choices made with diversity in mind were generally a boon to the show and to the lives of the actors. One black guy was cast who, under other conditions, not being a part of the campus theater community and being a rather contained fellow, would have been an unlikely choice—in other words, not being "one of the gang" would have worked against his being evaluated solely on his merits. However, not only was he up to the standard level of the other performers, but as it happened, the slightly "black" timing and facial expressions he naturally infused his role with created some of the nicest moments in the show. An Asian male was cast who was not only great, but on the basis of this was cast in subsequent campus productions, was picked up for one of the campus' leading a cappella groups, and last I heard had toured not only in *Miss Saigon* (where Asian performers have a natural leg up) but in *Rent*. Another Asian required some personal coaching, but ended up being a thoroughly charming presence and developed the confidence to join, and eventually solo in, a campus a cappella group; if she hadn't been cast in this show she would most likely never have discovered her talent.

Many affirmative-action advocates depict the policy as analogous to this *Nu Stu Revue* (I liked that title!) casting, thereby implying that criticism of such an obviously beneficial and innocent policy must be racist at heart. If the analogy were correct, then criticism of affirmative action would indeed be nitpicking at best, racist at worst, and usually the latter.

But the analogy is not correct. In real life, affirmative-action policies in admissions at all but the very top schools are as if the staff of the *Nu Stu Revue* had been forced to cast sharply lesser performers, baldly sacrificing merit for diversity. The reality here is unfortunate, but we cannot usefully evaluate the policy—or even understand why one would be necessary—without being aware of it.

As we have seen, the fraction of black students in America each year who make sterling scores on the SAT is a mere few hundred; selective schools typically have admitted black students with scores 150 points or more lower than whites' and Asians'. Among the twenty-eight schools Bowen and Bok examined in 1989, out of students who scored 1200 to 1249, 60 percent of the blacks were admitted as opposed to just 19 percent of whites; in the 1250–99 bracket, 75 percent of blacks and 24 percent of whites. However one feels about the appropriateness of SATs, those statistics show that we have not been dealing with a mere "thumb on the scale"—and the issue goes deeper than SATs into grades as well. For example, before affirmative action was repealed after the *Hopwood* case at the University of Texas, white students had been drawn from among the very best in the country while black students had had to be drawn from the bottom half of the national pool. At Lowell High School in San Francisco before the fall of 1998, black students constituted 5.6 percent of the student body as the result of an admissions policy which admitted minority students according to lower standards in test scores *and* grades. After the admissions committee was barred from using race in its decisions, the proportion of black students admitted fell by more than 50 percent, even despite consideration given to disadvantage and evidence of potential. This was not an unusual case, but a typical one. Bowen and Bok demonstrate through painstaking statistical analysis that to subtract race from the evaluation processes typical of selective schools would send the proportion of blacks and Latinos plunging, and the herculean efforts many universities are putting forth to maintain diversity after racial preferences have been prohibited is further and concrete demonstration that this is the case. Clearly race is hardly merely "one of many factors" in typical affirmative-action admissions policies; it tends strongly to be a factor of disproportionate weight.

The reason that this is the only way good schools can acquire a representative black population is that the culture is shot through so tragically with a wariness of school, but nevertheless the result is that on a great many campuses, the black student population admitted via set-asides are of perceptibly lesser qualification than the students around them.

Thus the question facing us regarding affirmative action in our times is not:

> Should we admit black students with top grades and scores over white students with the same credentials, given that racism keeps the numbers of such students low, and given that these students will perform as well as whites once admitted?

Who would have any problem with that? Only the occasional blinkered, hair-splitting letter-of-the-law addict, and surely not even enough of them to matter. However, unfortunately that formulation does not represent the true issue because its facts are wrong. Black students on average do not present grades and scores equivalent to other students'; racism plays·at best a background role in the disparity; and the students admitted do not generally perform at the level of white ones. Thus the actual question, and the one that I address in this section, is:

> Should we admit black students hindered from making top grades and test scores by a tendency to discourage one another from doing so, lent them as a legacy of segregation, with it given that these students will continue their substandard performance for this same reason once admitted?

I believe that the answer to that question is no, for the following four reasons, the last of which is particularly crucial.

## The Evils of Affirmative Action

### Affirmative Action Creates Private Doubt

White affirmative-action advocates often shrug "What's wrong with it when white students get in because their fathers went there or because they are good athletes?" This misses the point. Nepotism and favors (as well as dumb luck) play a large part in the trajectory of most lives, but these things are distributed randomly throughout the population, and most whites cannot rely upon them. As an *institutionalized* leg up, affirmative action leaves black Americans with the most systematically diluted responsibility for their fate of any group in America. The white student who gets a letter announcing his admission to Duke can go out and celebrate a signal achievement, although the luck of the draw almost always plays some role in a white or Asian person's admission to a school. Can the black middle manager's daughter getting the same letter have the same sense of achievement if her SAT scores and grades would have barred any white or Asian from admission? The truth is no—she can only celebrate having been good enough *among African-American students* to be admitted.

As I have mentioned, minority students often feel no overt stigma from affirmative action. However, the policy nevertheless inherently divests blacks and Latinos of the unalloyed sense of personal, individual responsibility for their accomplishments that other students so often can have. The fact that they tend not to be aware of this follows naturally from the fact that affirmative action bars it from their lives: You don't miss what you never had. However, its absence only nurtures the sense of separation from academic achievement, for the simple reason that so few minorities are allowed to know what it is like to truly attain high credentials and prestigious awards on their own merits. If more minority students were permitted to savor this feeling that we take as the birthright of any white person, then more minorities would likely begin to process quota-based set-asides as the dampeners of initiative that they are.

### Affirmative Action Makes Black People Look Unintelligent

With it widely known among a student body that most minority students were admitted with test scores and GPAs which would have barred white and Asian applicants from consideration, it is difficult for many white students to avoid beginning to question the basic mental competence of black people as a race. This is especially true when most black students are obviously of middle-class background, and even more so when one of the first lessons a white student learns from black students on campus is that it is an insult to assume that all black people grow up with their big brothers chugging forty-ounces of malt liquor in front of the TV set.

A white person need not be a racist to start wondering why black students need affirmative action even when growing up no poorer than they did. Black students could not help wondering the same thing about whites in a situation in which middle-class whites were almost all let in under the bar. Few white students will ever be in a position to key into the subtle cultural dynamics that hinder so many black students from performing at the highest levels on tests and earning the highest grades, especially given the reluctance of affirmative-action advocates to openly discuss such things. This can only leave many young whites with a private suspicion that blacks simply aren't as swift, which will in turn encourage suspicion in black students, and thus perpetuate interracial alienation on campus and undermine the mutual respect that successful integration requires.

Not one but two black friends of mine reported the searing experience of revealing, during one of those late-night freshman-year hallway group discussions, that their test scores and/or GPAs had been lower than the norm for white students, only to have an impolitic white student charge that they had taken someone's place. I could not help noticing that behind the indignation with which they recounted these events was the sad fact that in the end, neither had been able to effectively defend themselves. The old line about alumni children and athletes would only work on the off-chance that the accuser fit into one of these categories (in which case he would be unlikely to open his mouth anyway). Moreover, both of my friends were thoroughly middle class, products of two-parent homes and quality schooling, and thus neither could appeal to classrooms without textbooks or raising three siblings while their single mother cleaned houses. Few undergraduates—or even adults—command the spontaneous rhetorical resources to explain the subtle cultural barriers to scholarly achievement among *middle-class* black children; those with middle-class upbringings are generally barely even aware of these things on a conscious level; and few of those that were would be comfortable directly applying such an analysis to themselves.

Clearly, encounters like these subvert the goal of peaceful integration, and importantly, unexpressed renditions of these encounters lurk underneath interracial contacts campus-wide all year long.

The only way to get rid of the "dumb black" myth is by proving it false. Too often our response is simply to vilify whites as racists for subscribing to it. This, however, is like someone falsely accused by their spouse of adultery saying "Meanie!" instead of explaining why the charge could not be true. The sad fact is that as often as not these days, black people are left with no better response, because in almost all intellectual endeavors, their participation has been sanctioned on the basis of lesser performance than everyone else's.

## Affirmative Action for People Who Have Not Suffered Unique Disadvantage Is Unfair

When affirmative action was aimed at improving the lot of the disenfranchised, then its displacement of some qualified white applicants was thoroughly justifiable in the name of a greater good. However, when aimed at admitting middle-class black children, a great many of whom have suffered on no level any more than a great many white, or especially Asian, students, whites' complaints of reverse discrimination acquire more resonance. The defense that white athletes and children of the wealthy have always been admitted to elite universities under the bar is one thing coming from white people exempt from experiencing the policy themselves, but from black affirmative-action fans it is particularly weak. There is an obvious difference between set-asides for a small sliver of the white undergraduate population and set-asides for the vast majority of the black one—the former addresses certain subsets of the white population while the latter addresses the entire African-American race. Furthermore, the consensus has always held legacy students and subliterate athletes with B.A.s in bad odor, and thus to argue that minority students ought be allowed the same privilege does not put us in the best company—two wrongs do not make a right.

## Affirmative Action Hinders African Americans from Achieving Parity with Whites

Despite affirmative action having been introduced as a proactive policy aimed at uplifting the race, the fact is that today, it is no longer doing this. The black-white scholastic gap closed steadily until the late 1980s, but since then, black academic performance nationwide, including SAT scores, have plateaued.

### The Cause of the Plateau

Many might be tempted to suppose that the reason for this plateau is the persistence of societal racism. However, this point is extremely problematic. Inner-city schools have gotten worse since the 1980s, but few students from these schools take the SAT. Besides, in searching for an explanation of this plateau, we must also recall that many children with obvious handicaps to success, such as Asian immigrant children, manage to do excellently even in substandard schools. We must also keep in mind that this plateau is composed in part of the vast numbers of black students who continue to do poorly even with all possible support, such as in Shaker Heights or Evanston, Illinois.

I believe that this plateau is evidence that affirmative action has done all that it can to help close the black-white scholastic gap, and constitutes a demonstration that the remainder of the problem lies not in inequity of school funding or societal racism, but elsewhere. In seeking the cause of this plateau, what we seek is a factor that we would expect to disproportionately affect black children of all classes *who go to college*— not simply all black children. That factor is not poor inner-city schools, because that accounts for only a fraction of the black *college student* population, and it is not racism, because black students continue to lag behind even when there is too little racism in the context to be thought of as a barrier to achievement for a-human being with a basic endowment of spiritual resilience.

Along these lines, there is no factor which so obviously fulfills this requirement as the tendency for black students to hold schoolwork at half an arm's length—the Cultural Disconnect discussed in Chapter 3. In this light, what the plateau demonstrates is not racist backlash, but rather that while black students are certainly capable of making a showing, very few feel compelled to reach for the highest bar. This is not a pleasant conclusion, and it is not the one the reigning discourse trains us to give sustained attention to. However, how strongly a devaluation of school permeates black youth culture regardless of class has been so richly documented in academic studies, journalistic investigations, and endless personal anecdotes from black people across the country that one could only dismiss it as a factor—a *central* factor— out of a resistance to any but certain dictated factors as worthy of serious consideration.

### A Policy Working Against Itself

In this light, the maintenance of affirmative action nothing less than hinders the completion of the very task it was designed to accomplish, because it deprives black students of a basic incentive to reach for that highest bar. If every black student in the country knows that not even the most selective schools in the country require the very top grades or test scores of black students, that fine universities just below this level will readily admit them with even a B+/B dossier by virtue of their "leadership qualities" or "spark," and that even just a better-than-decent application file will grant them admission to solid second-tier selective schools, then what incentive is there for any but the occasional highly driven black student to devote his most deeply committed effort to school?

I can attest, for example, that in secondary school I quite deliberately refrained from working to my highest potential because I knew that I would be accepted to even top universities without doing so. Almost any black child knows from an early age that there is something called affirmative action which means that black students are admitted to schools under lower standards than white; I was aware of this at at least the age of ten. And so I was quite satisfied to make B+'s and A–'s rather than the A's and A+'s I could have made with a little extra time and effort. Granted, having the knack for school that I did, I was lucky that my less-than-optimum efforts still put me within reach of fine schools. However, there is no reason that the same sentiment would not operate even in black students who happen to be less nerdy than I was, especially given that a great many black students, just as a great many others, do not plan to attend top schools for financial and other reasons. It is also significant that one study has shown that black students (even middle-class ones) are less concerned that their school performance will affect their later chances in life than white ones. In general, one could think of few better ways to depress a race's propensity for pushing itself to do its best in school than a policy ensuring that less-than-best efforts will have a disproportionately high yield. Imagine telling a Martian who expressed an interest in American educational policy: "We allow whites in only if they have a GPA of 3.7 or above and an SAT of 1300 or above. We let blacks in with a GPA of 3.0 and an SAT of 900. Now, what we have been pondering for years now is why black students continue to submit higher grades and scores than this so rarely." Well, mercy me—what a perplexing problem!

It all comes down to this. Quite often we hear that black students underperform because teachers do not require enough of them. If this is true, then we must ask: Isn't it a direct contradiction of expecting the most of students to permanently exempt them from true competition? A response might be that when not enough has been expected of them, then colleges must adjust by "acknowledging" this. But even here: keeping college entrance requirements lowered is in itself a very part of educating young black children amidst lowered expectations!

### Pouring Water on a Drowning Man

I intend no criticism of black students in my argument here. As I have noted, the Anti-intellectual strain in black culture results from a race having spent centuries in poverty and disenfranchisement, all but denied education by the dominant group. This separation from the scholarly left the culture particularly susceptible to a rejection of school as "other," as Separatist ideology encouraged a focus upon what black culture already had, which unfortunately was only a marginal scholarly tradition, and a wariness of white culture, which unfortunately for us, included school. Hypotenuses, *Little Dorrit,* the opposite of *obfuscate*—to most students of any color these kinds of thing are not exactly comfort food. But to most black students, they are not only "school stuff," but "white stuff." That sentiment, even in a small dose, has a decisive impact.

There is nothing willful about black students' lesser school performance. That being the case, it remains that permanent affirmative action is *particularly* pernicious for a race with this particular history and this particular cultural baggage. Affirmative action has done a fine job of remedying the extent of the problem that was due to societal injustice. However, the increasing number of newspaper articles about middle-class black students clustering in the lowest percentiles of their high schools are telling us something, and it is not that the Klan still lurk behind every tree. What they are telling us is that to run that last mile, black American students need one simple thing, and that is the incentive to do so—especially in the context of the Cultural Disconnect from learning that distinguishes the race affirmative action was designed to help.

It is a general principle in life that in bringing a person up to par, there is a point at which the net must be taken away, because only then is one presented with an incentive vivid enough to spur the development of top-level skill. A parent often teaches a child to ride a bicycle without training wheels by holding the bike up and pushing the child along for a while. This gives the child a sense of the basic lay of the land, but as we all remember, there comes a point when Dad pushes you down the hill to ride by yourself for the first time. Then, and only then, do you master the subtle muscular poise that allows you to stay magically balanced and rolling along. Looking back, you realize that gaining that sense would have been quite impossible without having taken that first plunge; only when the danger of falling down looms do your mind and body avidly seek the interplay to avoid it. The only way that birds learn to fly is to be nudged gently out of the nest; they keep flapping and learn how to do it right because otherwise they fall. The only way to acquire true fluency in a foreign language is to immerse yourself in a situation where you must speak it all day long, where the only way to have meaningful human contact is to speak well. The level one achieves is lower to the extent that one has the opportunity to revert to one's native language when it becomes necessary to express a thought that requires a bit of effort to render. Along the same lines, black students simply cannot get beyond the average level they post today in a situation where Dad remains trotting alongside holding the bike.

It is for these reasons that affirmative action is best thought of as an emergency measure, doing great harm for the sake of a greater good just as the ravages of chemotherapy and radiation treatment are worth the benefit of killing a tumor. The harms of affirmative action—sowing self-doubt, giving the appearance of dimness, displacing equally qualified whites, and most importantly, the blunting of incentive—were worth giving black students access to earning power and contact with the mainstream in the aftermath of the Civil Rights revolution. However, the harms remain and are extremely unhealthy, and in the meantime, after thirty years, with black access to earning power and contact with the mainstream well established and in no danger of decreasing, affirmative action in university admissions has outlived its usefulness. It now interferes with a goal in the pursuit of equality every bit as important as earning power and interracial contact—closing the black-white scholastic gap.

## Benefits from Eliminating Affirmative Action

The demise of affirmative action is particularly crucial to the thesis I have explored in this book because in withdrawing the four evils above, it would be invaluable in working against all of the three currents I have discussed.

### Combatting Victimology

Victimology is at heart an expression of insecurity, which compensates for inner self-doubt by calling attention to faults in others. At heart, in a context of increasingly marginal victimization, to focus on this more than, or even as much as, upon progress only conveys satisfaction to a person whose pride is damaged to an extent that makes this more comfortable than active self-realization.

As we have seen, Victimology is particularly prevalent among black leaders, and leaders come disproportionately from the educated population. The elimination of affirmative action could, therefore, help to intercept Victimology at a crucial formative stage in future black leaders' lives. If every black student on a selective college campus were admitted according to the same criteria as other students, it would help to erode lingering feelings of inferiority to whites, and lessen the drive to assuage this by taking refuge in dwelling unduly upon vestiges of victimhood and passing this on to children. Black students often come to a selective campus wary that white students suspect them of being affirmative-action admits and thus not equally qualified. A simple solution would be to eliminate the policy that makes the white students' suspicion—let's face it—usually correct.

### Combatting Separatism

One of the many harms of affirmative action has always been that it reinforces the black cultural sense that to embrace school for more than utilitarian reasons is a "white" thing to do. Under affirmative action, most black students on a given campus have been admitted with grades and test scores that reflect, to some degree, this sense of separation from The Books. As a result, black communities on these campuses become a realm where high scholarly achievement is, if not devalued completely, weighted perceptibly less than on the rest of the campus. These students then graduate having been immersed in this cultural meme in the vital crucible during which they become adults, with this cultural meme living on even in black people of power and influence. The result is phenomena such as Afrocentric History and the Ebonics controversy.

A black student body where each student had been admitted with qualifications commensurate with other students' would be one where this sense of separation would not rule the day. Year after year of similar black student bodies on dozens of the nation' selective campuses would lead to an ever-growing black leadership class who operated free of this particular cultural baggage. Providing all black high-school students with the incentive to reach for the highest bar would work against the Separatist orientation toward school in general, by establishing a situation where to the extent that one gives in to this tendency, one's chances of admission to a good school are diminished to the same extent that they are for all students.

Furthermore, black students who have overcome the cultural barrier to school by having to devote themselves to it wholeheartedly are generally those who become less hardened in a sense that mainstream culture is an outside realm. I have known many black students, including myself, who have found it difficult to maintain a foothold in the campus' black community while also participating in mainstream activities like the general campus drama scene (as opposed to just the one or two black plays done each year), writing for the campus newspaper, or any activity outside of the expressly black-oriented realm. Not only is there a subtle pressure within the black community against such participation, but because so few black students take part in these activities, one's social circles gradually change by sheer force of frequency and depth of contact. A campus where black students were more open to a bicultural orientation would be one where this balkanization tendency would be lessened.

### Combatting Anti-intellectualism

If black students were finally required to submit the same quality of application to selective campuses as everyone else, then this incentive to immerse themselves in their work with the brand of commitment that earns top grades, would usher many of them out of the modes of thought that help to limit the race: a preference for inference based on established truths rather than "out of the box" innovation, and a leeriness of precision. Both of these factors are at the very heart of the purpose of education itself, and too often, black students are deprived of the incentive to become comfortable with this kind of thinking.

Claude Steele's work on black students' "stereotype threat," based on a study where black performance on tests suffered when requiring specification of race or when billed as measuring ability, is also pertinent here. This study has attracted a great deal of attention, and although I do not believe that confidence is the key issue here, for those who do, an important question is: What possible solution could there be to that particular problem? Here, for example, is Claude Steele's summation in one paper on "stereotype threat":

> To explain African American students' underachievement as a byproduct of either socioeconomic conditions or "black cul-

ture" offers little realistic basis for improving the situation. Our analysis uncovers a social and psychological predicament that is rife in the standardized testing environment, but, as our manipulations illustrate, is amenable to change.

The "manipulations" Steele refers to consist in large part of deemphasizing that the test measures ability (the race aspect of Steele's findings is actually but a fraction of the actual study). The question is how this translates from the realm of the psychological study into practice. In a quest to bring a race to parity with whites—and that is what we are, and must be, engaged in—is it really the most appropriate solution to *disaccustom* its members to competition rather than *accustom* them to it? It is unclear that the way to prepare a group to compete is to shield them from the fact that they are competing, and one cannot help but detect the Separatist sentiment that "black" is cosmically different here, as usual dehumanizing people of massive potential.

The only way to build confidence is to achieve, with no more but no fewer challenges to doing so than one's peers. It would be a relief if there were some other way, but there simply is not. Along those lines, to allow black students to compete would be the single most effective way of combatting whatever extent "stereotype threat" holds black students back—for the simple reason that there exists no other way. Even Claude Steele himself agrees "through the back door." In a recent article, he advises that "stereotype threat" be addressed by letting black students know that they are being subjected to high standards and that it is thought that they can reach them. Steele advises this as a specific corrective aimed at nudging black students away from a sense that teachers consider them unintelligent. I do not believe that this factor—i.e., racism—is significant in black students' overall performance, but Steele's proposed solution, regardless of its motivation, is not only the best one but the only one—call it a different path to the mountaintop.

## The Liberal Consensus on Affirmative Action: Back to Three-Fifths of a Man

### The Shape of the River Indeed

In my entire lifetime, I have never experienced anything more profoundly vexing than the thesis of William Bowen and Derek Bok's *The*

*Shape of the River,* namely that affirmative action has been proven to be a good policy worthy of open-ended preservation because most of its beneficiaries are now happy with their lives and content with their jobs. Every smug, fawning review I read of this book was as irritating as an eyelash in my eye, and reading the book I had to pause several times to avoid throwing it across the room.

Bowen and Bok breezily presume that the disadvantages I have mentioned—high-achieving blacks never sure whether they deserve their success and generally assumed not to, blacks looking and feeling stupid, blacks never knowing the test of real competition, blacks having no incentive to put forth their best efforts—are somehow unimportant in view of the fact that their interviewees who were admitted to universities under set-aside policies are now happy campers. Given their intent, however, Bowen and Bok ironically reveal an aspect of racism that does remain in our society, what I call the racism of neglect.

Indeed, only a fundamental sense that black people are somehow not whole, the sense that makes it so hard to imagine any black person representing "the American," can explain the blithe complacency of these authors and their fans in the face of the ills I and many others have described. It's easy to talk about permanent set-asides for people who are not your own. Only a sense that they are not "your own" could keep people from processing the blot, the stain that a policy like affirmative action is when restricted to a particular race, especially one too damaged by a sense of spiritual distance from learning for learning's sake to see the harm of it themselves.

Bowen and Bok, with their careful tables and dutiful acknowledgment of the black grade/score lag camouflaging the profound ideological bias of their approach, cannot imagine how it feels for me to read them telling me that the children I will have by 2020 ought be held to a lower academic standard because my father was not allowed to fly planes in the navy in 1944, because one or two white women will hold their purses closer as they pass, or because the occasional teacher won't call on them as much as they call on the perky white girl sitting next to them. Jews, offered such treatment in 1920, would have been insulted and would have made every effort to prove it unnecessary. Blacks tend not to, for reasons we have seen, but how are we to feel when the brightest, and supposedly most empathetic, of our country's leaders sanction this? Of course they consider their very take on all of this to demonstrate their empathy—but let's face it: A person you excuse from any genuine challenge is a person you do not truly respect.

One wants to ask people like Bowen and Bok: Could they say the same about their own children? Ronald Dworkin, erudite legal scholar, tells us in his review of the book in *The New York Review of Books* that the concerns of an elite minority amidst the group shouldn't matter—i.e., that my discomfort with affirmative action as a black who doesn't need it is unimportant compared to the benefits it offers most blacks. Very nice, but if Jews had been given affirmative action in the 1930s, just imagine having told American-born Jews of letters, chafing under the condescension inherent in affirmative action, that their sense of denigration was not to be heeded because immigrant Jews considered the policy to have "helped them" and made them feel "welcome"! (Interestingly, American-born working-class Jews would not have needed affirmative action to post representative numbers in good schools, because their history did not condition the emergence of a set of ideologies to turn Jews away from learning.) Dworkin says that even privileged blacks should be recruited under the bar to provide "diversity" even when they have few identifiable black cultural traits—because even this is a lesson for white students. Again, though, what about the meaning of this in the lives of these "diverse" people as individuals, as human beings? The withdrawal of incentive to succeed that this conditions in these "diverse" people? What about how this exemption from competition infects the psychology of a race? Suppose we told Ronald Dworkin that his children were to be admitted to all schools below their standards in order to serve as an object lesson to gentiles?

What Bowen, Bok, and Dworkin fail to address is this simple fact: Content and financially stable though their affirmative-action beneficiaries are, their children are continuing to post the lowest grades and test scores in the United States. Bowen and Bok appear aware that the middle-class status of these children would lead us to expect that they would no longer need the policy that their parents did, but they dwell upon this issue only briefly and consider it of little consequence. To justify the *institution* of affirmative action on the basis of how deeply established racism was in this country in the 1960s, as these authors do, is unexceptionable. However, in failing to even conceive as an issue worthy of address whether or not the policy should continue in an America so vastly different from that of the 1960s reveals nothing less than a concept of black people as essentially less than whole.

Another example of this kind of unintentional but pernicious dehumanization of the black American race is sociologist Nathan Glazer's widely touted *volte-face* on affirmative action in 1998, aired in several publications. Previously notorious for his disapproval of the policy long before California's Proposition 209 and similar movements this inspired in other states, Glazer announced that he had decided that the policy was justified on the basis that America "owes" black people exemption from serious competition as recompense for centuries of oppression.

To the extent that Glazer implies that most black Americans remain hindered from admission to good schools by concrete barriers of opportunity, he is operating according to the Victimologist perspective: the black America of 1965, a heartbeat away from institutionalized segregation and discrimination, is a place vastly different from the black America of 1998 three generations later. It is not enough to mention that ghettos persist or that more minority students go to poor schools than white ones. One would like to ask Glazer to take a look at the black students at his university, Harvard, and identify precisely what barriers—other than barriers suffered just as often by white students—they have encountered to doing their academic best.

To the extent that Glazer is urging us to impose a policy upon today's black students out of a desire to atone for what was done to their ancestors, he is dehumanizing these students, casting them as mythic victims on the basis of a historical legacy as if we were writing a play, rather than grappling with living, breathing human beings in the present tense. The question is not how we relieve good-thinking people like Glazer of their guilt for the historical misdeeds of their race, but how we bring present-day black people into equality with whites. The guiding mistake of people like Glazer is the misconception that these two things are one and the same. There is no logical guarantee that what accomplishes the former will also accomplish the latter, and given a choice, it is the latter that is our business at hand.

Despite the august credentials and beneficent intentions of scholars like William Bowen, Derek Bok, Ronald Dworkin, and Nathan Glazer, their positions on affirmative action are ultimately informed by what Shelby Steele in *A Dream Deferred* identifies as a drive to redeem themselves rather than help black people. *The Shape of the River* ultimately sounds uncomfortably like Charles Murray and Richard Herrnstein telling blacks to be satisfied with being athletes in *The Bell Curve*. Good, concerned white people: Do not turn human beings into pawns in a sociological experiment that will not personally affect any of your nearest and dearest. If you really believe black people are "fellow Americans," treat them as such. To people like William Bowen, Derek Bok, Ronald Dworkin, and Nathan Glazer, I say "Thank you for your concern, but you are selling us short."

*Diversity*

While my discussion of affirmative action has focused on grade/score disparity and the crucial issue of incentive, on the ground these are generally treated as background issues at best, with the dominant one being "diversity" on campus. Since the "diversity" justification was established with the *Regents of the University of California v. Bakke* decision in 1978, the affirmative-action issue has been couched so consistently and insistently on these terms that a generation of black students has grown up only dimly aware that the concept was developed as a rather strained apology for lowered standards.

The prioritization of this "Wee Pals" vision of multiethnicity is so deeply felt that, as I noted, the outside observer could easily miss in most public discussions of the issue that there is a performance gap between black and white students at all. However, within a context of evaluating the crucial issue of whether affirmative action is closing the black/white performance gap, this fig-leaf appropriation of a nominally innocent concept becomes a hindrance to intelligent and progressive engagement with the issue. The sad fact is that on top college campuses, "diversity" comes at a price: the levels of "diversity" to which we have become accustomed are impossible without admitting most minority students under the bar.

Many suppose that given a choice between consistent excellence and "diversity," the latter ought to win out. When most blacks faced true barriers to achievement, there was a case for this, and "diversity" helped for about twenty years: the black-white gap is narrower than it was in 1970. However, the gap stopped closing ten years ago, and as such, "diversity" is no longer serving our purpose and has thus fossilized into a manipulative and counterproductive fashion statement. To continue to argue for "diversity" as a *priority* reveals a lack of sincere interest in raising black students to the performance level of whites. It is time now to put excellence rather than headcounts first because exposing black students to serious competition is the only way to start them on the path to closing the black-white gap once and for all.

To be sure, there would be an unpleasant by-product of this approach. The number of minority students admitted to selective universities would at first go down. There is a strong tendency to frantically reject this prospect as "resegregation," but this hyperbole sells minority students short. The black-white scholastic lag is not small, but it is hardly so hideously vast that no minority students, or even just a handful, are eligible for admission to good schools. For example, the total of black students admitted to Berkeley after the ban on preferences took effect was 43 percent less than the previous year's. That is hardly a wonderful contrast, but it must be noted that the fall was by less than half. What's more, this same year, black admissions *increased* at three second-tier but solid University of California schools (Santa Cruz, Irvine, and Riverside). In general, after the bans on using racial preferences in admissions in California and Texas, minority admissions went down in only six out of seventy-four schools.

In the meantime, we must also avoid the "Yale or jail" myth, under which black students and professors indignantly defend black students' "right" to attend top schools with the implication that their ready admission to solid second-tier schools is a complete nonissue. The black students not admitted to the very top schools would easily be admitted to any number of solid second-tier ones. It is often argued that the top schools are virtually the only path to the most prestigious jobs, but this is not borne out by the facts. One does not wind up in a trailer park or working at Radio Shack because one attended Rutgers instead of Princeton; I, for example, got my B.A. from Rutgers and nevertheless have done pretty well for myself. More concretely, of today's African-American congressmen, army officers, people earning Ph.D.s from 1992 to 1996, MacArthur Foundation genius award winners of 1981 through 1988, and top fifty business officials, none but a sliver attended top-rated selective colleges. Surely Harvard connections do not hurt, but just as surely, such credentials are but one of several factors that determine the position in life one obtains.

## What I See: Affirmative Action as an Experience

Bowen and Bok associate affirmative action with the black managers and professionals filling out their questionnaires. Despite how deeply offended I have been by this book and its reception, I do, in my calmer moments, understand how they could feel this way, especially since for them, affirmative action has been a policy rather than an experience.

Affirmative action summons other associations in me, however. It is too easy to lose sight of the human aspect of this policy, so often do we see it discussed via charts, tables, thought experiments, musings on the nature of democracy, and fig-leaf defenses like "diversity." One sad story will illustrate how affirmative action perpetuates the very situation it was designed to address.

### Beyond the Checking Account: An Affirmative-Action Case Study

A black graduate student came to a prestigious university department as a visiting student under the wing of a new professor, who he had begun working with at another school. He was soon admitted officially to the department, but his work was consistently so below the standard of the other students' that it became sadly apparent that his admission had been a mistake. The usual practice in such cases was for a student to be asked to leave the program, but this was not done in this case. During the first year or two, there was perhaps a case for giving a black student a longer tether than usual, especially since it is not unheard of for a white graduate student to start slow but gradually blossom. However, the case became more tenuous as the years passed.

For one, his admission to the department had already been a second chance, his having come with the new professor because of having been asked to leave the department at the previous school. In any case, during the student's fifth year (and sixth in the field), while the other students who had come in at the same time were finishing their dissertations, the student was still working on one of the two test-run papers required for even being officially admitted to the stage of writing a dissertation, and a spoken presentation he gave based on the paper was extremely under-researched for someone who had been in the field for such a long time.

Yet at this very point this student was picked up for a tenure-track job in an African-American Studies department before even beginning his dissertation. Since (unlike the other students in his class) he had yet to publish any articles in journals and had yet to make any mark in his area, it was obvious that his hiring was based not on demonstrated ability but simply on his being a black student at a top school—when, recall, even his admission to the top school had itself not been based on having demonstrated ability commensurate with its standards. It is highly unlikely that a white person with so few credentials would be hired for a tenure-track position in any department. This African-American Studies faculty gave a stark demonstration of the sense of separation from the academic inherent to black American culture, which can lead even educated blacks to give academic qualification distinctly low weighting in the name of racial solidarity.

The student did not finish his dissertation until over three years into the professorial post, thus having required ten years to complete the doctoral program where most of the students in his class had required five, and the dissertation was less than half the average length of a dissertation in the field. Furthermore, while most graduate students begin attending conferences in their subfield as a vital part of becoming experts in their topic, this person at this writing has never attended a conference in his subfield, nor published an article about his chosen topic in a journal.

Yet this student was bright, and furthermore there were no indications that cultural conflict was the problem. He was of solidly middle-class background and quite comfortable in white company; in fact, his significant other was white. Neither was there anything in his work of a politically controversial nature which one might expect to skew outside judgments and expectations. However, if there is one thing that academic work requires, it is a brand of obsession with one's topic, and it was clear that what held this student back was simply that he lacked this obsession. One never got the sense that he had a burning interest in his work or a passion for the general subject; one would have been hard put to say of him that he was "crazy about linguistics." It is quite likely that the African-American sense of separation from "the book thing" was a major factor here as well. As I have said, this factor only expresses itself explicitly in the inner city; elsewhere, it exerts a subtler effect, but is often damning all the same. This student obviously had enough interest in the subject to apply to graduate programs; however, when push came to shove, cultural baggage played its hand and eternally tainted his genuine interest in reaching for the top. Indeed, I once heard that his family were not particularly supportive of his career plans. This is hard (members of my extended family weren't crazy about my career choice either), but the die was cast, and the fact remains: there are hundreds of things this person could have done with his life with glittering success, but the particular business of being an academic was obviously just not his bag.

It is white students in just this awkward position who are usually asked to leave graduate programs, and most report feeling, ultimately, relieved at having had an understandably difficult but necessary decision made for them after semesters of private doubt and pain. I strongly suspect this student would have felt similarly. I doubt if there was ever an explicit resolution by the department's faculty to grant this student a doctorate in the name of "diversity," but the sentiment was obviously decisive even if latent—a couple of white students during these years were asked to leave when it was clear that the program was not suited to them. More specifically, it is very likely that these well-intentioned and highly enlightened white people, Carefully Taught the Victimologist message as well as blacks often are, privately felt that to dismiss this student would render them "part of the problem."

As a result, they granted this student the status of being their peer. Yet the benefit of having exempted this student from the evaluation standards of other students in the name of "diversity" is unclear. Partly out of an inevitable sense of scholarly inferiority to the other students, the student kept to himself to the point of being a social unknown quantity to the department, never attending talks by invited speakers (another vital part of graduate training) or social gatherings. His work was too sparse and, unfortunately, poor to contribute "another perspective," or indeed any perspective, to the discipline. Furthermore, the low quality of this work cannot be said to have been the best source of ushering the white students in the department, or the white colleagues he will meet today, into accepting African Americans as intellectual equals. In addition, allowing this student to continue on the basis of substandard work prevented him from ever raising the quality of his work to the general standard, and his being nevertheless hired for a professional position before beginning his dissertation took him away from regular tutelage by advisers and thus froze him at this level.

Most seriously, however: As a professor in an African-American Studies department, this person, even with the best of intentions, cannot help but now pass along his level of competence and expectation to new *black* students—reinforcing them in the sense that top-level competence is somehow alien to blackness. Meanwhile, what will he contribute to showing his white and Asian students that black professors are as competent as others?

Of course, if this student's advisors had required suitable work from him before granting him a Ph.D., he would probably not have been up to it. I reiterate that the problem was not innate ability but a lifetime's cultural conditioning. In response, however, many might argue that our job is to "work with" students like this to override the effects of the culture. I would argue, however, that attempts to transform deeply ingrained cultural traits in matured individuals works too rarely to be a realistic social policy. Moreover, as we have seen, the motivation for reaching for the highest bar in college is mitigated in black students by the fact that postgraduate programs stand waiting to snap up any black student who has done better than okay. Our task is to work on the culture from the bottom up. Along these lines, the solution with this student was certainly not to simply grant him a hollow degree. Was the color of this student's skin really worth all of his pain, worth white faculty and students inevitably being reinforced in associating black people with scholarly mediocrity, or worth the fact that this person can now only perpetuate the very cause of the lag in black students' scholarly achievement?

It is extremely unpleasant to tell such a story. Most important, however, far from being static or marginal fallout, this story is by no means an unusual one in the affirmative-action climate in graduate schools since the late 1960s, as the result of the assumption that the categories of blackness and disadvantage overlap much more than they do, and that disadvantage is the only reason black children fail to excel in school. A great many university professors have similar tales to tell, and I have chosen only one of many I have seen or heard about. At least some such stories must be told for the greater good of assessing affirmative action in admissions with true honesty.

## Pulling the Ladder Up After Me?: Affirmative Action in My Life

One of the most damning condemnations of Supreme Court Justice Clarence Thomas's stance against affirmative action is considered to be that he benefited from it himself, but now wants to deny it to blacks who come after him. This has always struck me as a curious argument. Obviously Thomas came to disapprove of the policy as he matured. However, the consensus appears to be that having benefited from this policy somehow makes it immoral to openly give voice to logical conclusions that lead you in later life to question its wisdom, even if your reasons for questioning it are based on a concern for the well-being of the race. This simply does not follow, and what Thomas's detractors are demonstrating is a deafness to the very notion that affirmative action could be questioned; because they see it as a moral absolute, they can only see spitefulness in Thomas's opposition. Nevertheless, in stating my views I open myself to the same charge that I am "pulling the ladder up after me."

In response, I should note that despite my casual attitude toward affirmative action in secondary school, in college I came to feel diminished by the assumption that I had "struggled" thus far, given that I quite simply had not. I have been lucky enough to grow up in the post–Civil Rights Movement era, in a solidly middle-class home, attending excellent private schools. Certainly I have encountered racism here and there, but none that interfered with my advancement any more than any number of things interfered with that of most white people I know. As such, I do not consider myself to have jumped any sociological hurdles worth mentioning, and for this reason, the notion of being granted any position worth having on the basis of my pigment cells rather than my efforts strikes me as an insult. Furthermore, this is not a mere matter of abstract principle along the lines of avoiding eating beef as a protest against how cows are raised and killed. For me it has been a quite spontaneous and visceral sense of injury.

Yet affirmative action is almost impossible for an upwardly mobile black person to avoid, whatever their life circumstances have been. I was accepted into the Stanford linguistics program, for example, with a fellowship. As time went by, I learned that while I had been competitive within the top twenty out of about a hundred prospective students, that my lack of prior experience in the field and imprecise intentions of specialty at the time would have kept me from making the final cut under normal circumstances, and that my making the final cut of eight was due to my color. (I was told this by my black advisor, himself seeing this as healthy and unexceptional.) I also soon found out that my fellowship was a minority fellowship, which had also made the decision to admit me easier. Of course, I did make the top twenty, and that is not nothing at Stanford. However, all of this still meant that I had gotten a leg up in the name of my contribution to a headcount.

Now, of course, the best thing I could say is that once I found out that I had unwittingly allowed myself to be an affirmative-action beneficiary, I should have withdrawn from the department, packed my bags, and moved back across the country. However, at the time my opposition to affirmative action was not principled enough to lead me to weight my discomfort so heavily as to turn me away from such a valuable opportunity. Instead, I went ahead and earned my degree, but I was never able to be as proud of getting into Stanford as my classmates could be. After all, growing up as I did, how much of an achievement can I truly say it was to have been a good enough *black* person to be admitted, while my colleagues had been considered good enough *people* to be admitted?

The omnipresence of affirmative action makes it particularly difficult to avoid when one's livelihood and personal happiness are on the line. When I went out on the job market, prospects were extremely tight. In addition, as a big-city boy I feel hopelessly stranded in small towns, and for social reasons, at the time leaving California would have been extremely painful. As it happened, the only life choice available to me that would allow me to combine my career with spiritual contentment was applying for a postdoctoral fellowship at UC Berkeley dedicated to minorities. Especially given the grave thought of not getting any paid position, I went ahead and applied for this, and got it.

The problem here is that I was chosen not as one of the best applicants, but as one of the best minority applicants, and this is inherently a demotion. On paper, the minority fellowships are chosen according to standards as rigorous as the others, the goal being simply to make sure that minorities are proportionately represented among the grantees instead of their numbers having to depend on the vagaries of chance in the general pool, as they would even in the complete absence of racism. However, the very requirement that every year a certain number of grantees be minorities automatically renders the minority fellowship less competitive. In a given year there may well not be a minority application that would make the final cut in a general contest; a special minority fellowship guarantees that if no such application exists, then second-tier ones will be accepted alongside the first-tier ones from the general pool. Sure, this will be true some years, not true in others—but the general conclusion this leads to is that getting the minority fellowship does not require the grade of excellence that getting the general one does, at least not as consistently—and therefore, again, in general, not. Furthermore, competition was also lower within the minority pool simply because there were fewer applications from minorities. What all of this means is that I may well not have gotten a fellowship if I had applied within the general pool.

At this same time, I was also hired by the Linguistics Department at Cornell University (I postponed taking the position for a year while I did the postdoctoral fellowship). Even here, however, affirmative action got me a plum position I would not have gotten otherwise, leaving the ratio of luck to merit much higher in my appointment than it would have been for a white person. The faculty had originally wanted to hire one person, but found themselves split down the middle as to whether to hire me or someone else. Ordinarily they would either have hired no one or had to keep the tense dialogue going until they could finally get a substantial majority in favor of one of us (a mere tie-breaker would not have been sufficient). However, in this case they did not have to do either, because there was a salary fund specially earmarked for minorities. This allowed them to hire two new professors while only paying one salary out of department funds.

The faculty themselves are hardly to be blamed. But the fact that my hiring was made possible by a fund set aside for people of my skin color could not help but give my attainment of the post an air of the consolation prize. Many would tell me that I would not have been hired if I had not been deemed worthy of Cornell. But the fact is that everybody else on the faculty had been hired according to either unanimous, or at least close to unanimous, support from their colleagues. The minority salary fund was beneficial in allowing the faculty to satisfy everybody by hiring two people, but it also meant that I was hired without the usual level of support. In addition, it was obvious that if they had had to make one choice, the other professor, whose research focus fit theirs perfectly, would certainly have been hired over me, whose work was anticipated as helping add variety to the department's offerings.

True, it can be argued that the faculty's split was due to internal politics over what kind of linguist the department needed at the time rather than my inherent qualifications. But under ordinary circumstances, the person hired by an elite department is the one whose qualifications were deemed not only sufficient in themselves, but of such compelling value to that particular department that one side was committed enough to push their case hard enough to change most of the minds of the other side, and of enough value that those minds could be changed. Tales of how a compelling majority of department members were eventually swayed to vote for a particular professor's hiring are common on university grapevines.

My hiring at Cornell, however, was not one of those stories: Instead, the minority fund allowed me to satisfy the preferences of a subset of the faculty particularly committed to the department embarking on different tracks of the sort my work represented. As it happened, a few months into the school year I found myself in the center of a civil war along the fault line between this subset and the rest of the department, which led to an acrimonious administrative cleavage. My support, it turned out, had been part of a gradual preparation for the founding of a break-off department of questionable philosophical foundation, viewed by most observers in the field as a mistake, and which has since been reincorporated into the Linguistics Department proper. Okay, the people in this subdepartment may have valued me highly; the judgment calls here are rich and subtle. But ultimately, who would you rather be: the professor hired because the heart of an elite department saw him as a natural addition to their ranks, or me, the professor hired because his color allowed him, out of many people qualified, to be hired as a sop to a dissatisfied contingent, preparing to use him as capital in a vitriolic secession? Which one of we two applicants today, as human beings, can take more pride in his accomplishment?

Berkeley's Linguistics Department then hired me on a permanent basis, in a joint appointment with the African-American Studies Department. I can definitely say that my hiring was based on merit rather than the Linguistics Department's desire to have a black face around (there already was one if African counts as "black"), and naturally no such factor played a role in my hiring by the African-American Studies Department. However, the fact remains that the department would have had no way of coming to know me and my work without my having gotten the postdoctoral appointment.

So there I was in one of the top positions in American linguistics, with the moderate teaching load, vast library facilities, ample extra funding opportunities, summers off, and societal prestige inherent to such a job, and in the gorgeous and culturally rich Bay Area to boot. Meanwhile, I watched my white equivalents having to spend at least a year and often more in temporary positions in locations they would not have chosen, getting jobs with more required teaching and fewer perks than mine, or sometimes never being lucky enough to find a job at all. Everyone I know in linguistics is polite enough to refrain from pointing this out, but the fact is that no matter how you slice it, affirmative action repeatedly saved me from coping with the rigors of the job market.

When I mention my discomfort with these sequences of events, whites always affectionately dismiss this with, "Well, John, your work is certainly the equal of everyone else's." But this is not the point. Regardless of the sincere good intentions behind Stanford's, Cornell's, and Berkeley's affirmative-action policies, the simple fact is that if I were white, I would probably not have my current job. Granted, if I were not "of Berkeley caliber" as it is often put on campus, I would not have gotten the postdoctoral fellowship, and definitely would not have been hired. But there are plenty of white linguists out there of "Berkeley caliber" teaching four English composition classes a day at community colleges. Affirmative action neatly shielded me from at any point being judged *solely* on the basis of my "caliber" until Berkeley hired me permanently—Stanford accepted me as a "diverse" person and funded me with minority set-asides; the Berkeley postdoctoral fellowship separated minorities from the general pool; Cornell hired me along with someone else since I could be paid with minority set-aside funds. And then, Berkeley would never have known I was available to be hired if it were not for the postdoctoral fellowship. As such, affirmative action has spread its tentacles throughout my entire career, dulling my personal responsibility for my achievements by mixing jolly boosts into my life path while everybody else's fate was determined by the usual combination of competence and the eternal caprices of fate.

The racial preference policies that got me my job gave me help I did not deserve, while doing nothing to help black people whose lives really had barred them from doing their best. The very institution and preservation of these set-aside programs shows that racism no longer plays any significant role in admissions, and given that it does not, these policies needlessly shield black scholars from the highest grades of competition. Despite their beneficial intention, in the end, these policies serve but one purpose: validating the white faculty and administrators who promulgated them in their lack of racial prejudice. Certainly their deliberate intention is to help; I intend no cynicism in making that charge. But what has been lost sight of is that one does not help, but harms, a race by exempting its members from ever knowing the concrete and unalloyed sense of accomplishment that comes from winning as a result of one's best personal efforts.

I am often congratulated on my career, but the sad fact is that as much as I enjoy my job in many ways, I will never get beyond the sense of diminishment in having gotten it to such an extent "through the back door." I got tenure after four and a half years instead of seven, having been rather obsessively productive and having become rather well-known in my specialty. Yet it was perfectly obvious that in the back of most minds was "Of course he got tenure—they wouldn't dare deny tenure to a black person unless he was hopeless," and they were quite right. Especially after Proposition 209, most Berkeley faculty and administrators are devoted passionately to maintaining "minority representation" in all ways possible. This sense of "diversity" under siege cannot help but have played some part in evaluating my tenure file. After Proposition 209, to require anything but basic competence and then some of an African-American professor to give them tenure? Hello? For most young professors, getting tenure is a signal achievement calling for champagne. For me, frankly, it meant a nice raise, because I could have gotten tenure with a lot less work than I did and everybody knows it.

As it happens, I am secure in the fact that in the end I am qualified for my job, although this is something I must generate internally, since my having obtained my position was due so much less to this than it would have been if I were white. At the very least, my department did not hire me in an explicit search for a black professor. And the sad and simple fact is that, as anyone who knows me will attest, I was born to do this job—I cannot imagine what else I would do. However, it will always dampen my sense of accomplishment that my color played as much of a part in my getting here as my abilities. Today, I deeply regret having applied for that minority postdoctoral fellowship, and I consider it my duty to work against tokenism infecting the life trajectories of future members of my race as it has mine.

I am fully aware that my sentiments do not represent those of most black "beneficiaries" of affirmative action. Most middle-class black people with experiences similar to mine say that they are content simply knowing that they are competent and do not care what others may think, and perhaps consider their having been given boosts despite not having suffered significant obstacles as appropriate given their membership in a historically oppressed race. However, I submit that this ready acceptance of unnecessary head starts and lack of concern with how one, and one's race, is viewed as a result stem from the culture's ambivalence toward the scholarly, which we have seen even manifests itself in black academics. The issue is not an overt or complete rejection of the world of the book, but a conspicuously lesser weighting of one's competence in this arena as the measure of the (hu)man.

This becomes clear if we imagine how most black people would feel if it were decreed that affirmative action be instituted in realms in which blacks have traditionally excelled. If major-league basketball managers were directed to set aside spots not only for the best players in the country but also for those just short of this mark, or if the most prestigious jazz clubs were required to book not only black musical geniuses but also those a notch or two below them, black basketball players and jazz musicians, with all due compassion for the early life conditions of the runners-up in question, would feel justly insulted, with Jesse Jackson and the NAACP duly decrying the underestimation inherent to such a policy. Of course, this would be because black America has always so regularly produced a representative number of stars in these areas, such that black people are not seen to "need" affirmative action there.

As we have seen, most think that black America does not contribute a representative share of stars when it comes to school because black students are prevented by societal conditions from doing their best. This idea has an air of plausibility when it comes to poor or working-class black students, although I believe it to be mistaken. For example, while one might justifiably suppose that humble circumstances would hinder athletic ability less than scholastic, musical virtuosity requires the same concentration, practice, and attention to detail that schoolwork does, and yet jazz players have regularly come up from the slums (Louis Armstrong grew up in a violent ghetto quarter rife with substance abuse and illegitimacy, and was hardly unusual in this regard among his colleagues). However, for thoroughly middle-class black people who went to solid schools and do not even consider themselves to have suffered any appreciable racism, to feel no condescension in being boosted up academic ladders via set-asides demonstrates vestiges of a sense of the scholarly as a fundamentally separate realm. Most black people basically do not particularly mind being given set-asides in academia whether they needed them or not, because since the scholarly realm is processed as an area more visited than lived in, hitting the very highest note, and it being clear that one did, is considered less important than having made a decent showing.

As for me, after I submit this manuscript to my publisher, I have decided to take singing lessons and build a new wing onto my life as an opera singer. I have made this decision because the world of opera is one where the color of my skin will have no effect upon how I am judged, sink or swim, and I cannot bear the prospect of my entire life's accomplishments on this earth having been polluted with boosts premised upon the notion that I am fundamentally incapable of competition under any but ideal circumstances.

## Revisiting Lyndon Johnson

We have arrived at a point where closing the black-white gap will only be possible by allowing black students to spread their wings and compete with their peers of other races. Trying to accomplish this by letting them in under the bar and reconditioning them in college gives the appearance of being an alternate solution, but thirty years of programs of this kind have shown us conclusively that this will not solve the problem— because the lag persists. As Christopher Jencks has noted:

> By the time students apply to college, their minds have developed in particular ways: some neural paths have grown strong and others have atrophied. The mental differences among seventeen-year-olds do not completely determine their future, but neither are they easy to change. Those who have not yet heard any English can still learn to speak the language, but they will almost always speak with an accent, and some will never become fully fluent.

There are certainly strategies to be adopted other than repealing affirmative-action admissions policies. However, these strategies cannot be based upon the misconception that white racism, in its various manifestations, is the main problem to be addressed. To focus upon the fact that minorities are underrepresented in top-quality secondary schools, that some white teachers may be less likely to give top grades to black students, that black students may suffer from lack of confidence based on racist stereotypes, or on vestigial societal racism, are less proposals for solutions than capitulations, implying that black students simply cannot do their best until the elimination of broad sociological problems unlikely to disappear anytime soon. This would be an acceptable surrender if these problems were truly significant barriers to achievement, but since other students regularly surmount them, we must get out of the understandable habit of looking first to these things—on the pain of casting black people as innately weak and unintelligent.

Our interest, then, must be in helping black students to shed the true shackles of the Cultural Disconnect: a culture-internal wariness of school. In this vein, secondary schools would be well-advised to urge black children to form study groups, as these have been shown to raise minority students' performance via combining strengths, most importantly working against the sense that school is "not black" by immersing black students in situations of extended face-to-face interaction with fellow black students in activities devoted to classwork, with the inherent incentive lent by mutual dependence. Minority students ought also to be given standardized tests on a regular basis in all schools; even in a school with less-than-optimum resources, this alone will raise students' test scores given that one tends to perform better on such tests by learning their quirks as early as possible.

There are also strategies for encouraging "diversity" without reinforcing black students' sense of separation from school. Top universities ought to make some room for top-performing students from high schools that offer few or no advanced placement courses. This does involve taking a chance—as is readily acknowledged when only white and Asian students are in question, advanced placement courses are important in preparing a student for college-level work, and for every student without them who adjusts well in college, there will be another who suffers a permanent handicap. Yet in the interests of addressing the societal inequity of school quality, it is eminently defensible to take this chance, given that blacks are indeed disproportionately represented in such schools. However, although this will inherently increase minority representation, it must be a race-blind policy in itself. The variation some have urged in California—admitting all minority candidates who have done well in such schools but only some of other ethnicities—would return us to a situation where minority students were regularly admitted under lowered bars simply by virtue of the color of their skin rather than their individual circumstances or abilities. To imply that white students from such schools ought to be submitted to quality rankings while black students must not be would bring us back to reinforcing the idea among both blacks and whites that top-level effort is superhuman for the black student, and implying that black people have been so profoundly broken by their history that modern policy must treat them as eternal cripples.

Along these same lines, some universities also maintain a bias toward top-level high schools in their admissions policies; it would be in the interests of those committed to "diversity" to lessen, if not eliminate, this bias.

Berkeley has instituted the Berkeley Pledge, dedicated to helping minority students in secondary schools prepare for admission to college; other University of California schools have instituted similar programs. These efforts are aimed primarily at heavily minority schools in poorer areas. Predictably, Berkeley administrators are given to supposing that these students essentially embody "minority," but in fact such students are but a fraction of the minority students who apply to schools at Berkeley's level. Nevertheless, any effort that prepares black students to compete, rather than be let in the back door, is laudable because it helps to solve the problem at hand, and other states would benefit from instituting similar outreach policies.

However, none of these things will be as important as the crucial element of the incentive to do one's best, which is impossible in a situation in which there is any way to reach the top other than via one's best efforts. Moreover, maintaining permanently lowered standards at the end of the road will only subvert the intention of all of these bottom-up efforts.

In *The Bell Curve*, Charles Murray and Richard Herrnstein told us that we should eliminate affirmative action because black people are simply too dumb to do any better. This, however, will not do: My reason for opposing affirmative action in higher education is proactive. Namely, we must eliminate this obsolete program not for abstruse philosophical reasons, not because it can be rather laboriously interpreted as discrimination, but for a single, concrete reason: *It is obstructing African Americans from showing us that they are as capable as all other people.* The black-white scholastic gap will close, rather than simply sit unchanging, when top performance is required of black students. Under affirmative action, it quite simply is not, regardless of well-meaning but obstructive distractions such as appealing to the benefits of "diversity."

Many suppose that it is unrealistic to expect black children to perform at whites' and Asians' level. However, we must ask why we have come to consider it so otherworldly to expect a black child to do some eighth-grade math, draw some vocabulary analogies, solve a few logic problems in a set amount of time, and yes, do all of these things well. We must also ask why, to the extent that many of us can even begin to conceive of this, we imagine that it could only be under utopian conditions in which all teachers are utterly devoid of even the subtlest racial bias and all schools are awash in funding and equipment. What are we saying about black children to assume with such confidence that they are incapable of doing what poor Asians, and even Haitians and Jamaicans and Ethiopians are doing right alongside them every day?

I have faith in black American students. This is because I have seen nothing whatsoever in my life suggesting that black students are cognitively incapable of performing as well as anyone else in school, while, on the contrary, I have seen quite conclusively, year after year since I was four years old, that the linchpin of this problem is a cultural sense of separation from school that set-asides can only nurture, and that only concrete incentive can begin to undo.

Affirmative-action advocates are fond of quoting Lyndon Johnson's observation "You do not take a person who, for years, has been hobbled by chains and liberate him, bring him up to the starting line in a race and then say, 'you are free to compete with all the others,' and still justly believe that you have been completely fair." True. But thirty-five years have passed, and America has changed profoundly in ways that would shock Johnson if he were alive to see it. As such, today we must ask when you stop giving this runner a head start.

That time is now. When the person has become nicely muscled and acquits themselves quite nicely, then even if they are not yet at the highest level of musculature as the other runners, we are inclined to stop giving them that head start. After all, if the head start is eternal:

What possible way is there for the runner to finally achieve the capability of the other runners other than having to run the race without a head start?

Why should they try their best anyway?

How would we even know that they had? No matter how fast they run or how big they get, they will always have had that head start to dilute their achievement.

How compelling would we find it to have the runner say that the only way they will feel "welcome" in the race is to be given a head start forever?

If the runner is still not as confident as many of the runners, is giving them the head start forever the way to assuage this?

And finally, we all know in our heart of hearts that we will never feel that this runner is the equal of the other runners—or even the equal of the *lesser* runners—until they can make a showing without a head start.

## Onward and Upward

In the end, the most important thing for America as a whole to realize about the grip of Victimology, Separatism, and Anti-intellectualism upon today's black Americans is that whites cannot solve this problem in any other way but allowing black people the dignity of true competition. Whites have tried for almost forty years to assuage Victimology with their most altruistic efforts, only to see cries of "racism" remain at the same shrieking level. When whites try to bridge the separation between the races by adopting aspects of black culture, they are accused of co-optation; when they try to introduce their culture to blacks they are accused of cultural imperialism. Whites have tried to bring blacks into the academic arena with permanently lowered admissions standards, only to see black scholarly performance freeze at a substandard level, while black college students occupy administrators' offices crying "racism" at the very schools that admitted them with scores that would have barred any white student from admission.

### A Different World from the One You Come From

Indeed, as I and many others have noted, some of the resistance among many black Americans toward reaching the finish line stems from an underlying fear of becoming "white," black American cultural identity disappearing altogether with white people the ultimate victors. Of course, the fact is that if black culture did disappear altogether, one concomitant would be that whites and blacks would interbreed to an extent that the default American would be café-au-lait, not Beaver Cleaver pink. Nor would this be a mere matter of pigment—in the process, whites would incorporate a great deal of black culture. As Jim Sleeper notes, already Europeans are known to observe that white Americans walk and talk "black," and this is true. Of course, talk like that raises hackles in some black quarters as being about white cooptation and black cultural dilution. If you ask me, one man's cooptation or dilution is another man's cultural hybridization, and under any name, it is as inevitable as it is marvelous. For those who feel otherwise, though, I can only venture that the coffee-brown ideal that writers like Stanley Crouch sing of is one that strikes me as something so far in the future as to be more a matter of science fiction than sociology. For our purposes in this moment, despite the fact that we have already traveled a long way in coming together, racial differences are with us to stay. In that vein, it is important for us to realize that African-American culture can maintain a core distinctiveness without the three currents I have addressed.

One of the sweetest television pleasures I have ever experienced was the late, great series *A Different World.* I sat mesmerized through every single episode of this show chronicling the adventures of black students of all walks of life at the fictional all-black college Hillman, because here was depicted the black America of my dreams. Week after week, this marvelous little show kept alive my faith that there can and will be a black America alive with the music of black dialect, a compassionate sense of responsibility for the less fortunate, a spontaneous connection to music and dance, regular commemoration of the struggles and victories of the past, an electric sense of humor, and even a guest appearance by Jesse Jackson, yet combined with a dedication to personal advancement, a disinclination to fixate upon victimhood, an openness to cultural fusion, and a sense of school as an inextricable part of an American life. There is not a logical reason in the world why this could not be black America. We need only take a deep breath and re-examine what we have been conditioned to accept as political, intellectual, and cultural leadership, and allow ourselves to be granted the treasure of self-realization.

## Last Words

In this book I have done nothing less than call it as I see it. I'm not in anybody's pocket, and yes, both of my parents were African American. Yet I am quite aware that the response many black people will have to this book is that I am taking the line of the "other side," joining the whites who are "against us." Using the minor hellfire I endured during the Oakland Ebonics controversy as a guide, many will attack my book as "wrong" without seeing the need to actually address my arguments. The few who engage anything specific about what I wrote will refer only to excerpted passages stripped of their context. I will be told that I must think that I'm "too good" for black people; that expressing such opinions is a misuse of my authority as a college professor; that I am taking the white man's side just to make a buck. I will be accused of not being a Christian, and in general the party line will be that my book displays "no love for black people."

These people cannot help this. The stranglehold of Victimology, Separatism, and Anti-intellectualism upon the black community—and the illusion many whites labor under that this is healthy—will keep many from being able see my book in any other way, for reasons I have shown throughout these pages.

But here in real life it has become increasingly clear to me that I am not alone among black people in seeing the fallacy in the orthodoxy that the black American is eternally mired in a system set against them at every turn. An increasing number of black people are questioning the cognitive dissonance between the vast potential of their lives as post–Civil Rights Movement black Americans and the insistence of so many blacks around them that America remains a racist purgatory in which all black effort is a Sisyphean affair that renders even just keeping one's head above water a victory. There is a tendency in the black community, arising from the human quest for cultural fellowship, to classify people of the latter view as expressing "an alternate viewpoint," or even as "cool." The problem here is that these people are nothing less than an obstacle to the race's progress forward, from the dankest inner city to the poshest boardrooms. In closing, I ask those black Americans who find themselves unable to identify with the self-indulgent theatrics now forced upon us by whites and blacks alike to come out of hiding and start speaking up for real progress.

All of our lives we have seen the best and brightest black Americans, those we are told to emulate as role models, nimbly framing every aspect of American life as veiled racism, telling us that because of this vastly exaggerated scourge black Americans are exempt from criticism for even the most heinous of conduct, and that the good black person only uses school for financial gain or to acquire the credentials to chronicle how racist America was, is, and will be. But this is not the way it has to be. It only looks that way because it is all we have ever seen.

I know—believe me, I know!—that it is not easy to face the incredulous rage that speaking up for the truth arouses in so many of our fellow black Americans. Furthermore, I maintain that we have reached this state of affairs as an unintended result of the Civil Rights Act, which gave a demoralized group the keys to success by fiat rather than through the slow and agonizing avenue of working within the society, gradually eroding stereotypes and social barriers as Jews and the Irish did. We must have compassion for the black Americans who have unwittingly been disabled by this strange by-product of a good thing. However, our compassion must not let us allow this sociological excrescence to continue to condemn this race to eternal second-class status.

If we have true pride, we realize that we deserve better than this. When we hear the next black person say that blacks earn 61 percent of what whites do with the implication that the black manager pulling $60,000 a year regularly works next door to a white manager making $100,000, or that most black people live in the ghetto or might as well, or that most black people are being "pushed down the economic ladder," or that the Ancient Greeks stole their civilization from a "black" Egypt, or that black students cannot be expected to turn in top grades unless their parents subscribe to magazines, take this person no more seriously than you would someone who told you that the world was going to end tomorrow. That is, with politeness (because he can't help it), pity (because he is his own worst enemy), and private dismissal (because his message is a fiction with no relevance to our leading productive lives).

While not falling prey to the equally treacherous fiction that we have completely overcome, we must not be tempted by the seductions of underdoggism into turning a blind eye to how very close we are to the mountaintop. It is because this progress is so gloriously obvious that there are more and more black people out there with true pride. Not the manufactured pride of a strangely meaningless slogan like Black By Popular Demand; not a pride based on a mythical relationship to an Africa that never existed and that none of us would any longer even recognize as home—but a pride based on our personal achievements right here in our real home, these United States of America.

Inevitably and repeatedly, you will be told that to be truly proud—that is, to refuse to settle for wasting the brief time you are given on this earth playing victim and indulging in the half-assed logic that it requires—is to be "not one of us" or, more to the point, "white." Nothing could better point up that your accuser, driven by currents of history into mistaking an inferiority complex for nobility, lacks true pride herself. You are not "white" to be too proud to settle for this; you are human. Don't let such people's misinformed fury, sad and frightening as it is, mislead you into thinking otherwise.

Let Derrick Bell tell his "stories," but let's not join him at the Bottom of the Well. Pity Ralph Wiley walking down the street slapping at the "fire on his skin," but by no means let him convince you that this is what the rest of us Black People Should Do Now. As proud people, let's stop sitting silent as we are told that the Real Black Person wallows in defeat. Let's stop sitting silent as we are told that the Real Black Person doesn't like the people who will always surround us in the only country that is our home, and today usually mean us no harm. Let's stop sitting silent as we are told that the Real Black Person does not make better than a B+

average and does not dare crack 1000 on the SAT. Let's stop this run-away bus, this tripped-off car alarm, this eternal Passion Play, this self-defeating holding pattern miseducating generation after generation of black Americans into self-doubt and parochialism even when growing up in conditions that would be the envy of most people on earth.

More and more of us are realizing that the enshrinement of victim-hood as an identity and a focus upon tribalism over hybridicity has fallen out of step with our historical moment and become an obstacle to progress, and more and more of us are saying this out loud. There will remain those who can only see us as "sell-outs," but as barriers to black achievement continue to fall away by the month, we're going to keep coming, more every year, and I do not mean only a few black academics, but black people from all walks of life. The national dialogue is begin-ning to change already; indeed, I would not have written this book if I did not feel that I was part of a growing race-wide sentiment. To those black Americans out there who are tired of being told that to be black one must be a provincial, anti-intellectual underdog, I beseech you all to join in reviving the Struggle and getting back to making our way up the last few steps to the mountaintop. Don't be afraid. The ones calling the tune today will be curiosities in the history books tomorrow. We are the future. It's time for *us* to STAND UP!!!

# AFTERWORD

"What has the public response been to your book?" I'm always asked. Well, the verdict is in. The black intelligentsia and assorted comrades-in-arms have dutifully condemned my book and myself almost to a man. Every single criticism I predicted under "Last Words" near the end of the text has been leveled, most of them more than once.

But in truth, the black intelligentsia constitute only a fraction of the black reading public, and the merest sliver of the American reading public in general. Overall, the response to *Losing the Race* has been over-whelmingly positive—and no, not just from whites. I have received about fifty letters and e-mails per week since August 2000 about this little book, split about fifty-fifty between blacks and whites. All but a handful of the responses from whites have been positive, but more significantly, the black hate mails are but a trickle amid hundreds of responses from black Americans who are glad I wrote the book and wish me well.

I write this not to pat myself on the back; my sincere response to all of the well-wishes is a grateful but rather bemused sense that I am truly not worthy of it in the end. I am also fully aware that the reason I do not get more hate mail from blacks is because most readers of that sentiment consider me too beneath contempt to be worth writing to. However, what the positive responses from blacks show is that, even more than I realized when I wrote the book, there is a growing African-American movement against the enshrinement of victimhood as a cornerstone of what it means to be "black" in the United States. Many of my black critics predicate their responses upon an assumption that their assessment represents "*the* black response" to thoughts such as mine (most memorably, the black bookstore who began telling interested callers that the book was not worth buying and that this reflected "the opinion of the community"). But times have changed—all signs indicate that in 2100, the victimologist perspective on "blackness" in America is going to appear as quizzically counterproductive as the military follies of the Hundred Years' War do to us today. As I explain in the book, many of the assumptions about "black" and "white" that we take for granted are not destiny or truth, but the results of certain sociohistorical events of thirty-five years ago. And time is passing.

For this edition, I thought it might be useful to clarify some common misconceptions that *Losing the Race* appears to have raised, most of them certainly mea culpa.

## Losing the Race *Is Not Intended as a Criticism of Black Leadership*

My overriding goal in writing this book was to explain to white and black readers alike just why the black positions and ideologies we hear from most appear so disconnected from modern reality—and even irritating. My aim was not simply to lambaste the culture of victimology among blacks but to show that its ultimate origin is one which its victims cannot help. Centuries of slavery and segregation understandably fostered a group battered by low self-esteem, therefore seeking validation in reflexive and even fantastical indictments of the former oppressor.

Many readers, especially white conservatives, have read my book as one more decrying of black leaders as "poverty pimps" who purvey a sense of victimization upon blacks in a quest to keep them in their thrall. Certainly, "there's some of that"—Al Sharpton is a paradigm example, and it is becoming ever clearer in the increasingly callow theatrics of Jesse Jackson. However, it must be clear that I consider this a fringe phenomenon. It is not accidental that only very occasionally in *Losing the Race* do I attribute problems to black leaders misleading the black masses.

Victimology is in its essence not a political ploy, given that it is wielded just as fiercely by people with no interest in power or patronage. In most of its sufferers, the obsession with victimhood—and savage dismissal of blacks who point out the cracks in the plaster—is a direct response to the same insecurity about being black that led little black girls to choose white dolls over black ones. Seeing oneself as a perpetual underdog gives a sense of balm and healing to someone privately haunted by a sense of inferiority. I apparently did not stress this carefully enough in Chapter 1: *I believe that victimology would be just as prevalent among blacks even if operators like Sharpton and Jackson had never come on the scene.* The leaders merely take advantage of what was already there.

One need only read some of the negative reviews of *Losing the Race* from blacks on Amazon.com to see eloquently demonstrated how deeply victimology is felt regardless of patronage issues. These people are not putting on a show—they are sincerely disgusted at what they perceive as a black person denying a present-day Holocaust. To most of us, these reviews seem cruel and almost deliberately unreasoning. But while people of this kind of opinion test my patience at times, they ultimately do not deserve this reaction. Their responses are sad but predictable results of the very victimologist "virus" I describe in the book. Our job is less to work against the Al Sharptons, most of whom are losing sway in their fiefdoms as the futility of their message becomes painfully clear to increasing numbers of blacks, but to address the enshrinement of victimhood as a general ideological imperative.

## The Backbone of Losing the Race Is Not Its Anecdotes

Some critics have charged that Losing the Race is "anecdotal." In fact, I use anecdotes only to illustrate or bolster points defended with actual data and reportage. Not a single significant point in the book is based solely on "what I've seen."

Interestingly, this is not true of a great many books written by black thinkers of the victimologist camp, many of whom make no pretense of basing their books on anything but personal anecdote and impression. Ralph Wiley and bell hooks's work are typical examples. Here, the anecdotes are considered urgent and welcome—the black intelligentsia regularly lauds books of this sort as "vivid memoirs" and the like. Obviously, then, the problem with Losing the Race is not the anecdotes in themselves: what disturbs some readers is that I tell many stories that these critics would rather not hear.

Specifically, many feel that these anecdotes are not representative of the black experience, while others, allowing that the stories do represent common phenomena, complain that these stories neglect the good side of things which they feel ought be given equal weight in any discussion of black Americans.

Although I repeatedly note in the book, for example, that all blacks are certainly not going about incensed about the white man, or that there are a great many excellent African-American students in the United States, my thesis is that certain regrettable trends are indeed dominant in black thought. Of course the anecdotes I chose paint a negative overall picture; my point is that this negative picture is sadly accurate.

## Losing the Race *Does Not Claim*
## *That There Is No Racism in the United States*

A typical attack on *Losing the Race* asserts that I have claimed that there is "no" racism in the United States. This is not what I believe, as I attempt to make clear in Chapter 3 by recounting the racism I have encountered and seen in my own life. My claims are rather that 1) racism is quickly receding, and 2) to the extent that it still exists today, it is no longer a significant obstacle to black advancement or well-being.

Since the mid-1960s, black Americans have been encouraged to operate according to a tacit assumption that until all racism has disappeared, black success is too difficult to expect from anyone but the gifted or lucky. This, however, contradicts the experience of untold numbers of oppressed groups throughout world history who have achieved *despite* racism. Unlike some conservatives, I firmly support the societal assistance that blacks received from the Civil Rights Act and Affirmative Action (although I maintain that the latter should have been discontinued in education at least fifteen years ago). However, especially with these supports granted, it is simply unempirical to suppose that black achievement is decisively hobbled until there is not a drop of racism in any white person's heart, until every television show's cast is 13 percent black, and until every police officer in the country is a candidate for sainthood. The African-American who feels that racism is at all times "what we really need to be talking about" reveals themselves to have been taken in by the Zeitgeist that has reigned in black American thought over the past thirty-five years. What we really need to be talking about is teaching underclass blacks how to open small businesses and gradually purchase their communities.

The contrast between how racism was processed by black thinkers in the pre–Civil Rights era versus today is neatly encapsulated by a historical event covered in the media since I wrote the book. Early in the previous century, black Tulsans—just decades removed from slavery—had founded their own thriving business quarter, where blacks, barred from the mainstream except as menials, re-created and enjoyed all of the resources and luxuries available to whites. In the early 1920s, in response to a false rumor that a black man had accosted a white woman, whites burned the quarter to the ground and killed hundreds of blacks.

Today in the black community, the Tulsa story has been treated as a call to remember that whites could turn the hoses on us again at any time. Yet the Tulsa story contains a much more important and useful message: if black people could create a business quarter like that in an era of racism so naked that lynchings were ordinary and most whites were hostilely closed to anything but passing social contact with black people, then this shows that today, black people could certainly build self-sustaining communities of their own along the same lines. (Yes, one bank might be subtly disinclined to give blacks small business loans. But other banks will not be, and surely some bank will grant the loan—all it takes is one. How many white banks of any kind were granting black Tulsans loans?)

That the Tulsa story is processed as a "watch out" story rather than a "here's how" story is not accidental. We divert our primary energies to affirming the obvious—that racism still exists—rather than teaching the black underclass how to take over their communities.

### Anti-intellectualism versus Valuing Education

My book naturally elicits the sharpest ire for my argument that anti intellectualism has become entrenched as a decisive facet of "black identity." Many readers have read this as a claim that black Americans simply do not value education itself.

Yet as I stress in the book, in the overt sense, blacks value education quite highly. The outright devaluation of a college degree is about equally distributed among blacks and whites. I will never forget when I was about ten hearing a working-class white cashier scornfully asserting "I didn't want college." Faculty brat that I was, this was the first time that I had heard anyone openly deride going beyond high school.

The problem arises once black students are *in* school. There remains no more urgent testimony to this than the widespread problems in school performance among black students even in middle-class school districts. In *Losing the Race*, I described this phenomenon in Shaker Heights, Ohio, but since then, similar phenomena have been reported in several other school districts such as Nyack, New York, and Prince George's County, Maryland. Our problem is not that black parents do not send their children to school; it is that once they are there, too often their performance is depressed by a charge leveled by their peers that doing well is "selling out." As I say in the book, there are plenty of black students who try their hardest in school. But the reason so few of them perform at the highest level is that this sense of school as an "add-on" rather than a "mix-in" hinders them from developing the particular necessary skills to the extent that other students do. This problem continues to express itself throughout college and postgraduate programs, and I believe it is the primary factor creating the increasingly discussed black-white gap not only in test scores but in grades.

One may disagree with this thesis—but tallies of how many black young people are attending or graduating from college, or observations that black parents tend to be in favor of school vouchers, do not constitute logical refutations. Not only do I not deny these facts, but they are irrelevant to the issue.

## Anti-intellectualism Is Not Restricted to Black Americans but Is a More Pervasive Problem Among Us

I am often reminded that anti-intellectualism is hardly restricted to black people, and I heartily agree. My life has offered me generous exposure to rampant anti-intellectualism among whites, and I am quite aware that the charge has been leveled at American culture as a whole, most memorably by Richard Hofstadter. Rutgers University of the mid-1980s, where I earned by B.A., was dominated by whites of a provenance roughly depicted in the television gem *Married with Children*, many the first generation in their family to go to college, and most more concerned with partying and mating than learning. Seemingly every second undergraduate was majoring in economics, a subject they had no interest in except as a conduit to a lucrative job. Anti-intellectualism has also been documented among white Appalachians, some working-class British communities, etc.

Yet I maintain that the anti-intellectual mind-set plays its hand more prominently among blacks as a whole. If I wrote the book again, I might term "The Cult of Anti-Intellectualism" the "Cultural Disconnect" from learning for its own sake, as this more accurately parses the nature of the problem and sounds less like a condemnation. My interest is in why even thoroughly middle-class black students lag behind in school at all levels. Given that the usual explanations adduced for this do not, in my opinion, withstand scrutiny, I argue carefully in *Losing the Race* that the culprit is a culturally determined sense of distance from the scholarly endeavor. This sense of distance is precisely what I have perhaps unfelicitously termed "anti-intellectualism."

My framing of anti-intellectualism as a black *cultural* (rather than occasional or class-based) trait is also based on what I have seen in black academia. Specifically, in black culture, anti-intellectualism is not infrequent even among the caste assigned to be the standard bearers of the highest level of thought in the race. This is hardly a matter of stupidity but yet another outgrowth of "victimology." In literary studies and the social sciences, black academic work tends strongly to be based on "doing the right thing," which translates as celebrating blackness or defending black behavior. But since black Americans have always co-existed intimately with whites, to parse a black cultural or historical phenomenon almost always requires paying as assiduous attention to "general" as "black" data. However, the Separatist imperative tends to render "general" data uninteresting or irrelevant, and if that data by chance interferes with the sociopolitical argument one desires, then too often this data is actively dismissed. I attempt to illustrate this in the chapter about my experiences during the Ebonics controversy, bolstered by observations about "Afrocentric history"; Randall Kennedy has noted a similar problem in legal studies. Whatever the moral good of the intentions of work of this kind, the result is an acceptance of substandard argumentation, and thus, a fundamentally anti-intellectual approach.

Of course, in the larger sense, this is an outgrowth of the infection of academia as a whole by leftist ideology, so pervasively at this point that many leftist academics are sincerely unaware that their claims are anything but logic and morality incarnate. Certainly the work of legions of white leftist academics is equally blind to the full range of data relevant to the area addressed. This confusion of ideology with truth affects the body of black academic work in the humanities and social sciences so pervasively, however, because the victimologist position is itself fundamentally leftist, although again, very few black academics would actively and consciously parse themselves as such.

### Immigrants' "Self-Selection" Does Not Render Their Children's School Performance Irrelevant to a Discussion About African-Americans

Many respondents have also said that to compare black Americans' school performance with that of the children of immigrants is inappropriate because immigrants' initiative in relocating to the United States makes it natural that they would inculcate their children with a commitment to educational achievement.

In fact, the equation between the initiative to emigrate and scholarly achievement is a false one. What demonstrates this are Latinos: here are immigrants to America whose children are second only to blacks in lagging grades and test scores—and just as with blacks, this problem continues even in the middle class, among students who speak English natively. These students' parents certainly possessed the initiative to emigrate—and yet a problem similar to that of black American students prevails nevertheless. Here, few would disagree that culture is the decisive factor: a sense among many Latinos, reinforced by the Civil Rights movement ideology, that school and other mainstream institutions are the "gringo's" game. Latino students who excel report being teased by their Latino peers for "acting white" just as their black equivalents do.

What this shows, then, is that culture is a powerful determining factor in school performance, which can even trump immigrant initiative. My claim is simply that culture is the determining factor with black students as well.

## The Cult of Anti-intellectualism Is Largely an Outgrowth of the Mid-1960s

Many black readers have resented my charge of anti-intellectualism against a people who, after all, were enslaved and denied access to education for centuries. My point, which I did not emphasize sufficiently in *Losing the Race*, is that this problem became particularly serious in the mid-1960s, as a natural outgrowth of the particular circumstances of that era.

Before then, all indications are that after Emancipation, blacks were as hungry for education as any American group: anti-intellectualism was largely a class issue just as it has been in the white community.

It appears to have been precisely around 1966 that black children began teasing black peers who embraced school with taunts of "acting white." Since the publication of *Losing the Race*, I have received well over a hundred unsolicited testimonials from black Americans who report having either suffered teasing of this kind or seen it happen, as well as about one hundred similarly unsolicited reports from black and white teachers who have observed the phenomenon. With only one exception (and that one slightly ambiguous), all of these incidents occurred in the late 1960s or afterward. Blacks who came of age before this report that they were teased just for being a nerd, as American children of all colors have always been, but not for "acting white" (similarly, in the late 1940s in Atlanta, my mother was teased by black children for being "a walking encyclopedia" but not for thinking she was white). One black man remembers being teased for being "smart" in the early 1960s, but then saw his younger siblings and cousins being teased for "acting white" in the late 1960s. Obviously, these letters and e-mails hardly constitute a scientifically authoritative record; however, the volume and consistency of these testimonials is highly indicative.

By no means, then, are "the souls of black folk" inherently anti-intellectual. Our problem is one specific to our era, a counterproductive outgrowth of an attempt at self-definition in an era when white malevolence was clearer and more present.

### The Black-White Performance Gap Is Not a Myth Once We Adjust for Class, Income, and School Funding

After reading almost one hundred letters and messages from concerned teachers of middle school through college, as many black as white, describing how black students are often held back from excelling in school by the "acting white" charge or how black students lag behind in their classes regardless of background, it becomes utterly impossible to imagine that Jonathan Kozol's "savage inequalities" are anything approaching a complete, or even primary, explanation for the problem we face.

Again and again, one reads of black boys, in particular, telling guidance counselors that they simply cannot do well in school because they "don't know how my friends would treat me." Contrary to what some might suppose, it is extremely difficult to glean any evidence from these descriptions that the white teachers are closet racists, or that the black ones have "turned against their own kind." All of these teachers are sincerely concerned yet frustrated people reporting on a very real phenomenon that has distressed them for years. And almost none of the teachers I have heard from teach in poor neighborhoods.

Again, I make no claim that the correspondence I have received carries the weight of an academic survey. However, if I had one hundred letters attesting to the pervasiveness of racism in all black lives, a great many people black and white would warmly accept these documents as "vivid confirmation" of same. In this light, I consider these testimonials—and the dozens that keep coming—useful evidence, bolstering that which I brought to bear in this book.

### The Difference in the Black Students I Have Seen Has Not Been an Artifact of My Own Bias and Low Expectations

Some black college professors have angrily asserted that they have never seen evidence of a sense of distance from the scholarly endeavor in their black students. I fully acknowledge the validity of what they have experienced, and yet these reports contrast sharply with the testimonials to the contrary I have received from teachers as well as various adults' recountings of their experiences as students.

In most cases, it is clear that the dissenters teach "black" subjects. The overriding aim of most college courses along the lines of "Race and the Media" or "Black Feminist Literature" is to reinforce students' sense of victimhood, as a sincerely intended brand of "education." Topics such as these are, in themselves, urgent ones which I have no objection to in theory. But if the professor's main imperative—even if not explicitly stated—is to instruct students in the history and covert persistence of racism in American life, then it is not surprising that black students are "connected" and committed in such classes in a way that they may not be in other classes. The contours of post–Civil Rights black American culture combine with the insecurity inherent in being a young human being to ensure this.

## Affirmative Action Does Not Cause the "Cultural Disconnect" but Nurtures It

From my argument that Affirmative Action in education has outlived its usefulness, I have apparently given the impression that I consider Affirmative Action to be the *cause* of the "cultural disconnect." On the contrary, Affirmative Action is an "enabler" of the problem. When history has hindered a group from top performance by conditioning a sense that school is a hoop one jumps through for "whitey" (except when utilized for earning power or to celebrate identity or cry for one's people), then a policy requiring only "pretty darned good" performance from any black person regardless of their circumstances hinders the dissolution of the performance lag in question. In other words, if we are to solve the problem, and we all agree that the dominant theme in the solution is to be "high standards," then a set-aside policy, regardless of its good intentions, is in the brute logical sense antithetical to our goals. Incentive is key to top performance in any endeavor—this is a fact well known to psychologists and economists. My argument is simply that there is no logical basis for supposing that this truth is somehow suspendable when it comes to black students in school, black students being human, something which no amount of historic racism, or even present remnants of it, can belie.

## The "Black Conservative" Stereotype

In the consciousness of the black wing of what Gore Vidal has called "the chattering classes," there is a bogeyman figure, the "black conservative" who criticizes the black race out of desire to make money and be on TV, the media presumably frothing at the mouth to fete him. I sense that I am supposed to refuse to dignify this charge with any acknowledgment, but I am not very good at that kind of thing, and thus will venture a response.

Indeed, *Losing the Race* has been quite widely covered. However, there are few things more bizarre than reading cries that "black conservatives" are *favored* by the media. For one, Derrick Bell, June Jordan, Cornel West, Patricia Williams, and Lani Guinier are hardly hurting for media coverage, as well as bookstore readings and speaking engagements.

More to the point, black conservatives encounter quite a bit of ill treatment from the mainstream media, of a sort Lani Guinier will never encounter. Larry Elder's *The Ten Things You Can't Say in America* has sold much better than this book and was on view in seemingly every bookstore in the country in the fall of 2000, right down to ones in airports and shopping malls. Yet there were almost no mainstream reviews of Elder's book, nor was he sought for television appearances. I have more than once had media representatives take up hours of my time with interviews only to not air them when my views proved to be too politically incorrect. This has included one black interviewer who cheerfully admitted after grilling me for an hour that she had hoped to "get" me. Having not been able to catch me short on a question, she never aired the interview, despite having spent large sums of a major network's money to bring a crew to Berkeley to tape the segment. The notion that "black conservatives" somehow have an easier ride waiting for them in the media than other black writers is a myth.

Then there is the opinion that it is somehow inappropriate for me and black writers who agree with me to be paid for our work or have it publicized. Yet those making this charge have no problem with people like Nathan McCall and June Jordan getting book advances, exposure, and speaking gigs (in their case much more lucrative than anything a Thomas Sowell gets). The idea that I am suddenly a "hustler" under the same conditions is based on a conviction—sincere, not just a put-on—that I spend my evenings poring entrancedly over my Ishmael Reed but then go out on the stump declaiming about "victimology" to line my pockets and point gleefully at myself sitting in a suit on *Politically Incorrect*.

I can only say that I most certainly fervently believe everything that I wrote, and wrote it to help foster understanding and change. Whenever I read one more writer earnestly dismissing me as some kind of self-hating opportunist, I always have to remind myself that it is actually me and my book the person is leveling this charge at. This cartoon figure is someone neither I nor any of my friends and family recognize in me.

The fact that so many intelligent and sensitive black American thinkers can in all seriousness espouse a scenario so psychologically counterintuitive when it comes to the careers of certain black authors is tragic testimony to how decisively the victimologist impulse has perverted too many fine minds in this country. The "black conservative" stock figure is nothing less than a stereotype, joining the several negative ones created by whites that we already labor under. To have such a stereotype lobbed at me hardly makes me question whether I should have written the book, but instead reminds why I wrote it.

Most important, a great many African-Americans agree with what I wrote—I am even beginning to suspect most of them do. The leftist convictions of the black intelligentsia are not representative of the race; it only appears that way because such people are disproportionately numerous in academia and are also almost always the people asked by the media to review black books. A great many African-Americans are increasingly aware that the Ishmael Reeds among us are more performers than activists, coming to town walking through the same tired old melodramatic period piece year after year, having long ago run out of anything to tell us that will create change or improve black American lives. The only thing holding black America back from more openly embracing truly progessive values is a contemporary variation on the "divided consciousness" that W. E. B. Du Bois wrote about.

Millions of black people in America are engaged in being the best that they can be and are fully aware that racism is at best a marginal affair in their lives. However, we are too often taught that we are not to say this outside the confines of all-black settings, that instead our public face must be one of victimhood. As one caller on a black radio show I appeared on said, "Man, these people don't disagree with you—they're just mad at you because you're saying it where white people can hear it." Right on—every single thing I write in this book is a fairly easy topic at a black barbecue; bring these things up and you are almost sure to have at least half the room agreeing and the two or three professional victimologists among the group coming away feeling on the defensive. The victimologist standpoint is particularly uncommon among blacks older than about sixty-five, who came of age before the ideological tide turned and have been perplexed ever since as to just what led us from Thurgood Marshall and Adam Clayton Powell, Jr., to Jesse Jackson and Al Sharpton. However, when asked about race issues when whites are present the next day, the same people who sounded a lot like Larry Elder or Shelby Steele the night before can often be seen to pause for a moment and then carefully dredge up episodes of possible racism they may have encountered in their lives, claim that there aren't enough positive images of blacks in the media, and give the same old support to the official verdict that racism still dominates American life, and is what "we really need to be talking about."

This "bilingual" perspective on what being black means today comes from a fear that white America ought be kept on its toes, that there is an ever present danger that we may slide back to the horrors of the past. I wrote *Losing the Race* because I sense that we have passed the point where we need fear this anymore, and that on the contrary, today we serve our interests best by being honest with ourselves as well as with mainstream America about the progress that has been made and the opportunities available to all of us. If I turn out to be wrong, I will be the first person to admit it openly—and promise to even donate to the N.A.A.C.P. all the money I "hustle" in doing so.

*Oakland, January, 2001*

# Notes

Abbreviated sources:

BB   William G. Bowen and Derek Bok, *The Shape of the River* (Princeton: Princeton University Press, 1998).

JP   Christopher Jencks and Meredith Phillips, eds., *The Black-White Test Score Gap* (Washington, D.C.: Brookings Institution Press, 1998).

P   John Perazzo, *The Myths That Divide Us* (Briarcliff Manor, NY: World Studies Books, 1998).

S   Fred Siegel, *The Future Once Happened Here* (New York: Free Press, 1997).

ST   Laurence Steinberg, *Beyond the Classroom* (New York: Touchstone, 1996).

T   Stephan Thernstrom and Abigail Thernstrom, *America in Black and White* (New York: Simon & Schuster, 1997).

## INTRODUCTION

*Niggardly* episode: e.g., "Race Mix-Up Raises Havoc for Capital," *New York Times*, January 29, 1999.

Perception that three in four blacks are poor inner-city residents: *Newsweek* poll, April 26, 1991, cited in T pp. 183–84.

One in five blacks live in inner city: U.S. Bureau of the Census, Current Population Reports, pp. 20–471, *The Black Population in the United States: March 1992* (Washington, D.C.: U.S. Government Printing Office, 1993), table 15, cited in T, p. 581.

## CHAPTER ONE: THE CULT OF VICTIMOLOGY

Marcus Garvey School incident: S, pp. 110–11.

Black America in 1960 versus 2000: BB, pp. 1–10, except:

New York City mayoral report, S, p. 26; proportion of blacks born in New York in 1964, S, p. 47.

A quarter of blacks are poor: U.S. Bureau of the Census, Current Population Reports, P, pp. 60–194, *Poverty in the United States: 1995* (Washington, D.C.: U.S. Government Printing Office, 1993), table C-3, cited in T, p. 233, cf. also Orlando Patterson, *The Ordeal of Integration* (Washington, D.C.: Civitas/Counterpoint, 1997), pp. 27–28.

Progress of black middle class: T, p. 196 (derived in part from U.S. Bureau of the Census, Current Population Reports, P, pp. 60–194, *Poverty in the United States: 1995* [Washington, D.C.: U.S. Government Printing Office, 1993], table 2).

Interracial marriage rates: Douglas J. Besharov and Timothy Sullivan, "One Flesh: America is Experiencing an Unprecedented Increase in Black-White Intermarriage," *New Democrat*, July–August 1996, p. 21, cited in T, p. 526, cf. also

Orlando Patterson, *The Ordeal of Integration* (Washington, D.C.: Civitas/Counterpoint, 1997), p. 195.

Decline of housing segregation, black attitudes toward: P, pp. 42–48.

Perception that three in four blacks are poor inner-city residents: *Newsweek* poll, April 26, 1991, cited in T, pp. 183–84.

One in five blacks live in inner city: U.S. Bureau of the Census, Current Population Reports, P, pp. 20–471, *The Black Population in the United States: March 1992* (Washington, D.C.: U.S. Government Printing Office, 1993), table 15, cited in T, p. 581.

Contribution of unwed mothers to child poverty statistic: Orlando Patterson, *The Ordeal of Integration* (Washington, D.C.: Civitas/Counterpoint, 1997), p. 29.

Black income compared to white: T, pp. 196–97, P, pp. 389–92.

Black church burnings: P, pp. 379–82.

Numbers of black men involved with justice system: Marc Mauer and Tracy Huling, *Young Black Americans and the Criminal Justice System: Five Years Later* (Washington, D.C.: The Sentencing Project, 1995), p. 1.

Black crime rates: *Sourcebook of Criminal Justice Statistics* (Washington, D.C.: Department of Justice, 1997), p. 384, table 4.10 (cited in P, p. 67).

Blacks on death row: P, p. 90, from *Sourcebook of Criminal Justice Statistics* (Washington, D.C.: Department of Justice, 1994), p. 90, and William Wilbanks, *The Myth of a Racist Criminal Justice System* (Monterey, CA: Brooks/Cole Publishing, 1987), p. 17.

The Congressional Black Caucus and crack laws: John DiLulio, Jr., "My Black Crime Problem, and Ours," *City Journal* (Spring 1996), p. 19, cited in P, p. 89.

Laxness of New York police force in 1970s and 1980s: S, pp. 188–89.

Port Authority drug search: "Police Say Drug-Program Files are not Biased," *New York Times*, April 26, 1990, cited in P, pp. 348.

Rise in New York crime rates after Diallo killing: "The Diallo Shooting: The Statistics," *New York Times*, March 29, 1999.

"I mean, you're a cop": Jeffrey Goldberg, "The Color of Suspicion," *The New York Times Magazine*, June 20, 1999, p. 55.

"The problem with black politicians is . . .": Ibid.

New Jersey highway stop statistics: e.g., "Whitman Says Troopers Used Racial Profiling," *New York Times*, April 21, 1999.

Police brutality and the racist whites blacks are likely to meet: Orlando Patterson, *The Ordeal of Integration* (Washington, D.C.: Civitas/Counterpoint, 1997), pp. 61–64.

Improvement in the LAPD: S, p. 161.

Adam Clayton Powell and the New York Police Department: Will Haygood, *King of the Cats* (Boston: Houghton Mifflin, 1993), pp. 179–80.

Sharpton after Amadou Diallo's death: "Battle-tested Sharpton Slips into Familiar Role," *New York Times*, February 13, 1999.

Black high-school and college students on government drug conspiracy: Jennifer L. Hochschild, *Facing Up to the American Dream: Race, Class, and the Soul of the*

*Nation* (Princeton: Princeton University Press, 1995), table 5.1, p. 106, cited in T, pp. 515–16.

Carby on Danny Glover: Hazel V. Carby, *Race Men* (Cambridge: Harvard University Press, 1998), pp. 182–91.

Christopher Edley: Jason Zengerle, "The Gatekeeper," *The New Republic,* March 22, 1999.

"You always have such people": John Hope Franklin, *The Color Line: Legacy for the 21st Century* (Columbia: University of Missouri Press, 1993).

Stanford black students' perceptions of racism: see David O. Sacks and Peter A. Thiel, *The Diversity Myth: "Multiculturalism" and the Politics of Intolerance at Stanford* (Oakland: The Independent Institute, 1995).

June Jordan pieces: Jordan, June. 1995. "Where I Live Now." *The Progressive,* January 1995; "The Street Where I Live," *The Progressive,* December 1995.

June Jordan poem: "Break the Law!," *Affirmative Acts* (New York: Anchor, 1998), p. 264.

Poll on Louis Farrakhan: P., p. 17.

Tupac Shakur's background: Armond White, *Rebel for the Hell of It* (New York: Thunder's Mouth Press, 1997).

"He was a thug, but . . .": Kim Greene quoted in Devlin Barrett and Andy Geller, "Rapper Shakur Dead," *New York Post,* September 14, 1996.

Lichelle Laws: S, p. 144.

New York "squeegee men": S, p. 194.

Maxine Waters dancing with gang members: S, p. 141.

Ralph Ellison quote: Letter to Horace Porter, December 22, 1976, John F. Callahan, "American Culture is of a Whole": From the Letters of Ralph Ellison, *The New Republic,* March 1, 1999, p. 44.

*Niggardly* episode at University of Wisconsin: Ethan Bronner, "Big Brother Is Listening," *New York Times* (Education Life section), April 4, 1999.

## CHAPTER TWO: THE CULT OF SEPARATISM

Manning Marable: Manning Marable, "A Plea that Scholars Act Upon, Not just Interpret, Events," *New York Times,* April 14, 1998.

Afrocentric History and argumentation: see Mary Lefkowitz, *Not Out of Africa* (New York: Basic Books, 1997 edition).

"When we see a mainstream work, and a black actor enters": "The Right Thing, in Brooklyn," *New York Times,* November 4, 1999.

Cleaver quote: Eldridge Cleaver, *Soul on Ice* (New York: McGraw-Hill, 1968), p. 58.

Evidence in the Simpson case: Vincent Bugliosi, *Outrage* (New York: Norton, 1996).

Elijah Muhammad biography: Claude Andrew Clegg III, *An Original Man: The Life and Times of Elijah Muhammad* (New York: St. Martin's, 1997).

Damian Williams and comrades in L.A. riots: S, pp. 138–41.

Kenneth Clark: S, p. 7.

"High-spirited nonconformists": S, p. 38.

The Columbia radicals and welfare: S, pp. 49–54.

Richard Delgado and Critical Race Theory: Richard Delgado, *The Coming Race War?* (New York: New York University Press, 1996), p. 29.

Will Marion Cook and Bob Cole: Allen Woll, *Black Musical Theatre: From Coontown to Dreamgirls* (New York: Da Capo, 1989), pp. 6–31.

"There's a black culture. . . .": S, p. 11.

Evidence in the Brawley case: see "From Fiber and Smudges, Questions in Brawley Case," *New York Times,* March 10, 1988; "Key Findings in the Report," (New York) *Daily News,* October 7, 1988.

Sharpton as articulate and smart: "Battle-Tested Sharpton Slips into Familiar Role," *New York Times,* February 13, 1999.

Columbia law school graduate: "Prosecutors Detail Columbia Law Student's Secret Life as a Criminal," *New York Times,* December 21, 1998.

CHAPTER THREE: THE CULT OF ANTI-INTELLECTUALISM

White versus black SAT scores: BB, p. 20.

Black students' SAT scores at Berkeley: T, pp. 406–7, citing Robert Lerner and Althea K. Nigai. *Racial Preferences in Undergraduate Enrollment at the University of California, Berkeley, 1993–1995: A Preliminary Report* (Washington, D.C.: Center for Equal Opportunity, 1996), charts 4, 5.

Black SAT scores according to class: T, pp. 404–5, citing College Entrance Examination Board, Profiles, College-Bound Seniors, 1981, and College Entrance Examination Board, National Ethnic/Sex Data, 1995.

184 black students: T, p. 399 (citing same two sources as above).

Black SATs compared to general average scores in 1951: BB, p. 30.

Correlation of SAT scores with college performance: BB, pp. 74–75.

Class ranks in classes of '89: BB, p. 77; two other studies with same conclusion about predictive value of SAT scores: Frederick E. Vars and William G. Bowen, "Scholastic Aptitude Test Scores, Race, and Academic Performance in Selective Colleges and Universities," JP, pp. 457–79; Leonard Ramist, Charles Lewis, and Laura McCamley-Jenkins, "Student Group Differences in Predicting College Grades: Sex, Language, and Ethnic Groups," *College Board Report* 93–1, 1994.

SATs overpredict black performance: T, p. 638 citing Robert Klitgard, *Choosing Elites* (New York: Basic Books, 1985), pp. 160–65, 187–88.

Black and Latino high school performance: ST, pp. 83–88.

B+ versus straight-A average: "Affirmative Action Under Attack on Campus Where It Worked," *New York Times,* June 4, 1995, cited in T, p. 406.

Black law students and professional school exams: Stephen Thernstrom and Abigail Thernstrom, "Reflections on *The Shape of the River,*" *UCLA Law Review* 46 (1995), pp. 1610–12.

"Whether it is the loneliness": Beverly Daniel Tatum, *Why Are All the Black Kids Sitting Together in the Cafeteria?* (New York: Basic Books, 1997), p. 78.

Teacher bias and minority students: ST, pp. 88–89.

Studies on black teachers and black student performance: summarized in Ronald Ferguson, "Can Schools Narrow the Black-White Test Score Gap?," JP, pp. 347–50.

Cape Verdean sophomore: "Public Schools are Forced to Confront Issue of Preferences," *New York Times,* November 29, 1998.

"Stereotype Threat" studies: Claude M. Steele, "Race and the Schooling of Black America," *Atlantic Monthly,* April 1992; Claude M. Steele, "Thin Ice: "Stereotype Threat" and Black College Students," *Atlantic Monthly,* August 1999; Claude M. Steele and Joshua Aronson, "Stereotype Threat and the Intellectual Test Performance of African Americans," *Journal of Personality and Social Psychology* 69: 797–811; Claude M. Steele and Joshua Aronson, "Stereotype Threat and the Test Performance of Academically Successful African Americans," JP, pp. 401–27.

School funding: *Digest of Educational Statistics: 1995* (Washington, D.C.: U.S. Government Printing Office, 1996); "How Much Does D.C. Really Spend Per Pupil?" *Washington Post* August 3, 1995, cited in T, pp. 349–50.

More Effective Schools program: S, p. 37.

Southeast Asian academic achievement: Nathan Caplan, Marcella H. Choy, and John K. Whitmore, *The Boat People and Achievement in America: A Study of Family Life, Hard Work, and Cultural Values* (Ann Arbor: University of Michigan Press, 1989); Nathan Caplan, Marcella H. Choy, and John K. Whitmore, "Indochinese Refugee Families and Academic Achievement," *Scientific American,* February 1992.

Lack of racial bias in tracking: Michael S. Garet and Brian Delaney, "Students, Courses and Stratification," *Sociology of Education* 61 (1988); Adam Gamoran and Robert G. Mare, "Secondary School Tracking and Educational Inequality: Compensation, Reinforcement, or Neutrality?," *American Journal of Sociology* 94 (1989); Karl Alexander and Michael Cook, "Curricula and Coursework: A Surprise Ending to a Familiar Story," *American Sociological Review* 47 (1982); Ronald Ferguson, "Can Schools Narrow the Black-White Test Score Gap?," JP, p. 366.

Tracking at Berkeley High: Chris Thompson, "The Most Integrated School in America," *The East Bay Express,* June 11, 1999, p. 12.

Shaker Heights: Michael A. Fletcher, "A Mystery: Good Schools but Bad Grades," *The Washington Post,* November 2, 1998.

Fordham & Ogbu study: Signithia Fordham and John U. Ogbu, "Black Students' School Success: Coping with the Burden of 'Acting White,'" *Urban Review* 18 (1986).

Evanston, Ill.: "Reason is Sought for Lag by Blacks in School Effort," *New York Times,* July 4, 1999.

*Examiner* series: "How Race Colors Learning," *San Francisco Examiner,* June 7, 1998, followed by three continuations, June 8–10, 1998.

Berkeley High quotes: Chris Thompson, "The Most Integrated School in America," *The East Bay Express,* June 11, 1999, p. 12.

Minority parents' expectations: ST, p. 161.

Black dropout rates: BB, pp. 55–65.

Minority student engagement: S, p. 87.

Sociologist dismissing cultural explanation: Chris Thompson, "The Most Integrated School in America," *The East Bay Express,* June 11, 1999, p. 11.

CHAPTER FOUR: THE ROOTS OF THE CULTURE OF ANTI-INTELLECTUALISM

"When I walk in that gate every morning . . .": Chris Thompson, "The Most Integrated School in America," *The East Bay Express,* June 11, 1999, p. 11.

New York State Board of Regents booklet: "Learning Style of Minorities to Be Studied," *New York Times,* November 21, 1987, cited in T, p. 364.

Black parenting styles' effect on learning: "Stacked Odds," second of four part series in *The San Francisco Examiner,* June 8, 1998.

Private school in Washington, D.C.: Eleanor Orr, *Twice as Less* (New York: Norton, 1987).

Casteel study: Clifton Casteel, "Attitudes of African American and Caucasian Eighth Grade Students about Praises, Rewards, and Punishments," *Elementary School Guidance and Counseling* 31 (1997).

"There's this guy who works with my mom . . .": Chris Thompson, "The Most Integrated School in America," *The East Bay Express,* June 11, 1999, p. 11.

"The anger and resentment": Beverly Daniel Tatum, *Why Are All the Black Kids Sitting Together in the Cafeteria?* (New York: Basic Books, 1997), p. 60.

Mickelson study: Roslyn A. Mickelson, "The Attitude-Achievement Paradox among Black Adolescents," *Sociology of Education* 63 (1990).

Ralph Ellison quote: Letter to Horace Porter, December 22, 1976, John F. Callahan, "American Culture Is of a Whole": From the Letters of Ralph Ellison, *The New Republic,* March 1, 1999, p. 43.

Black students at orientation at Berkeley High: Chris Thompson, "The Most Integrated School in America," *The East Bay Express,* June 11, 1999, p. 12.

CHAPTER FIVE: AFRICAN-AMERICAN SELF-SABOTAGE IN ACTION:
THE AFFIRMATIVE-ACTION DEBATE

"Minority students look around . . .": James Traub, "The Class of Prop. 209," *The New York Times Magazine,* May 2, 1999, p. 76.

Berkeley student figures courtesy of the UC Berkeley Office of Public Records.

Socioeconomic profile of black students at selective universities: BB, pp. 46–50.

Black graduation rates: BB, pp. 55–59 (my "three times" figure derived from adjusting base comparison [75 percent black versus 94 percent white graduating] for proportion of blacks BB calculates left one school but graduated from another).

Lack of stigma: James Traub, "The Class of Prop. 209," *The New York Times Magazine,* May 2, 1999, p. 76.

Berkeley black recruitment officer: "Black Students May Prefer to Say No to Berkeley," *New York Times,* May 2, 1998.

CHAPTER SIX: AFRICAN-AMERICAN SELF-SABOTAGE IN ACTION:
THE EBONICS CONTROVERSY

Tucker Carlson: cited in Wayne O'Neil, "If Ebonics Isn't a Language, Then Tell Me What Is?," *The Real Ebonics Debate: Power, Language, and the Education of African-American Children,* ed. Theresa Perry and Lisa Delpit (Boston: Beacon Press, 1998), p. 43.

Anthology: ibid.

List of media treatments of Ebonics: ibid.

Success for All: Ronald Ferguson, "Can Schools Narrow the Black-White Test Score Gap?," JP, pp. 343–46; Nicholas Lemann, "Ready, Read!," *Atlantic Monthly,* November 1998.

Oakland School Board Resolution: *The Real Ebonics Debate: Power, Language, and the Education of African-American Children,* ed. Theresa Perry and Lisa Delpit (Boston: Beacon Press, 1998), p. 143.

"Distracting noises": Theresa Perry, "I Don't Know Why They Be Trippin'," ibid., p. 4.

"The mayor may be a . . .": Carl Rowan, "The Barry Verdict: A Victory for No One," *Washington Post,* August 15, 1990.

CHAPTER SEVEN: HOW CAN WE SAVE THE AFRICAN-AMERICAN RACE?

Manning Marable: Manning Marable, "A Plea that Scholars Act Upon, Not Just Interpret, Events," *New York Times,* April 4, 1998.

Proportion of black high scorers admitted to selective universities: BB, pp. 26–27.

University of Texas before Hopwood: Stephen Thernstrom and Abigail Thernstrom, "Reflections on *The Shape of the River,*" *UCLA Law Review* 46 (1995), p. 1585.

Lowell High School: "Public Schools are Forced to Confront Issue of Preferences," *New York Times,* November 29, 1998.

The weight of race in admissions policies: BB, pp. 46–50.

Plateau in black SAT scores: BB, p. 21; in general academic performance: T, pp. 357–59.

Steele quote: Claude M. Steele and Joshua Aronson, "Stereotype Threat and the Test Performance of Academically Successful African Americans," JP, pp. 425–26.

Steele article advising high standards: Claude M. Steele, "Thin Ice: "Stereotype Threat" and Black College Students," *Atlantic Monthly,* August 1999.

Dworkin review: Ronald Dworkin, "Affirming Affirmative Action," *The New York Review of Books,* October 22, 1998, pp. 91–102.

Increases in minority enrollment at three UC schools: Stephen Thernstrom and Abigail Thernstrom, "Reflections on *The Shape of the River,*" *UCLA Law Review* 46 (1995), pp. 1626–27.

Minority admissions down in six out of seventy-four schools: James Traub, "The Class of Prop. 209," *The New York Times Magazine,* May 2, 1999, p. 50.

Successful blacks and elite schools: ibid., pp. 1618–20.

Jencks quote: Christopher Jencks, "Racial Bias in Testing," JP, p. 73.

Sleeper observation: Jim Sleeper, "Toward an End of Blackness," *Harper's,* May 1997, p. 44.

# ACKNOWLEDGMENTS

For reasons probably not entirely unclear, writing this book has been a largely private endeavor, slipped between the cracks of a life spent primarily researching, teaching, and sometimes performing. Thanks are due, however, to my sister Holly, who while certainly not agreeing with everything I have written, helped to keep me grounded in reality. Ashlee Bailey read the manuscript as well, and furnished innumerable helpful articles and sources; the book would be a lesser one without her contributions. Stephan and Abigail Thernstrom have been inestimably helpful in providing information and feedback. Special thanks also to Katinka Matson for believing in me, and to John Brockman for soliciting the essay that eventually grew into a book I never suspected I would write.

# INDEX